SAMUEL

Son and Successor of
REES HOWELLS

Director of the Bible College of Wales
– A Biography –

RICHARD MATON

Samuel, Son and Successor of Rees Howells: Director of the Bible College of Wales – A Biography – by Richard A. Maton
Copyright © Richard A. Maton 2012, 2014, 2016, 2017, 2018.

Scripture quotations unless otherwise stated are taken from the Holy Bible, the New International Version®. NIV®. Copyright © 1973, 1978, 1984 by International Bible Society. Used by permission of Zondervan. All rights reserved.

Other versions used:
- (AV) – Authorised Version (also known as the King James Version)
- (NASB) – New American Standard Bible
- (NCV) – New Century Version

All rights reserved. No part of this publication may be reproduced, stored in a retrieval system, or transmitted in any form or by any means – electronically, mechanically, photocopying, recording, or any other (except for brief quotations in printed or official website reviews with full accreditation) without the prior permission of the Publisher, ByFaith Media – (Mathew Backholer) – www.ByFaith.org. Uploading or downloading this work from the internet (in whole or in part) is illegal, as is unauthorised translations. For requests for Translation Rights, please contact ByFaith Media.

References to deity are capitalised. As is the nature of the internet, web pages can disappear and ownership of domain names can change. Those stated within this book were valid at the time of first publication in June 2012.

Cover design, images, photos, design layout and content, copyright © 2012, 2014, 2016 and 2017, 2018, Mathew Backholer – ByFaith Media

ISBN 978-1-907066-14-6 (paperback)
ISBN 978-1-907066-36-8 (hardback)
ISBN 978-1-907066-28-3 (eBook ePub)

British Library Cataloguing In Publication Data. A Record of this Publication is available from the British Library
Richard Alexander Maton: born September 1932
First published in 2012 by ByFaith Media, updated in 2014, February 2016, August 2017 and January 2018.

- Jesus Christ is Lord -

*Yet it pleased the Lord
to bruise Him; He hath put
Him to grief: when Thou shalt make
His soul an offering for sin, He shall see
His seed, He shall prolong His days, and the
pleasure of the Lord shall prosper in His hand. He
shall see of the travail of His soul, and shall be satisfied:
by His knowledge shall My righteous Servant justify
many; for He shall bear their iniquities.* Isaiah 53:10-11 (AV)

And He said unto them, "Go ye into all the world, and preach the Gospel to EVERY CREATURE." Mark 16:15 (AV)

I exhort therefore, that, first of all, supplications, prayers, intercessions, and giving of thanks be made for all men; for kings, and for all that are in authority; that we may lead a quiet and peaceable life in all godliness and honesty. For this is good and acceptable in the sight of God our Saviour; who will have all men to be saved, and to come unto the knowledge of the truth.
1 Timothy 2:1-4 (AV)

God said, "And I sought for a man among them, that should make up the hedge, and stand in the gap before Me for the land..."

I heard the voice of the Lord saying, "Whom shall I send, and who will go for Us?" Then said I, "Here am I; send me."
Ezekiel 22:30 and Isaiah 6:8 (AV)

Contents

Page   Chapter

5.	Contents	
7.	Contents of Photos	
11.	Foreword	
13.	Preface	
15.	Introduction	
25.	The Hidden Years	1.
32.	Early Days	2.
53.	War in Europe	3.
62.	The Venture Begins	4.
68.	The Silver Thread	5.
72.	Progress on Every Front	6.
88.	The College Stirs Again	7.
96.	The School of Faith	8.
104.	Challenges at Home	9.
115.	Kingdom Prayers	10.
127.	Easter and Whitsun	11.
139.	New Faces	12.
144.	Give Ye Them to Eat	13.
153.	Second Missionary Journey	14.
160.	The Congo Crisis	15.
165.	The Spectre of Communism	16.
176.	At the Helm	17.
180.	The Stormy Sixties and Seventies	18.
194.	A Resolute Stand Amidst Gathering Clouds	19.
206.	The Daily Walk	20.
214.	The Landing	21.
220.	Saturdays	22.
233.	The Young Generation	23.
240.	The French Connection	24.
247.	The Wall Comes Tumbling Down	25.
258.	Victory in South Africa	26.
262.	Retired!	27.
276.	Ethiopia	28.

Contents

Page		Chapter
287.	Operation Desert Storm	29.
298.	New Developments	30.
307.	The Achilles Heel	31.
315.	Handing Over the Baton	32.
324.	Epilogue	33.
326.	The Views of Two Visitors	
336.	The Every Creature Conferences	
337.	Bible College Students and Publications	
338.	Global Horizons	
339.	Sources and Notes	
352.	ByFaith Media Books	
357.	ByFaith Media DVDs	

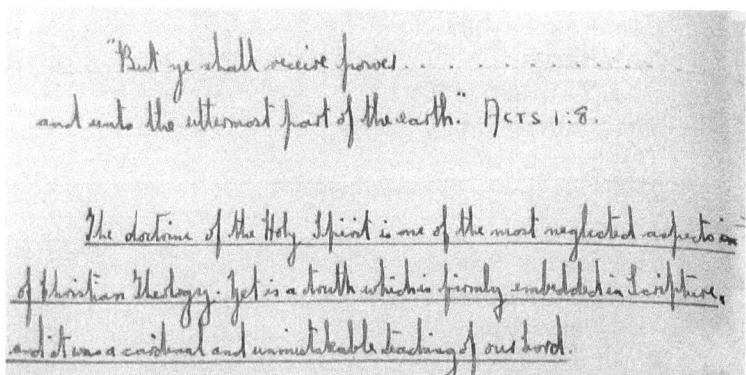

The beginning of a sermon by Samuel Howells from the late 1930s. The text reads: *"But ye shall receive power...and unto the uttermost part of the earth."* Acts 1:8.

The doctrine of the Holy Spirit is one of the most neglected aspects of Christian theology. Yet is a truth which is firmly embedded in Scripture and it was cardinal and unmistakable teaching of our Lord.

Contents of Photos

Abbreviation:
C. = circa, meaning approximately

Page

4. Samuel Rees Howells in his early 20s – c.1933
6. A section of a sermon by Samuel Rees Howells
10. Faith for a Bible College April 1923
14. Richard and Kristine Maton in 2011
20. Rees and Lizzie Hannah Howells 1910
21. Rees and Lizzie Hannah Howells in Africa c.1917
28. Rees Howells' coffin in front of Derwen Fawr House
31. Samuel Howells and staff members of BCW in 1950
33. Rees and Lizzie Howells with baby Samuel 1913
34. Moses Rees and Samuel Rees Howells, age 3, 1915
35. Moses Rees' Piano Stores and Stationery, Garnant
39. Samuel Rees Howells age 4, 1916
40. Samuel Howells with his cousin c.1918
41. Samuel at School in Garnant c.1919
43. Glynderwen House – Samuel's weekday home
44. Glynderwen House and El-Shaddai Building c.1935
50. Samuel's first property, Twyn y Mynydd
52. Samuel Howells as a lecturer c.1946
54. Penllergaer Mansion (the Big House) 1939
57. Rees and Lizzie Howells and Derwen Fawr House
58. Sketty House (front view)
58. Sketty House (back view)
61. Mount Pleasant Baptist Church and bomb damage
65. Aerial view of Derwen Fawr and Sketty Isaf House
71. New erected buildings on all three estates 1936
75. Ieuan Jones as a Bible College student
76. David Davies, Samuel Howells and Arthur Neil, 80s
77. The Howells family c.1940
78. Mrs Lizzie Howells in the Holy Land 1937
79. The Paris Team with the Howells in Swansea
81. The Middle East Team c.1954
84. Samuel Howells in Beirut, Lebanon, 1951

Contents of Photos

Abbreviation:
C. = circa, meaning approximately

Page

86. Mr V. Atchinak and Samuel Howells in Beirut, 1962
87. Student Day, November 1963 (men staff & students)
88. Samuel Rees Howells with his foster parents c.1922
89. Duncan Campbell at Derwen Fawr c.1955
92. Samuel Howells with Tobias 'Toby' Bergin c.1980s
95. Aerial view of Derwen Fawr Estate early 1950s
97. The Howells family – Faith Is Substance c.1930
100. Moses Rees and fashionable Samuel Howells
103. Gravestone of George Müller, Arnos Vale Cemetery
104. Mrs Howells' and Samuel Howells' thank you card
111. Rees and Samuel Howells with Miss Alice Townsend
112. Rees and Lizzie Howells in America, 1922
116. Kitchen Garden 1970s
118. Samuel Howells at Derwen Fawr early 1970s
119. Courtyard of Derwen Fawr; ladies' and men's hostels
120. Ebenezer on the courtyard wall at Derwen Fawr
121. Italian Gardens in the grounds of Derwen Fawr
126. Samuel Howells in the early 1960s
128. Samuel preaching c. late 1980s
134. Llandrindod Wells Convention, Wales, c.1930
135. Mrs Howells, Samuel and Alice Townsend c.1921
136. 1939-Whitsun Meeting, Rees Howells preaching
137. Whitsun (Pentecost) meeting 7 June 1938
138. The College Motto – BCW prospectus 1935
140. BCW staff, late 1950s with Samuel Howells (centre)
146. Llewellyn family at Penllergaer c.1915
155. Samuel Howells on Black Mountain c. late 1970s
158. Samuel Howells in Istanbul, Turkey, 1962
158. Samuel Howells at Dachau Concentration Camp
159. Samuel Howells in 1951 (unknown location)
162. Congo Newspaper headline clipping 1964
164. Congo Newspaper headline clipping 1964

Contents of Photos

Abbreviation:
C. = circa, meaning approximately

Page

166. Derwen Fawr Road 2011
167. Derwen Fawr Road 2011
168. The Howells family late 1940s
174. Gladys Aylward newspaper caricature 1950s
177. Samuel looking out of his bedroom window 1980s
179. Top section of the Italian Gardens at Derwen Fawr
183. Billy Graham preaching at Wembley Stadium 1954
191. First 'No Sneers' Russian Bible in nearly 50 years
196. Samuel working in his bedroom / office 1980s
202. Reinhard Bonnke and Peggy Coulthard c.1970s
203. Thank you note – Millions of Russians for Christ
204. Rees Howells trekking in Zululand 1917
205. Booklet found in Samuel Howells' Bible
207. Samuel Howells on the veranda of Derwen Fawr
208. Samuel Howells having a picnic in the countryside
215. Samuel Howells with his mother 1965
218. Samuel Howells in the Blue Room 1995
219. Samuel Howells at Philippi, Greece, 1962
231. Samuel Howells' signature
232. Samuel Howells recuperating c.1970s
233. Some of the BCW ladies staff, July 1981
238. Samuel Howells with Sam Matthews on the bridge
239. Prayer list of countries and Bible distribution
241. Maison de l'Evangile (The Gospel House) in France
242. Samuel Howells in Paris, France, c.1962
249. Samuel Howells relaxed and happy mid 1980s
250. Derwen Fawr Road after a blizzard, January 1982
251. View from the veranda of Derwen Fawr 1982
259. Church at Rusitu, Gazaland where revival broke out
263. Emmanuel Grammar School 1980s
264. Primrose Thomas, Mair Davies and Dr. K. Priddy
267. Aerial view of Emmanuel Grammar School c.1955

Contents of Photos

Abbreviation:
C. = circa, meaning approximately

Page

268. Emmanuel School badge
269. Bible College School Inter-House Work Shield
275. Entry of a death in Samuel's pocket diary 1987
277. The Howells family with Haile Selassie 1939
285. Coptic Christians reading the Holy Bible
286. Bible Society of Ethiopia, Addis Ababa
292. Rees Howells in 1949, six months before his death
299. Lizzie Howells 1965
302. Samuel celebrates 50 years as Honorary Director
303. Samuel Howells with Richard Maton February 2000
306. Entrance to Derwen Fawr Estate c.1940
308. Schoolchildren at Emmanuel Grammar c.1955
310. Samuel Howells at the grave of his parents 1973
314. Samuel Howells with Norman Grubb c.1975
320. The Howells family grave in St. David's churchyard
323. Samuel Howells as a young man c.1929
335. The College Vision – Go ye... from a 1937 booklet

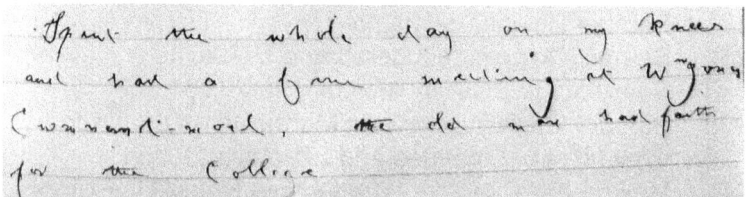

First recorded reference to start a Bible College by Rees Howells, from his notebook, dated 6 April 1923: Spent the whole day on my knees and had a prayer meeting at Wm (William) Jones — the old man had faith for the College.

Foreword

The life of Samuel Howells and the story of the Bible College of Wales (BCW) have touched the lives of innumerable people around the world. When Richard Maton told my brother and me that he was writing a book about the life of Samuel Howells, the son of Rees, we were very excited. A few years later, Alan Scotland, the successor of Samuel Howells as Director of BCW contacted us and asked if we (ByFaith Media) would publish Richard's book. After reviewing the manuscript, we realised that Richard had written a wonderful biography of the life of Samuel Howells, with in-depth details concerning the inner life and workings of the Bible College of Wales; its staff, students and friends. Samuel lived a full and long life and delved deep into the intercessory ministry. With this in mind, we proposed that we would publish two versions of the book with the intention of delving deeper into the ministry of intercession of Samuel Howells that was not possible in the larger manuscript. Richard Maton's original manuscript is the life of Samuel Howells and the history of BCW, a biography: *Samuel, Son and Successor of Rees Howells: Director of the Bible College of Wales – A Biography*. The other book focuses on Samuel's life of prayer, ministry of intercession and includes many new chapters, with additional facts, quotes and testimonies sourced from the BCW archives and elsewhere. This is called: *Samuel Rees Howells: A Life of Intercession*.

Richard Maton spent fifty-two years of his life at BCW and worked closely alongside Samuel for more than twenty years. He was the most loyal ministry friend that Samuel had in the last two decades of his life and Samuel trusted many secrets to no other person. My brother and I spent a combined seven years at Bible College as students and then staff members. To us, Richard was the 'face' of BCW, not only a lecturer, but a trustee, dean and the Principal. Throughout those critical final years of Samuel's life, Richard worked unearthly hours, yet remained accessible, patient, and practised the presence of Christ. Richard is married to Kristine and between them, they have served the Lord under the ministry of Samuel Howells for more than a century! Without Richard and Kristine Maton's years of research and labour, the story of Samuel Howells could never have been told. We are all indebted to them.

On an editorial note, the information within this book has been collated and collected from the original sources and notes from the BCW archives. Richard has also drawn from personal memory, the experiences of others and cited other sources. The publishers have spent several months delving into these archives pouring over thousands of documents, letters and handwritten notes. Any similarity to the other two books about Rees Howells in previous decades has arisen because they too were sourced from these archives.

Some former BCW students mentioned within this book have had their surnames omitted as they are ministering in sensitive countries, others may eventually do so. Some testimonial letters were not signed, for the same reason and have been left blank. Where a name has been changed, this is noted within the text.

Within this book, alongside the values in British Pound Sterling (£) is the *approximate* value in American Dollars ($) based on £1 to $1.6. Please note: inflation has not been calculated into the values except where noted.[1]

This book contains a number of Welsh words and phrases, (a language rich in consonants) which is very different from English.

As you read this book, we hope that you too will learn that God is able to use any person who is willing to surrender his or her life, fully and unconditionally to Him.

> *I beseech you therefore, brethren, by the mercies of God, that ye present your bodies a living sacrifice, holy, acceptable unto God, which is your reasonable service.* Romans 12:1 (AV).

Mathew and Paul Backholer
ByFaith Media
www.ByFaith.org

Preface

Writing a book was never something I imagined possible, but this is a record of impossibilities, so perhaps it is appropriate that I should be part of one, after all.

God touched my life in my early twenties and gave me the privilege of sitting under the ministry of Rev. Samuel Howells, son of Rees Howells, Director of the Bible College of Wales, Swansea, UK, for forty-seven years. In a spiritual environment of faith and prayer, nurtured since 1924, there was much to learn. These spiritual lessons can only be learnt through a close personal walk with God and are certainly not easy, as indicated by Jesus in Matt. 16:24-25.

Then Jesus said to His disciples, "If anyone would come after Me, he must deny himself and take up his cross and follow Me. For whoever wants to save his life will lose it, but whoever loses his life for Me will find it."

Although a quiet, reserved man, Samuel shared his heart on many aspects of Christian living and there is a legacy of tape-recorded ministry of prayer sessions and Bible Studies that he left.

The facts and matters concerning the life of Samuel Howells that are included in this book are drawn from events which I witnessed personally, from observations and stories which have been related to me, and from the documentary evidence that is currently in the possession of the trustees of Global Horizons. As such, it represents a true record of the main stages of the development of Samuel Howells' ministry.

I have tried to paint a true picture of this very gracious man of God whose influence on world events during the latter half of the twentieth century cannot be truly assessed. In addition, I have traced the major events of the Bible College history, through its various decades. It is difficult to do so without including the names of many other key players whose dedicated and sacrificial living meant everything to Samuel. It was certainly a team effort, an example of the Body of Christ functioning as it should, working through relationship situations which community living presents, to maintain the *unity of the Spirit in the bond of peace.* Ephesians 4:3.

Many personal contributions from former students and friends of Samuel have added to the intimacy of the biography, and permission to access the Bible College archives has ensured its accuracy. I am deeply indebted to my dear wife, Kristine, who was also privileged to sit under Samuel's ministry and some of Rees Howells'. Her wisdom, encouragement and practical contributions have helped maintain a balance. I am also grateful for close friends who have reviewed early drafts and encouraged me to move forward. I mention especially Rev. Geoffrey Fewkes with his knowledge of the Welsh background and culture of which Samuel Howells was part, and finally Steve and Kathy Coupe from *Nations*, Llanelli, with their own busy schedule for world vision, who have so kindly spent many, many hours editing and reviewing, searching for accuracy and a clear presentation. It is difficult to express my appreciation adequately.

If someone, somewhere, at some time is challenged or encouraged through reading this simple narrative, my venture will have been well worthwhile.

R. M. 2012

Richard and Kristine Maton in 2011

Introduction

This intriguing biography carves its unmistakable pathway through twentieth century history and clearly shows what God can do through the lives of individuals totally surrendered to Him.

The quality and depth of Samuel Howells' ministry as Honorary Director of the Bible College of Wales in Swansea from 1950 to 2002 was greatly shaped and moulded through his years spent under the ministry of his father, Rees Howells. The title 'Honorary Director' was not a position without any responsibilities, quite the contrary. It was initially used to distinguish him from his father, the Director, who founded the College, and the title stuck. For some who may not be familiar with the story of Rees' experience with God in the early part of the twentieth century, let me outline it briefly. Then, as my narrative unfolds, I will refer often to specific spiritual lessons learnt by Samuel from those years of intense preparation.

It began in the hillside village of Brynaman, a close knit community in South Wales on 10th October 1879, when Margaret Howells gave birth to another son, Rees. In their small white-walled stone cottage, now named 'Waunhelygen' in Llandeilo Road, lived eleven children with their parents. For Thomas, the father of this happy household, life was a constant struggle, as low wages barely met the essentials for his growing family. Such was life for the lower stratum in a two-tiered Victorian society.

Young Rees Howells started work at the age of twelve years in the local tin mill. Although not a committed Christian, he was deeply religious, as so many were in a land which had experienced spiritual awakenings, in 1759 and 1859. Along with other young men of his age however, eager to better themselves, Rees emigrated to the United States of America in 1901 to seek his fortune, sailing from Liverpool on the White Star Liner, *Oceanic 2*. God had other plans for his life and, confronted with the fear of death for the first time, having contracted typhoid fever, he was wonderfully converted. He met the risen Saviour and with his life completely changed, he returned home in 1904 just as revival blessing was sweeping the land through the anointed ministry of Evan Roberts from nearby Loughor. It was then, in a Convention at Llandrindod Wells in 1906 to foster the spiritual growth of young Christians, that Rees experienced a unique encounter with God, who revealed Himself to him in a manner similar to that of Moses at the burning bush in the wilderness near Mt. Horeb (Exodus 3:1-6).

Rees Howells would constantly refer back to that life-transforming encounter with the living God which became the bedrock of the amazing ministry that was to follow. Quoting from Rees Howells' own words the experience is described.[1]

"The meeting with the Holy Ghost was just as real to me as my meeting with the Saviour those years before. I saw Him as a Person apart from flesh and blood, and He said to me, 'As the Saviour had a body, so I dwell in the cleansed temple of the believer. I am a Person. I am God, and I am come to ask you to give your body to Me that I may work through it. I need a body for My Temple (1 Corinthians 6:19-20), but it must belong to Me without reserve, for two persons with different wills can never live in the same body. Will you give me yours? (Romans 12:1). But if I come in, I come as God, and you must go out (Colossians 3:2-3). I shall not mix Myself with your self.'

"He made it very plain that He would never share my life. I saw the honour He gave me in offering to indwell me, but there were many things very dear to me, and I knew He wouldn't keep one of them. The change He would make was very clear. It meant every bit of my fallen nature was to go to the cross, and He would bring in His own life and His own nature."

It was unconditional surrender. From the meeting, Rees went out into a field where he cried his heart out because, as he said,

"I had received a sentence of death, as really as a prisoner in the dock. I had lived in my body for twenty-six years, and could I easily give it up? Who could give his life up to another in an hour? Why does a man struggle when death comes, if it is easy to die? I knew that the only place fit for the old nature was on the cross. Paul makes that very plain in Romans 6. But once this is done in reality, it is done for ever. I could not run into this. I intended to do it, but oh, the cost! I wept for days. I lost seven pounds (3.18 kg) in weight, just because I saw what He was offering me. How I wished I had never seen it! One thing He reminded me of was that He had only come to take what I had already promised the Saviour, not in part, but the whole.

"Since He died for me, I had died in Him, and I knew that the new life was His and not mine. That had been clear in my mind for three years; so He had only come to take what was His own. I saw that only the Holy Ghost in me could live like the Saviour. Everything He told me appealed to me; it was only a question of the loss there would be in doing it. I didn't give my answer in a moment, and He didn't want me to."

It took five days to make the decision, days that were spent alone with God.

"Like Isaiah, I saw the holiness of God," Rees said, "and seeing Him, I saw my own corrupt nature. It wasn't sins that I saw, but nature touched by the Fall. I was corrupt to the core. I knew I had to be cleansed; I saw there was as much difference between the Holy Ghost and myself as between light and darkness.

"Nothing is more real to me than the process I went through for that whole week. The Holy Spirit went on dealing with me, exposing the root of my nature which was self, and you can only get out of a thing what is in its root. Sin was cancelled, and it wasn't sin He was dealing with; it was self, that thing which came from the Fall. He was not going to take any superficial surrender. He put His finger on each part of my self-life such as my love of money, my ambition, my reputation, and I had to decide in cold blood. He could never take a thing away until I gave my consent. Then the moment I gave it, some purging took place (Isaiah 6:5-7) and I could never touch that thing again. It was not *saying* I was purged and the thing still having a hold on me; no, it was a breaking, and the Holy Ghost taking control. Day-by-day the dealing went on. He was coming in as God, and I had lived as a man, and what is permissible to an ordinary man, He told me, will not be permissible to you."

The Holy Spirit finally summed up the position for him,

"On no account will I allow you to bring in a crosscurrent. Where I send you, you will go; what I say to you, you will do."

It was the final battle of the will.

"I asked Him for more time," Rees continued, "but He said I would not have a minute after six o' clock. When I heard that, it was exactly as if a wild beast was roused in me. You gave me a free will and now You force me to give it up."

"I do not force you," He replied, "but for three years have you not been saying that you are not your own, and that you wanted to give your life back to the Saviour as completely as He gave His for you?"

"I climbed down in a second," recalled Rees. "The way I had said it was an insult to the Trinity. I am sorry, I told Him, I didn't mean what I said."

"You are not forced to give up your will," He said again, "but at six o' clock I will take your decision. After that you will never get another chance."

It was my last offer; my last chance! I saw

the Throne (Revelation 3:21) and all my future for eternity going. I said, "Please forgive me, I *want* to do it."

Once more the question came, "Are you willing?" It was ten minutes to six. I wanted to do it, but I could not. Your mind is keen when you are tested, and in a flash it came to me, how can self be willing to give up self? Five to six came. I was afraid of those last five minutes. I could count the ticks of the clock. Then the Spirit spoke again. "If you can't be willing, would you like Me to help you? Are you willing to be made willing?"

"Take care," the enemy whispered, "when a stronger person than yourself is on the other side, to be willing to be made willing is just the same as to be willing."

As I was thinking upon this point, I looked at the clock. It was one minute to six. I bowed my head and said,

"Lord, I am willing."

Within an hour, the Third Person of the Godhead had come in. He gave Rees the verse, Hebrews 10:19 (AV).

Having therefore, brethren, boldness to enter into the holiest by the blood of Jesus.

"Immediately," said Rees, "I was transported into another realm, within that sacred veil where the Father, the Saviour and the Holy Spirit live. There I heard God speaking to me, and I have lived there ever since. When the Holy Ghost enters, He comes in to abide for ever. To the blood be the glory!

"How I adored the grace of God! It is God who goes so far as to give us repentance. It was God who helped me to give up my will. There were some things He had asked for during the week that I was able to give, because I was master of them; but when He asked me to give up my self and my will, I found I could not – until He pulled me through."

An eyewitness tells us that no words can describe the

little meeting in the house that night; the glory of God came down. Rees started singing the chorus, "There's power in the blood," and they couldn't stop singing for two hours! Then from 9pm to 2:30am, it was "nothing but the Holy Ghost speaking things I had never dreamed of and exalting the Saviour."[2]

Rees and Lizzie Hannah Howells 1910

Samuel Howells, his son and successor as the Honorary Director of the Bible College of Wales from 1950 to 2002, also endeavoured to stress the importance of receiving the Person, and not just the blessings of the Holy Spirit, in the foundation and future of the College. At certain periods in history God had met individuals in a similar way. The God of Glory had appeared to Abram in Ur of the Chaldees. Through subsequent visions, an eternal covenant was forged for the future blessing of a nation and every family in the world, to be made possible through his 'Seed' – the Redeemer of mankind. That promise was to be tested in Isaac but Abraham had not wavered, even to believing for the resurrection from the dead. The book of Hebrews lists others who experienced Divine encounters, and there were the Prophets as well as Jesus' disciples themselves. The Apostle Paul on the road to Damascus was blinded by the heavenly vision and subsequently left his fingerprints upon the course of history. Each one played their part in their day as the Holy Spirit took full possession of them, dominating their minds and actions. Rees Howells' experience was as radical as theirs and should not be underestimated as we proceed in our narrative.

For several years, Rees Howells was kept in the seclusion of his home environment as the Holy Spirit taught him the principles of gaining positions of authority in Christ through the ministry of intercession. He married a local Christian lady, Elizabeth Hannah Jones, in 1910, crossing the strong denominational divide that existed in those days. Rees' family attended Gibea Chapel which dominated the village and was the mother chapel of several Congregational causes in the district. With regular attendance of eight hundred on Sundays, the worship was led by music provided by a beautiful pipe organ. Further down the road, Siloam Chapel near the Working Men's Hall, was the home of the Baptists, where Hannah Jones' family attended.

Mr Rees and Mrs Lizzie Hannah Howells in Africa c.1917

Rees carried the presence of God wherever he went, so much so that when he finally left Tairgwaith Colliery in Lower Brynaman, where he had worked at the coal face since his return from America, his fellow miners wept and implored him to stay as they felt so safe with him. Feeling God's call upon their lives to serve as missionaries, Rees and Hannah commenced training, Rees first at the Presbyterian College in Carmarthen then, for both, further medical courses in Edinburgh and London.

Eventually, following six years of fruitful ministry in Africa as missionaries, where they saw thousands of people converted through fresh moves of the Holy Spirit, Rees and his wife Hannah returned to Wales in 1920. They were offered the opportunity to travel the world and speak about revival to thousands of people but during a further visit to the Llandrindod Wells Convention in 1922, in mid Wales, they were invited by Rev. G. H. Lunn to join a prayer meeting for the opening of a College in Wales to teach young Christians more about the Bible. God spoke to them that He wanted them to be responsible for its establishment, relinquishing the prospect of the world tour. Scheduled to visit the USA, they asked the Lord for, and received, the full fare and more, the rest as a seal. The Bible College of Wales was opened in 1924. This was for the specific purpose of passing on the spiritual lessons, which had made their ministry so fruitful, to others who would take the Gospel around the world.

In Rees Howells' intercessory walk with God through the years, the Holy Spirit had demonstrated through him that He had absolute and complete power over the devil in finances, sickness and deliverance. Through the spiritual conflict resulting in the purchase of Glynderwen Estate, the Holy Spirit also broke the power of the Church of Rome, which had at that time hindered the progress of the Gospel in so many countries of the world, as Rees had experienced firsthand in Africa. In one public meeting, he declared that it would never again wield the same control in the world as it had in previous generations. This was a very powerful ministry. Then in 1934, God met with him again and challenged him concerning the need for someone to believe that the Saviour really meant that the Gospel would be preached to all nations before His return. Rees accepted that challenge personally. He knew it would require much finance and that it would require a company of men and women, filled and totally sold out to the Holy Spirit, as were the first Apostles, and Rees Howells was prepared, not just to talk and preach about it but to become personally responsible for it. I must repeat and emphasise the phrase, 'This was a very powerful ministry.'

Throughout his ministry, Rees Howells was always reaching out in the Holy Spirit to raise the standard in the Church to that of the early Church, when the *greater works* (John 14:12) were performed as a clear testimony to the world of that time. This fresh Vision from God steered the College ministry forward and many of the staff and students were prepared to follow on too, committing their lives to whatever God wanted for them, at any price. The Vision and their personal commitment were put to the test during World War II, when Rees led the College in a prolonged intercession for the demise of the Nazi threat to dominate the world, as Hitler aimed to eradicate the Jews and to stop the spread of the Gospel.

The believing and faith that the Holy Spirit gave at that time enabled Rees Howells to declare publicly, the complete defeat of Hitler, and that Divine power and authority were available for the overthrow of all spiritual powers restricting the proclamation of the Gospel in every country of the world, for the fulfilment of the Vision. This was given to Rees Howells on 26th December 1934.[3] In accordance with Jesus' proclamation, the Gospel would be preached in all nations and then the end would come. Those present in meetings at the height of World War II spoke of the exceptional light and revelation that was shed upon the Scriptures concerning these issues. Then on 10th October 1943, the Jewish Day of Atonement, in the course of his 3pm ministry in a College prayer meeting, Rees Howells speaking from Jeremiah 32:27 and from 33:3 said,

> "I believe that today is the beginning of this, as nine years ago was the beginning of the Vision. From today on the Holy Spirit will begin to make intercession for the Jewish people. If you ask what man can do, what about that young man in Midian (referring to Moses – Exodus 3). It is not sheep I have to look after, but men and women! If the devil says, 'I can't do this,' I shall

say, 'What did Moses do?' and the Holy Spirit was not given then. There are millions of Jews all over the earth today crying to God for this to happen. I want God to look down on the Jewish Nation and remember these things."

This was to prove the last major intercession that Rees Howells was to engage in and it gripped him during the final seven years of his earthly life. After much travail, the State of Israel was established in 1948 and Rees Howells had assurance concerning the future blessing of the whole nation. The outworking of the Vision, for an outpouring of the Holy Spirit on every nation in the world before the Lord's return, continued. As the College resumed after the war, its ministry was focussed upon providing a sending base for young men and women into the nations, and continuing in the intercessory ministry.

In the 9:30am service of 17th October 1945, Rees Howells mentioned a mental picture that he had.

"I saw a field of intercession that will circle the world, and as the Moravians prayed the clock around, we are to pray while others preach. I am going back to spend my days in intercession to ensure the blessing in every nation."

He appreciated that the outpouring of blessing would be accompanied by much persecution but stressed that the tribulation and martyrdom was only to be a stepping stone to glory! Having experienced so much opposition and oppression in his own ministry, he spoke with real authority.

The details of Rees Howells' life and ministry are recorded accurately in two well-publicised books, *Rees Howells Intercessor* (1952) by Norman Grubb and *The Intercessions of Rees Howells* (1983) by Doris Ruscoe.

It was into this profound legacy that Samuel, their only son, was called and, through a fresh anointing from the Holy Spirit, continued to follow the unfolding of God's plan and to remain true to the revelations given through his father, through fifty hidden years of ministry until the turn of the century. He died on 18th March 2004 and is buried with his parents in an inauspicious corner of Penllergaer Church graveyard, on the outskirts of Swansea, South Wales, UK.

Chapter One

The Hidden Years

'It was a dark day,' quoting from his own words, for Samuel Howells – affectionately known as Mr Samuel to everyone at the Bible College of Wales (BCW) – when his father Rees Howells, who founded BCW in 1924, died on 13th February 1950. Despite the enormity of the task that lay ahead, to continue in the intercessions for the world, (the Every Creature Commission for world evangelisation) which had gripped Rees Howells in his later years, and also to oversee the ongoing ministry of the Bible College in its training of young men and women for Christian service, Samuel had been well prepared for the task and carried a deep peace which God was giving him. In fact, he had not once been free to pray for his father's recovery for several weeks since his father had spoken personally to him one evening. It followed a memorable 9pm Sunday service in the College prayer room on 15th January 1950, when Rees Howells had a clear witness that the Holy Spirit in him had finished the work the Lord had given him to do on earth. He had just read the Songs of Moses and David (Exodus 15 and from the Psalms of David). Then he declared with such a ring of certainty,

> "Every Creature will hear the Gospel, the finance of the Vision is safe and the King will come back."

He also added that he had the assurance that the Lord would give the promised £100,000 ($160,000) for which he had believed. The £100,000 was a considerable sum of money in 1950 and in 2012 would be worth approximately £2,700,000 ($4,320,000).[1] The £100,000 was to be a seal from God that He would provide all the finances necessary for the Gospel to be preached throughout all nations in the world before His return. As with Rees Howells, unlimited resources could be tapped through the exercise of faith in

God, rather than through making appeals or raising funds by other means.

Rees Howells' final services were at 9am on 8th February 1950, when his ministry centred around John 11, and at 7pm when the need for the faith of God was again stressed through Mark 11:22-26 and Luke 12:27-31. He always pointed out, as did Samuel, years later, that the more accurate translation, particularly in Mark 11 should be – *faith of God*. This conveys the true meaning of the word 'faith,' which is not some nebulous feeling but a quality of God's own nature which can be appropriated through our response to Him. All the time he drew from his vast experience of proving the Lord's ability and willingness to operate in the realm of the impossible, in response to faith.

"Pray that we will be delivered tomorrow," he said, "as the delay does not put a doubt in us."

The service had concluded with the singing of *Away Over Jordan With My Blessed Jesus*, a popular chorus at that time. Those who were in the late service that night realised that the Holy Spirit was speaking through Rees Howells, and it certainly left a deep and lasting impression on everyone.

There had been several meetings taken by Rees Howells when the Holy Spirit had spoken like that before, and Samuel often referred to them while preaching himself. One had been in 1936 when, as a young man just out of university, Samuel sat transfixed in his favourite seat at the back of the room in the Sunday afternoon service. Adolf Hitler had sent his soldiers into the Rhineland and the situation in Europe looked very bleak indeed. The College had engaged in fervent prayer for several weeks to no avail. Then on that memorable afternoon of 29th March, when the crisis reached its height, Rees Howells used words the staff and students had never heard before. They certainly rang in Samuel's ears for the rest of his life.

"Prayer has failed. We are on slippery ground. Only intercession will avail. God is calling for intercessors."

It was then that they had the opportunity of entering into the realm of intercession.

Fourteen years later, several days after the final

services in February 1950, Samuel happened to be in his father's room. Rees Howells turned and said,

"Samuel, I want to speak to you and I want you to promise in the presence of the Lord that you will do two things after I have been taken."

He had never spoken like that before and those words had a shattering effect on Samuel. He knew that moment that the ministry on earth of the Founder (as Rees Howells was often known) was over. Then Rees Howells paused and just looked at Samuel with those piercing eyes of his. That experience would remain with him to the end of his life. Very solemnly, Samuel promised that he would do anything to fulfil his father's desire, despite an overwhelming sense of inadequacy.

Then Rees Howells continued,

"I want you to promise me solemnly in the name of the Lord, today, that you will carry on the leadership of this work in exactly the same way as I have done and that, in the Holy Spirit, you will become responsible for everything and that you will in no sense turn away from the principles, whatever the cost. You will be tested to the hilt as I have been but the Holy Spirit will never fail you if you stand true to Him. I am not asking you to do this because you are my son, although I know that God gave you to me and that is why I gave you back to Him, and as you know I have had no natural claim on you ever since. I believe it is God Himself who has appointed you to this work, and you will then give me your word that you will carry it on as I have done. If you do this, the Holy Spirit will be with you every step of the way."

Samuel told his father, that although he felt that he was the last person on earth to follow him as Director – and Samuel never lost that personal conviction – yet he believed that it was the Lord's will and he was prepared to accept the commission despite its enormity.

The Founder continued,

"There is one thing I want you to promise me, that you will see that the £100,000 ($160,000)

will be given away to the countries of the world as I have believed and desired to do, because the intercession for world blessing is wrapped up in that sign. You will not let it go, will you?"

Samuel reminded his father that he did not have the faith for such a large sum, nor even a much smaller one, but he promised that he would not let it go, whatever happened. With deep emotion the Founder then turned and said,

"The Lord will bless you, Samuel."

Samuel was prepared and commissioned. The days ahead were to prove very difficult, but a fresh anointing from God came upon him, evident to all in the College. The severe stammer that had coloured his public speaking for many years, disappeared overnight. His tongue was loosed and he spoke with a fluency to be admired by many an aspiring preacher.

Rees Howells' coffin in front of Derwen Fawr House 1950

Samuel did not participate in the Service of Commemoration on Thursday, 16th February 1950, when senior staff members, Dr. Kenneth Symonds and Dr.

Kingsley Priddy spoke on behalf of all those who knew Rees Howells well, and Henry Griffiths, a great friend from Llanelli, a well-known town eight miles west of Swansea, paid a fine tribute too.

The standard left for all those who would be involved in taking the work forward was expressed through Dr. Kingsley Priddy's words,

> "This man will be called great in the Kingdom of Heaven because he never compromised, he taught the standard of Jesus Christ to the full and he would not lower it, he would not pander to the flesh. He said, 'You come up to it.' I have witnessed that wonderful life. Didn't he shower his love upon us and upon the world? That burden crushed him because his love was the love of the Spirit. Didn't his joy infect us? Everyone who came in touch with him was blessed. Peace – didn't he have peace, in the darkest hours of the war, in finance, in death? Love, joy, goodness, longsuffering, meekness, temperance, they were the virtues he showed, no matter how much people came against him. He walked in the Spirit, not desiring vain glory. His life was the commandments of God, and he lived them one hundred percent."

Letters of sympathy poured in from all over the world to encourage Samuel and Mrs Howells, and all of the Bible College community. Norman Grubb, writing from the Worldwide Evangelisation Crusade in Ibambi, Belgian Congo on 14th February 1950, expressed the loss in his own inimitable way.

> Mr Howells has grown into my life these twenty years as my father in God, and he has meant all these years to me, my closest spiritual bond on earth. I can hardly imagine that he is now the other side of the veil till we all meet. If I feel my dreadful human loss, what must you feel, his intimate family in Christ on earth. I can only praise with my whole heart what the Lord has revealed to me of Himself, the Person within, through Mr Howells and the streams of blessing

these years, and I could not begin to put into words my love for him, a love which will bind us together through all eternity, but it does leave a deeply empty space here on earth which one must just accept from the Lord.
My very great love and deep bonds in Christ.
Norman.

As Samuel shared privately with staff members in later years, a fresh sense of God's presence swept over him as he stood over the open grave at Penllergaer Church graveyard and a new strength gripped hold of him.

He expressed the change that had taken place in his own life when he spoke to all the staff in the College service on 17th February from Luke 2:25-35 and Luke 23:39-43. In both passages, it was a revelation that had filled first the vision of the aged Simeon in the Temple, and second, the vision of the penitent thief on the cross. They both had a revelation of Jesus as He really was, although there was nothing outwardly to indicate it, and they were introduced to another realm. Samuel spoke with great confidence referring to the death of his father.

"Outwardly it is the greatest failure, but we (speaking about himself) have had the revelation – now it is the greatest glory. We knew we were striving all the time, but now the striving is gone. We knew we were not changed. I believe that was the greatest revelation that God gave to the thief, that the Person who was hanging there was God. There was nothing outwardly in the Saviour at that point but failure, but the thief saw that He was God. I believe this is the greatest revelation in the New Testament. Something like this has happened in these days. We have striven for fifteen years for that change (referring to Boxing Day 1934, when the Vision was given to the Founder), but we have changed this week because of the revelation. If we strove before to believe – we know it is coming today. This weekend is the most vital weekend – we have to ensure the character and position of this place. I told the Lord today that nothing is to be changed – if it is, it will be over my dead body. The work is to continue as the Leader would wish."

These were very strong words and were to be challenged on several occasions during ensuing years, but prayer, faith and intercession remained the bedrock of the ministry under Samuel's inspired, anointed ministry.

Some of the staff members of the Bible College of Wales in 1950. Back row (from left to right): Archie Jones, John Rocha, Toby Bergin, Charles Ridgers, David Rees, Leslie Lee, Geoffrey Crane, Dr. Kenneth Symonds, Rev. Ieuan Jones, Norman Madoc. Centre row (from left to right): Judy Jenkins, Jessie Harris, Judith FitzHerbert, Olwen Evans Tommy Howells (no relation), Samuel Howells, Dr. Kingsley Priddy, Valerie Sherwood, Audrey Potter, Olive Raven, Ceturah 'Kitty' Morgan, Hanns Gross. Front row (from left to right): Eva Stuart, Mary Henderson, Winifred Jones, Doris Ruscoe, Matron Roderick, Mrs Lizzie Howells, Margaret Williams, Scottie (Miss Scott), Gwladys Thomas, Dr. Joan Davies.

Chapter Two

Early Days

Samuel rarely spoke of himself or his early days spent in the mining village of Garnant, twenty miles north from Swansea at the head of the Swansea Valley. It was a straggling village with sturdy stone-walled, slate-roofed houses lining Cwmamman Road which followed the River Amman along its winding path through the valley. Travellers from Llandeilo or Ammanford to Pontardawe and Neath would pass that way, but they were few and far between. Occasionally a venturer would cross the Betws Mountain south to Morriston and Swansea, but only on a clear summer's day. That route was usually reserved for the miners working the coal deposits in the hills. Welsh anthracite coal was the best in the world in those days. Garnant was a close-knit community, used to the bleating of sheep on the nearby hills and the bleak winters when the snows came.

Before his birth on 31st August 1912, the Lord gave the name of Samuel to his parents Rees Howells and his wife Hannah (always known as Lizzie). His parents were called to Africa by the Lord, to be missionaries with the South Africa General Mission (SAGM) in 1915, so Samuel was given into the care of foster parents, Uncle Moses Rees and his wife, Elizabeth. In a letter to Samuel once, Rees Howells wrote: 'I am more indebted to them than to any people on the face of the earth.' Uncle Moses ran a general provisions and newspaper store in the village, called the Piano Stores, and the family lived over the shop. Elizabeth was head teacher of the local Primary School, Glanaman Junior, so they were provided for, and Samuel was given the very best of everything. While Mrs Rees was at school and Uncle Moses tended the store, a young lady, Miss Alice Townsend, watched over him and coached him at home until he was old enough to attend the school himself.

At times Samuel was allowed to help in the store. He would often reflect upon those sheltered days cocooned in the religious environment of the Welsh-speaking village of Garnant with its neighbouring mining communities of Brynaman and Gwaun-Cae-Gurwen (known locally as GCG), homes of his parents.

Rees and Lizzie Howells with baby Samuel 1913

Moses Rees and three-year-old Samuel Rees Howells outside Moses Rees' shop and home 1915

Life revolved around the chapels which were always full to capacity on Sundays, and the Rees family attended the Welsh Congregational Chapel next door to their store. With its lovingly polished rows of wooden pews, and steep gallery for the more agile, the chapel carried its own atmosphere of awe and respect. The 'big seat' at the front was reserved for the elders who sat facing the preacher, and turned to overlook the congregation for the singing of the hymns, which were always sung in harmony. On a raised level, usually with a railing around it, was the magnificent preaching lectern with its large-print Welsh Bible, from which the preacher or preachers would unfold the deep truths of the Scriptures. Many were very eloquent, possessing the skill of raising the pitch of their voice into a song, known as a 'hywl' (rhymes with oil). This Welsh word has its own special meaning describing the sail of a ship which has caught the full wind, as the preacher spoke with strict poetic Welsh metre in a musical, intoned and theatrical manner. It really was quite a skill.

Moses Rees' Piano Stores and Stationery, Garnant

From an early age, children memorised the Scriptures, and Sunday School included adult classes too. It has been described as a nourishing, religious upbringing. The influence of the 1904 Revival, which commenced in Loughor, only twenty miles away under the ministry of Evan Roberts, was still strong. In later years, Evan would visit Rees Howells at the College on a friendly basis.

Samuel's childhood memories of several special incidents, gleaned from reliable sources, help to paint the picture of a young man curious to investigate all that life had to offer his generation. On one occasion, Samuel was refused permission by Mr and Mrs Rees, his foster parents, to view a film at a local hall. The cinematograph was the up-and-coming form of entertainment, especially for a rural Welsh village. What a temptation! When Samuel was not to be found at home that day as usual, Moses Rees marched straight down and hauled the young offender out of the building and back home, suitably reprimanded. This was possibly the last time that Samuel would ever visit a 'cinema' in his life. A similar tale tells of smoke rising from cracks in the garden shed, inviting an investigation, only to reveal a young man experimenting with a pipe, but who can separate fact from fiction?!

There was one story which he recounted on more than one occasion, that of the 'killing of the pig' in the village, witnessed by some of the children. It had a profound effect upon this sensitive young man, as every stage of the gory tale was recounted in detail, which may explain why Samuel always refused to eat bacon or pork to the end of his life. It was actually a custom for families in Wales to fatten up two pigs during the year, and Glanaman was obviously no exception. One pig was for Christmas, its offal being made into faggots which were shared with neighbours. The second was to pay off any debts which had accrued during the year.

At the bottom of the garden and up the embankment ran the local railway line, and Samuel could vaguely recall being asked to wave to his parents on 10th July 1915, just before his third birthday, as the train puffed its way along the track, taking them to Llanelli, on their journey to Southern Africa to become missionaries.

They had left Garnant having bought tickets only as far as Llanelli, the Lord not having at that point supplied the full fare to London. In Llanelli and still without the money, Rees and Hannah his wife joined the queue – a real test of obedience and faith, rewarded by a last minute deliverance from one of the singing crowd who had gathered to see them off. This was not an act of bravado to be copied but emerged from their experience of the faithfulness of God gained through a walk of complete dependence on His promises over several years. Before they left the station on their journey to London and beyond, they were showered with further gifts at Llanelli, enough to cover their expenses for the whole trip. They sent postcards to Samuel regularly on their journey, one of the steam ship *Walmer Castle*. They had been able to assure the captain of a safe passage through U-boat infested waters because God was taking them to Africa to serve Him.

That it cost them dearly to take this step is reflected in an article headed 'Little Samuel' published in a SAGM missionary magazine called *Diamonds from South Africa* in 1915.

> We want the children who read *Diamonds* to follow us in thought and prayer to Gazaland. We want them also to pray for our little boy Samuel, who has been left behind in Wales. There is a very interesting story about little Samuel. The very month he was born we were called to Africa. We prayed to the Lord for a name and He led us to call him Samuel, after the Samuel of old. As Hannah dedicated her little boy Samuel so did we ours, with very little thought at the time that the Lord would call us to give him altogether back to Him, just as Hannah did her child. Months passed and we loved Samuel more daily, such a nice little boy he was, who always made the home happy. But one day the Lord said, as He did to Abraham, "I want thy son whom thou lovest." He showed us that He wanted us to go to South Africa (the south of the continent of Africa) and leave little Samuel at home. We remembered how God

had given His only begotten Son for us and that the Son gave His life. We then prayed that the Lord would open up a home for Samuel and He answered our prayer, and because of that answer we feel that we shall have the 'hundredfold,' and that we can claim the promise in Matthew 19:29 and expect from the Lord deliverance for many little African boys and girls, because we obeyed His word. Now we ask you to pray that the Lord will lead little Samuel to walk in the footsteps of the one after whom he is named, and that he shall some day be a prophet of the Lord.
Rees Howells.

It was a painful wrench for Rees and Hannah Howells, to leave their two-year-old son in Wales as evidenced by a number of poignant postcards. Each had its love expressed, which Mrs Elizabeth Rees will have read out carefully to her young charge and talked about the typically African pictures on each card. One dated the 5 August 1915 reads:

Dear Howell,
This is just a card to greet you on your third birthday (31st August). We have sent you a little present from Durban. Hope it will arrive in time... Rees and Lizzie

A series of postcards were sent to Samuel in 1918 on the 15th, 18th and 27th July, also from Durban, South Africa. One from the following month, 16th August 1918, reads:

My dear little Howell,
I just remembered that your birthday is this month. I hope you will have a nice day and lots of cakes. What do you think of the lovely picture? (Boksbury Lake, Johannesburg). Wouldn't it be nice if you could spend your holiday here. How is Uncle Joe and all at Pentwyn?
With best love to all, from Nana (Lizzie).

All these cards were treasured memories for Samuel all his life as he, too, felt the enormous pain of this costly obedience by his parents. Out of it, of course, were to emerge waves of revival blessing in Southern Africa wherever they were to minister.

Samuel Rees Howells age four, 1916

These deep wishes for Samuel were to be fulfilled one day, but there is always the price of obedience to pay. In some ways, he was kept in isolation from the mainstream village youth. He was re-named Samuel Rees, home schooled by Elizabeth Rees, the headmistress, with the assistance of Alice, then sent to the local village school. There were the good days at school and the not so good – days of boyish fun and days of tears, ink blots on his exercise book, playtimes missed for work not completed, class lectures from the teacher, hands on heads and, in Samuel's case, every misdemeanour relayed to Elizabeth, followed by the inevitable lecture at home and early to bed! Samuel always seemed to empathise with young school boys – and with a smile!

Samuel Rees Howells with his cousin c.1918

In this predominantly Welsh environment, where even many adults struggled to express themselves easily in

English, school life too was filled with the rich sounds of this beautiful language. Samuel was very fluent and revelled in the traditions and stories handed down from his forefathers. Gone were the days of the 'Welsh Not,' a small wooden pendant inscribed 'WN' (meaning Welsh not, English to be spoken), hung round the neck of any child heard speaking Welsh in the classroom or playground. The Welsh called it 'cwstom' meaning Welsh stick. At the end of the school day, the unfortunate victim wearing the pendant was thrashed before going home. This naturally engendered intense bitterness throughout the ensuing years. Of course, there were the romantic tales like Twm Sion Cati, the sixteenth century Welsh Robin Hood whose daring exploits brought him much fame. Then there was the collection of Welsh folk lore enshrined in the *Mabinogion* manuscripts. All was eclipsed by the extensive knowledge of the Bible, which the children received at school, Sunday School, as well as at home, and an awareness of the rich spiritual heritage gained through revival movements in Wales.

Samuel Rees Howells at school in Garnant c.1919

Of all the stories that Samuel loved the most, to which he occasionally referred later in his life, was that of Mary Jones from the little-known village of Llanfihangel, tucked away in the shadows of Cader Idris Mountain in North Wales. She was born in 1784 to poor parents, her father, Jacob, being a weaver who was assisted by his wife, Mary

(Molly to distinguish her from her daughter). They earned just enough to survive, helped by young Mary, who looked after their few hens and some bees. None in the humble household could read. When a school was opened two miles away in the village of Abergynolwyn, Mary was given the opportunity to attend, rising early to complete her work and walking barefoot each day to her lessons. She had been promised that she could read neighbouring Farmer Evans' Bible once she mastered the art of reading. That dream was finally fulfilled, but the next was more difficult – to own her own Bible. Six years of working hard and saving every farthing and halfpenny earned, ended with a triumphant twenty-five mile walk across the mountains – shoes hanging over her shoulders – to Bala, where Thomas Charles stocked Bibles for sale. There were none. Mary's violent sobbing deeply moved Thomas Charles to give one copy, earmarked for someone else, to Mary, before she returned cross-country to her home. It was that moving incident which led Thomas Charles to form the British and Foreign Bible Society, internationally acclaimed as a leading promoter of the Bible. This moving story obviously captured young Samuel's imagination and fuelled his passion to support all those involved in the printing and distribution of Scriptures throughout the world.

Samuel was then transferred to Miss Pinkham's school in Oystermouth, just outside Swansea, perhaps to hone his English, and later to Greggs' private preparatory school in Uplands, Swansea. This seemed rather an intense regime as Samuel prepared for Matriculation (the school-leaving exam), and could help to explain the shyness and limp handshake by which many remember him. Yet Samuel remained a keen student, able to busy himself in books. His exercise books were kept neatly, a product of those stiff training days at home, and he developed an even, well-connected cursive style of handwriting with distinct tall, slender loops. Graphologists would certainly place significance on this and recognise a young man eager to reach spiritual heights.[1]

At weekends, he took the train home to Garnant – as he was still living with his foster parents – and escaped into his beloved hills. Samuel had opened his heart to the Lord as his Saviour at the age of twelve, while listening to an open-air service conducted by the Salvation Army in their village every Sunday, and he attended all the chapel services with fresh understanding of the rich ministry each Sunday. During the week he slept in Glynderwen House, Swansea, a newly-acquired eight-acre estate, once owned by Sir Charles Eden, uncle of the British Prime Minister Sir Anthony Eden, overlooking Swansea Bay at Blackpill, where his parents, Rees and Lizzie Howells, had opened the Bible College of Wales in 1924. Although just a twelve-year-old lad at the time, the events leading up to its purchase – an impressive victory of faith told more fully later in this book – were carefully related to him by Moses and Elizabeth Rees.

Glynderwen House – where Samuel stayed during weekdays (Opening day of the Bible College of Wales 1924)

Samuel rather liked this imposing mansion, set in a commanding position. He was given a large bedroom facing the sea and was made to feel very special as he glided down the main stairs onto the polished parquetry floor of the hall below.

The rooms were spacious, a number with French windows opening out to the lawns and flowerbeds, and a steep grassed slope with several magnificent trees. Beyond was the Cwm Stream which ran through the grounds to the sea. It took some time for Samuel to get used to his first taste of communal living, as he mingled with the first batch of Bible College students and found a space in the bathroom for his cold early morning wash. The clatter of wooden chairs on the wooden dining room floor, a vast expanse it seemed too, disturbed him a little. He was encouraged to help with the washing-up (cleaning the dishes) afterwards in the tiled kitchen. Gradually he felt more at home and discovered the wine cellar, accessed through a trap door, used then only by the cooks for storing apples and vegetables. The curiosity of this intelligent but shy young man knew no bounds as he investigated every corner and, in later years, he could always discuss with people matters relating to Glynderwen House with considerable insight. He soon earned the affection of everyone else in residence. However, Glanaman was Samuel's home.[2]

Glynderwen House (left) with ivy removed and El-Shaddai Building (right) c.1935

It was often with a sigh of relief that Samuel was able to step out of the train at the little station at Glanaman each Friday. He would time himself as he strode down the slope and over the railway crossing and into his familiar territory once more.

The influence of those foundational days spent in the Bible College would strengthen Samuel in the 1950s, as he was now carrying the yoke of responsibility for the whole College himself, and for furthering the work of the Gospel worldwide in whatever way he could.

At a tender age, God challenged Samuel to set aside his personal ambition of becoming a doctor to go as a medical missionary, which Moses and Elizabeth Rees would have loved. In the early 1930s, he made preparations, with much persuasion it seems, to take on the challenge of gaining an Oxford University degree in Theology. Having known Samuel for so many years later on in his life, the author realises that this giant step of faith would not have been taken without much trepidation, certainly much prayer. However, on Tuesday, 27th March 1934, he slipped a letter into the post box and was pleasantly surprised to receive a prompt reply from Wolsey Hall dated 29th March. Enclosed also was a complete prospectus of all courses, with instructions to peruse pages 45 to 51 covering the theological courses offered. There was an enrolment form with the added incentive of a free 40th Anniversary Gift of a mottled brown fountain pen specially made for Wolsey Hall by a well-known London firm. This offer was made solely to each student who enrolled with the College in 1934.

The courses of study selected were General Church History (70-451 AD), English Church History up to 1714, the Philosophy of Religion and Comparative Religions; quite a formidable challenge. A list of textbooks recommended was received, most of which will have been either discovered in the second-hand bookshops or found in university libraries. Samuel too was opting for tuition offered by Wolsey Hall for the princely sum of £6. 6s. 6d, for sixty lessons![3]

Final acceptance was received, enabling Samuel to go to Oxford, with its dreaming spires, domes and weatherworn towers, as an external student living with Herbert Lambourne and his wife, a gentle couple who were very kind and understanding. Herbert Lambourne actually worked at Brasenose College, Oxford, and won respect by his unashamed loyalty to Christ. "This is my department, sir, and we don't have bad language here," he once told a student. On hearing of Herbert's death in 1949, Samuel wrote a letter of sympathy to his family, remarking on all the kindness and encouragement the Lambournes had shown to this young stranger from Wales in the 1930s. A letter of thanks in reply mentions a victorious funeral service.

Now in accepting a place to study at Oxford, this was quite a challenge for one who, even at that stage in his spiritual life, was learning to trust the Lord for his day-to-day expenses. In their preliminary remarks, Wolsey Hall offered advice to their prospective students, including the following, which Samuel must have mused over often:

> It is essential that the student should not only know his subject, but be able to set down his knowledge in a clear and orderly fashion, and this cannot be done without much practice. Also, you have no need to worry about the syllabus, the lessons cover that. Your success depends on strength of will and persistence.

Samuel worked diligently at his studies and received regular letters of encouragement from Elizabeth Rees, whom he knew as 'Mam.' Lizzie Hannah Howells (his mother) was referred to as 'Nana.'

> Dear Howell, Lizzie wrote to Samuel during his examination period: It was nice to have your letter this morning with all the good news, especially that you are getting on with your good work. We hope you will keep well until the ordeal is over.

The following note reads:

> Be brave tomorrow morning, don't mind the examination and keep your wits about you. Hope to see you soon and trust you will get what you want.

Another week passed and it is evident that Samuel had not forgotten to keep in touch with his Glanaman foster parents. Mam writes once more:

> We are glad to have your postcards and to know that you have got over the papers, whatever the result. It does not matter how it turns out, you have worked hard and done your best. Keep a good heart tomorrow morning and don't mind whatever happens. It will all come

right in the end.

Samuel received letters of encouragement from his father, Rees Howells, and from his friends at the College. They all sought to whet his appetite to return as soon as possible to the spiritual atmosphere and prayer meetings at the College.

22nd October 1936
My dear Samuel,
Delighted with your letter yesterday. Yes, the place of intercession over the Treasury has been gained; in a moment the Lord can command the donors to give way, as He commanded the widow woman to sustain Elijah, (1 Kings 17:7-16). I am getting wonderful times with the Lord in the mornings. It's like old times when I had no care in the world. The meetings are as good as ever.
Cofion goreu (Best regards). Rees.

10th November 1936
My dear Samuel,
We are having wonderful times. We are still gazing at the intercession over the Treasury. When you think, after climbing up for two years, putting it all at the feet of the Master, and I am sure it will all come back on its hundredfold. Every step has been walked so well, first the Vision of Every Creature, then the Every Creature Conference. We have great longings to build colleges in these different countries, or to help those who are building them. It seems that the world has become our parish in a day, there is such a scope in the Vision.... At the College here they are all in good form, fighting to the man. They are wonderful people and they revel in the intercession.
Cofion goreu. Rees.

Staying at the Bible College during that period was a dear lady, Mrs Charles Cowman who, with her husband, had founded the Oriental Missionary Society in 1901, that great Missionary organisation of the twentieth century, out of which was birthed World Gospel Crusades in 1949. One of her most well known books is the daily devotional, *Streams in the Desert*. Samuel had been deeply impressed by her ministry and her thoughts on prayer, which he found most encouraging during his challenging days in Oxford.

Mrs Cowman herself was quite a creative person and Rees refers to her in a letter to Samuel in Oxford. In it, he mentions a meeting when she produced national flags from different Northern European countries for which she felt Rees should take responsibility in deep intercessory prayer. Quite a challenge for one who had to stand up in the meeting each time a new flag was produced! Of course, being responsible for something in Rees' vocabulary meant a financial implication for which he was willing. Samuel appreciated the sentiments and must have smiled when he read it.

> The best scene of all was that I had to stand up while she was presenting me with the flag, just as you have seen some of the officers do when they present a flag of their regiment to the king. The first was the flag of Finland and a Bible which had written inside, "We have been captured by the Vision and we are ready to put a Bible in every home in Finland." Then she spoke about Estonia and I was called to stand up again and go through the same ordeal. The third and fourth flags came, so before the end she made me responsible for seven countries. It was a wonderful scene so then I saw why the Lord had called me to give back the £10,000 ($16,000) to Him because it is no use sending envoys to countries unless we are able to follow the work on. We saw last evening what the Lord is going to do.

Usually these treasured letters and postcards, which Samuel kept all his life, included family news or amusing incidents, reflecting the wonderful sense of humour which he was to inherit. Rees Howells had established many close friendships with Christian leaders and missionaries working all over the world, as letters from La Maréchele, the notable evangelist to France indicate.[4] Samuel was acquainted with them all so he was already very knowledgeable of worldwide missionary endeavours. This would build an excellent platform for his future ministry.

Samuel graduated in theology in 1936. With limited financial resources, he had lived carefully, and followed his usual disciplined regime that included a very simple diet. The prophet Daniel and his three young friends in Babylon, Shadrach, Meshach and Abednego – could well have inspired him to do this. Although he became very fond of the ancient city, steeped in its classical traditions, and paused often by the stone cross near Martyrs' Memorial in Broad Street, Oxford, and checked his watch tucked away in his waistcoat pocket regularly with the chimes of College clocks, Samuel experienced what is understood by every true Welshman – 'hiraeth' – his longing for home. Homesickness for the hills of Wales became very real in that cloistered academic upper-crust environment, but the Lord took him through. He sometimes spoke of times when his fundamentalist beliefs were questioned by his Oxford tutors in what was a generally liberal atmosphere. Both his natural parents and his foster parents were very proud of his academic success.

It is evident from correspondence that Moses and Elizabeth Rees were having a bungalow built at Twyn y Mynydd, on a parcel of ground near the home of Uncle Dick. Uncle Dick was Rees Howells' invalid uncle, who lived in a stone walled cottage called Pentwyn on the side of the Black Mountain overlooking Garnant. Samuel often referred to Uncle Dick, with whom his father had great fellowship during his years of preparation in the school of intercession. Uncle Dick had surrendered his whole life and body to the Holy Spirit and knew the consequent infilling that resulted as the new Master took control of his life. Samuel often remarked that very few really make that degree of surrender. It was no surprise that on Whit-Sunday 1910 the Holy Spirit had completely healed Uncle Dick, following a word from the Lord given through Rees Howells as to the exact date when the miracle would take place. It proved a real test of faith in the power of the spoken word of God in a given situation, and the resulting miracle strengthened the testimony in the district from then on. God was at work.

Samuel's first property, Twyn y Mynydd (there was no loft / attic conversion when Samuel owned the property)

So, for Samuel to have a bungalow prepared for him was a wonderful provision.

> It will be nice when it is finished (Elizabeth Rees wrote to Samuel) but we are in no hurry. I think it will be a good place for you; the air is better and it is an easier sort of place to be in; but of course we like this because we are used to it.

The Rees family were making provision for Samuel and this newly-built bungalow overlooking the valley was to become his home for the future. Samuel eventually placed it on the altar and the proceeds were used for the Kingdom. It was a further leading from God that he then joined the staff of the Bible College – lecturing in New Testament, Church History and Greek, caring for men students and acting as Assistant Director. Those who sat in his lectures remember him as a gentle encourager, with a keen sense of humour which helped to lift everyone when they were flagging during afternoon sessions. They will also remember his open style of questions set in examination papers.

> The Life of Christ. Examination
> Wednesday afternoon
> Time: 1½ hours
> Answer any three questions.
> 1. Write notes on all of the following:
>   a) The Presentation in the Temple.
>   b) The Flight into Egypt.
>   c) Nazareth.
>   d) Herod Antipas.
> 2. Give an account of our Lord's Baptism and Temptations.
> 3. Discuss the significance of these two great events in our Lord's life.
> 4. What do you know about the opening stages of our Lord's Galilean ministry?
> 5. Give the context of all the following passages and explain.
>   a) *And he shall go before Him in the spirit and power of Elias.*
>   b) *My Father worketh hitherto, and I work.*
>   c) *And all that heard Him were astonished at His understanding and answers.*
>   d) *Go thy way, show thyself to the priest.*

(The author hopes his readers could manage that one in style!).

Samuel's clear teaching style certainly characterised his ministry during the prayer meetings, when anointed exposition of the Scriptures always laid a solid foundation for purposeful prayer.

These were certainly early days, and Samuel was conscious of the great challenges that lay ahead, particularly for the generation of young men and women of which he was part, to live solely for the great Vision to reach every nation with the Gospel. In the intense spiritual environment of faith and prayer in which he was being reared at the College under Rees Howells' ministry, he was ready to play his part. It had been a good beginning, if not rugged at times, so he was full of confidence that the Holy Spirit would lead them all through to a glorious victory, but spiritual victories are not gained without much travail and intense conflict as the young generation were about to discover.

> *Put on the full armour of God so that you can take your stand against the devil's schemes. For our struggle is not against flesh and blood, but against the rulers, against the authorities, against the powers of this dark world and against the spiritual forces of evil in the heavenly realms.* Ephesians 6:11-12.

Samuel Howells as a lecturer c.1946

Chapter Three

War in Europe

As with everyone else throughout the country, Samuel's life was rudely interrupted and shaped for the remainder of his years by the declaration of war on 3rd September 1939. This came to be known as World War II. Everyone at the College had huddled round a wireless (radio) as Neville Chamberlain spelt out those fateful words to the British people, that a state of war existed between their nation and Germany, following the German invasion of Poland.

No one in the College anticipated that events would go so far in Europe, and this is referred to in greater detail later in our narrative, but the facts were real and everyone, including Samuel, had to face what it would mean to them personally.

Immediately, identity cards were issued and the male population required to register for military service, which would be mandatory for certain age groups. For Samuel and others at the College the age-old ethical question of whether or not it was right to carry arms in the military service had to be considered very seriously. Anyone who had personal objections had to present themselves to a tribunal in the Civic Centre, Swansea. Samuel's case, as a minister of religion, with his pastoral responsibilities at the College and preaching ministry in the locality, was accepted, although he remained diligent in his fire watching duties and in the disciplines which Rees Howells imposed upon any who remained in the College throughout the ensuing years. These included no holidays or going home, except for compassionate reasons, and accepting a very austere lifestyle. It was rigorous!

The College staff were redeployed in other ways during the war. Some were members of the National Fire Service, others were drafted into the Forestry Commission to act as lumberjacks at the Penllergaer Estate which had been acquired by Rees Howells in late 1938. The vast estate was originally the home of John Llewellyn whose daughter, Mary, married Lewis Weston Dillwyn in 1807. Their son, John Dillwyn Llewellyn, a renowned photographer of his time, undertook an extensive restoration project on the mansion and grounds, and had married Emma Thomasina Talbot. It was their second son, Sir John Talbot Dillwyn Llewellyn, who carved his name into the fabric of Swansea's history. An archaeologist[1] and founder member of both the Glamorgan Cricket Club and the Welsh Rugby Union in 1885. Sir John was voted Mayor of Swansea in 1891 and Honourable Member of Parliament from 1895 to 1900. When he died at Penllergaer House in 1927 at the age of 81, the Dillwyn Llewellyn family chose not to use it as a family home. Apart from assisting to accommodate refugees during the Spanish Civil War, it fell into disrepair.

Penllergaer Mansion (the Big House) 1939

College staff also served in non-combatant roles in the armed services during the war, as paramedics or in bomb disposal units. At least one was drafted into the Secret Service with its underground base somewhere in the Gower, ready to operate in case of invasion.

The ladies, too, were all involved in serving in one way or another. Several performed vital roles in the Military Services. Others served as nurses at Madame Patti's home, converted to Craig y Nos TB Sanatorium, near Ystradgynlais in the Swansea Valley, or taught in Emmanuel School, or helped with cooking, cleaning and fire watching. By 1943, ninety percent of Britain's single women were at work! Emmanuel School had been opened by Rees Howells in September 1933, originally as the Bible College School. It provided a home and education for children of missionaries and home workers, and by the advent of the war it had opened its doors to day children.

Gradually the effects of the war impinged on daily life. Food rationing for butter, bananas and sugar was introduced in January 1940, and later extended to tea, margarine, lard and cheese with ration books issued, while each person received sixty-six clothing coupons per year. The ladies in the College became experts with Singer sewing machines, while the cooks contrived a variety of meals with the National dried milk, reconstituted eggs and tins of Fray Bentos prepared beef, flavoured with Oxo cubes and Daddies' sauce! An interesting wartime statistic was that the nation's health greatly benefited from the quantity of fresh vegetables consumed each day. Allotments sprang up all over the country, and the College found its enclosed kitchen garden very useful.

Around Swansea, deprived of its street signs for security reasons, new posters appeared such as 'Dig For Victory,' 'Is Your Journey Really Necessary?' and 'Walls Have Ears.' The most common, of course, was the Morse code sign 'dot-dot-dot-dash V for Victory,' which was sounded out over the wireless (a radio) to send coded messages to the Underground Movement operating on the Continent. The soothing strains of Vera Lynn's voice with 'We'll meet again,' or the lively strains of the bubbly Gracie Fields, frequently wafted over distant loudspeakers. Many music hall stars including Arthur Askey and George Formby, toured the battlefields, seeking to raise the morale of the Allied troops around the world.

Unless a person has actually lived through a war it is difficult to convey the sense of apprehension and uncertainty that it instils, but gradually the nation adjusted and bonded together, exhibiting its characteristic quiet determination to see the war through, whatever it meant.

The stark realities of what war really would mean soon came much closer to Swansea, after the regulation 7pm blackout clothed the town in comparative darkness on the night of 27th June 1940, when the chilling wail of sirens filled the still air. This was to be the first of forty-four bombing raids by the German Air Force, the Luftwaffe, including six blitz type attacks.

The worst of these lasted for three long nights of concentrated bombing, as Hitler turned his targets away from blitzed London to cities and ports around Britain. The menacing drone of the Dornier Do 172 and Heinkel 111 engines, a characteristic of German bombers, approached Swansea Bay. The planes were picked up by a searchlight battery on St. Helen's Rugby Ground. The concentrated barrage of anti-aircraft (ack-ack) guns around the Bay shattered the whole air. Soon the sky was ablaze with light, as shells from the 3.7 inch QF (quick firing) gun burst around the aircraft and tracers guided crews in search of planes. There is still a 3.7 QF gun mounted by the bridge crossing the River Tawe as a tribute to all those who defended Swansea during those bitter days.

The first of the German parachute flares then descended over strategic targets to assist the aircrews. Showers of incendiary devices and deadly high-explosive bombs brought devastation on the town below. In this prolonged fourteen hours of assault on Swansea, 1,273 high explosive bombs and 56,000 incendiaries rained down on the centre of town, killing 203 people and injuring 409 others. There was widespread damage to property.

Samuel spent those three nights in prayer while on fire watch duty on the veranda of Derwen Fawr House.

"There was no time for sleep," he once said in private, "when people's lives were in mortal danger."

Derwen Fawr House has an interesting history. It was once one of the large Victorian-style properties, owned by the local gentry, which were features of West Swansea, in what was then rich countryside. The original property on the site, one of several in what was known as Lower Sketty Farm (Sketty Isha), was called Waun Kysha and belonged to Sir Francis Holbourne in the eighteenth century, and then to the Rosser family. Later, it was purchased by Charles Henry Smith, a Llansamlet colliery owner and squire of Gwernllwynchwydd (pronounced Gwernlwinkwith). It stood on both sides of a re-routed tree-lined lane, known as Bryn Road, which wound its way from Blackpill up to Sketty Green, bypassing magnificent Sketty Park, built by Sir John Morris of Clasemont. He was the son of the renowned industrialist, Robert Morris, after whom the village (now town) of Morriston was named. Sir John Morris developed Swansea's famous copper-smelting and brass-wire mill industries.

Rees and Lizzie Howells on the lawn in front of Derwen Fawr House, Derwen Fawr Estate c.1935

The main building had been named Hendderwen (the old oak tree) in 1808, after the venerable oak tree, the girth of which was reputed to be 31 feet, 10 inches (9.7 metres). Charles Henry Smith built himself a splendid new mansion on the south side of Bryn Road, with land in front stretching down to the sea, and renamed it Derwen Fawr Road. The farm across the road was rebuilt and named Sketty Isha; its house was called Sketty Isaf. The 17 acre Derwen Fawr

Estate eventually passed into the hands of Sir Charles Ruthen, Director of Housing for the Ministry of Health, and Samuel's father had bought it for £3,000 ($4,800) in 1934.

Sketty House, on the Sketty Isaf Estate. View is of the front of the House, however it was used as the back entrance

Back to the war years. On the fields and sand dunes below the College were batteries of 3.7 inch QFs and the larger 4.5 inch guns, not so effective because of their longer range but nevertheless very menacing. The whole earth trembled and the air was filled with the smell of cordite from the spent cartridges. War had certainly reached Swansea. There was widespread devastation to at least eight of the town centre's main streets before the escaping aircraft scurried off down the Bristol Channel to their bases in France. Swansea suffered more air attacks than any other port of Wales.

Rees Howells had been exercised to believe for complete protection for the properties that he was responsible for, so that people from Swansea sought refuge in the College classrooms overnight, and they were all welcome. A deep sense of peace descended over the College and in the prayer meetings taken by Rees Howells some of the greatest revelations were given concerning these last days. No air raid shelters were built in the grounds of Derwen Fawr, not even the Anderson shelters which families sank into their gardens, covering them with twenty inches of soil.[2]

As Samuel walked silently with his father through the rubble past the old gutted market in Oxford Street, after the bombing, both men were moved to their depths, and renewed their determination to give everything in their cooperation with the Holy Spirit in the intercessions the Lord had laid upon the staff remaining in the College.

Sketty House. View is of the back of the House (with its spacious lawn), however it was known as the 'front' as students and staff entered the House through the 'tradesmen' entrance, along a stone hallway and up a narrow 'servants' stairway onto the first floor.

One great lesson which Samuel learnt during those dark and austere days of the war, was that of careful use of money which the Lord had entrusted to him. He often received much criticism for what seemed like a short-sighted view. Having lived through many winters without heating in his room, his philosophy was to wear adequate warm clothing, which he revelled in even during the summer months, but any waste of water and electricity was anathema to him.[3] This policy did 'ruffle a few feathers' in some staff and visitors, but Samuel could cope with that. He once shared privately,

"Some people have called me stubborn, but I am stubborn for the Kingdom."

In short, in modern terms, "Tough!"

One particular story which found the pages of the *London Gazette* and caught Samuel's attention was an award of the George Medal made to a Swansea Air Raid Precaution (ARP) messenger. His devotion to duty epitomised the valour of the men and women living in Swansea during those raids, and reflected another side to Samuel's own character in the face of overwhelming odds which he would face when he eventually became Director of the Bible College. The messenger, William Joseph Jenkins, was instructed to take a message to the Control Room, a distance of about three miles. Avoiding falling debris and burst gas mains, he got to within three quarters of a mile of the Control Room. Then he was thrown off his motorbike by falling bricks. Temporarily dazed, he remounted, was blown off his machine by a bomb and rendered unconscious. When he recovered he insisted on continuing and, despite being blown off his machine again, finished the remainder of the journey, about half a mile, although his tyres had been burst by the explosions. Jenkins later returned to his post for further duty.

No wonder Winston Churchill, on a surprise visit to Swansea on 11th April 1941, was able to reply to a Swansea newspaper reporter of the *Evening Post*, who asked if he had any message for the town, "There is a grand spirit in the town. It is standing up to it well. It will be a long pull but we will get there in the end." Later, in the Mayor's parlour, he commented that he was very appreciative of the tremendous spirit of the people of 'battered Swansea,' their patience and their willingness to play their part. On several occasions during the war, Winston Churchill was sent letters of faith and encouragement from Rees Howells. They included mention of the unceasing prayers being offered at the College for the final victory over Adolf Hitler and the Nazi regime.

Samuel's own determination to fight through was sensed in his slow and deliberate reading of Philippians 3:13-14 one day.

> *Brothers, I do not consider myself yet to have taken hold of it* (been made perfect). *But one thing I do: Forgetting what is behind and*

straining towards what is ahead, I press on towards the mark for the prize of the high calling of God in Christ Jesus.

The final air raid on Swansea occurred in 1943, when twenty planes from Unit KG2 of the German Air Force launched a surprise attack on the town centre. By then, bombs had become even more lethal and included their 'Sprengbrade' (firebombs), and one exploded on the entrance of Swansea Hospital, killing thirty-four patients and staff. After that Hitler unleashed his venom on Britain through his V1 (Doodlebugs!) and V2 rockets but, by then, his grip in the war was weakening.

Throughout the war years uninterrupted prayer was maintained at the College, as the Holy Spirit fought spiritual battles one after another through the bodies which had been consecrated for that purpose during the 1930s, and Samuel was totally involved. It shaped and sharpened his ministry, and aspects of that process will be mentioned later on in the book.

Mount Pleasant Baptist Church (right) on the Kingsway, Swansea city centre after a blitz in 1942. This Church is approximately three miles from the Bible College of Wales and is still a house of worship. A Wesley Chapel in College Street was destroyed on the 21st Feb. 1941 (its basement had been used as a bomb shelter for around one hundred people). St. Mary's Church of England on St Marys Street was also destroyed, in Feb. 1941, but rebuilt in 1959.

Chapter Four

The Venture Begins

The deep spiritual experiences of World War II, when Rees Howells led the staff through those years of intercession, strengthened Samuel often during his later intercessory battles. Rees Howells had been a real role model for Samuel in his future ministry.

Pondering the past silent years in his own spiritual journey, and feeling this overwhelming sense of personal inadequacy, Samuel was greatly encouraged by the knowledge that he had the support of a team of staff members who had walked the pathway of the cross through those dark war years and who had also learnt the principles of faith and prayer. They too had given their lives for the Vision for world blessing and the fulfilment of the Great Commission of Matthew 28:19-20.

Jesus said, *"Therefore go and make disciples of all nations, baptising them in the name of the Father and of the Son and of the Holy Spirit, and teaching them to obey everything I have commanded you. And surely I am with you always, to the very end of the age."*

It was his regular practice, during his early years as Honorary Director, to visit each member of staff personally for a discussion about their work and to encourage them, often slipping into their hands some pound notes tucked in the top pocket of his suit. That pocket seemed to be a never-ending gold mine to those looking to God for every penny to meet their personal needs. These were his loyal friends and he cared for them in the Lord. During the winter months, especially as he was older, personal chats were confined to his room at prearranged times when his bright searching eyes were focused on his visitor.

One immediate and distinct evidence of God's hand resting upon the new spiritual leader of the Bible College, now still only thirty-eight years old, was that in the pulpit with a complete command of English, Samuel spoke with quiet authority and displayed a deep understanding of the Scriptures. A cameo picture of Samuel in those early days at the College is provided by a former student and one-time staff member, who died in Texas in 2007 – George Oakes. George became one of Samuel's close friends and visited the College regularly through the years.

Having received a call to foreign missions, I was led to the Bible College of Wales in Swansea in 1936. The morning and evening meetings were directed by Mr Rees Howells and attended by staff and students. During his messages, the Director (also known as the Founder or Leader) would often mention Samuel, his son, who was studying at Oxford University. During vacations, Samuel visited the College and we were delighted to make his acquaintance. Samuel was very reserved and soft spoken. After completing his MA degree at Oxford he returned to the College and became part of the teaching staff. I remember even the tone of his voice in his first lecture in New Testament Greek.

During my second year as a student, my mother passed away and I was at home in Liverpool for a month. On my return, I was frequently asked to drive the College car for Mr and Mrs Howells. I became closely acquainted with Samuel through this contact, and began to recognise his tenderness and grace, his spirituality and attitude impressing me. He had lived a very sheltered life in the home of his adopted aunt and uncle while his parents were missionaries. Life in the College was different as he was involved with staff and students, and with the responsibilities of lecturing.

Samuel became almost like a brother to me, and this work-relationship was a blessed experience. We often joked about things as he showed his humorous side. He was eighteen months older than I was but I would tell him that one day I would catch up with him! We had great times visiting the family or taking visitors on tours. The declaration of war against Germany in 1939 became a tremendous challenge to us all, and the College became a spiritual battleground as we spent days in prayer on our knees.

The death of Rees Howells in February 1950 was a tremendous shock, and I will never forget the meeting Samuel called to give us the news, and challenge us to unite together to carry on the work of the College, and the Vision to reach the world with the Gospel. He must have faced the future with fear and trembling but was in constant communion with God, and from that time forward he carried the burden of the world and of the College. At the pulpit, Samuel spoke with authority and power and became bold and forceful in his preaching.

In 1951 I was called to Brazil to work as a missionary. In Language School I met Charlene and we were led of the Lord to unite our lives in marriage. On our first furlough we stayed in the College with our son, Philip. I remember Samuel *romping around with him (*to play boisterously). He loved children. We admired him and enjoyed fellowship and prayer together. Samuel had a very sweet nature and had a passion and love for the Lord and His people, and his vision was worldwide. I have felt the loss of this great man of God.

Throughout his lifetime, Samuel perfected his style of public speaking, never hurried, and with a careful choice of descriptive vocabulary. He would advise nervous preachers to realise they were speaking to individuals only, assuring them that he would pray for them. He prayed for everyone, friend or foe.

The College services had been held in a number of rooms during the years, but Samuel preferred what was to be called the 'prayer room' in Derwen Fawr House. It was also used as a dining room each day, so there was a well rehearsed drill before each morning and evening service, to move long wooden dining tables and arrange chairs. Sunday services were held in the Conference Hall, an elongated red corrugated-roofed building in the College grounds, with a speakers' platform at one end and a gold lettered text 'All One In Christ Jesus' overhead.

Aerial view from the 1950s of Derwen Fawr House (middle) and spacious lawns. Across the road is Sketty Isaf House. Houses have since been built on the top left field whilst bungalows have been built on the bottom far right field.

Central heating systems in the College relied on coal-fired boilers, stoked by students by night and day. To run a boiler efficiently required considerable skill, not always easily acquired. A boiler burning too quickly produced clinker so that the water tank never heated the circulating water. Winter prayer meetings, even in the prayer room, often saw the congregation wearing overcoats and wrapped in scarves. In later years when more efficient radiators were installed, trapped air in the system produced similar results.

Congregations always went down on their knees on the

bare wooden floorboards for prayer times, often for over an hour at a time. Prayer cushions were later provided for the not-so-young. Long hours were spent each week seeking the face of God (for world situations) but these were always preceded by anointed ministry from the Scriptures, when the lives and ministries of the heroes of faith were studied carefully. God's presence was very real in these sessions. It was one such Friday evening on 24th March 1950 when Samuel opened his heart to the College staff and students.

"These dealings you have with the Holy Spirit – it is very difficult to put them into words. It seems that He has been speaking to me all day long and one has felt within oneself (Samuel often referred to himself as 'one') the travail of the Holy Spirit for a lost world. One doesn't want to bring a message but to go back to God. The pressure upon us must be increased if anything. One believes that the Holy Spirit has been searching for a hundred years to find a man to take this Commission. Is it right that millions should be lost? He did find one man who was willing to take it up and we all know what it cost him."

Samuel was referring to the Founder, Rees Howells.

"These past fifteen years have meant a broken body. We knew if the Holy Spirit didn't relieve the pressure he couldn't go on. No one knows what liability is unless he has walked it. All these things came upon him. Although it was the Holy Spirit that carried them in him, but his was a human body, and it was too much for that body. What has come to one today, even if prayers are answered, is that there is a world to reach and it is only to be reached by prevailing prayer. We are coming tonight to meet God, to cry to Him to fulfil the task. Millions of souls tonight are unsaved and it is only through human channels He can reach them, and we are praying these prayers because they are wholly and entirely for the Kingdom. You know the illustrations the Saviour gave to show what it meant to pray with importunity."

Samuel read and then referred to the parables of the Unjust Judge (Luke 18:1-8) and the Friend at Midnight (Luke 11:5-10).

"When He gave these parables it wasn't only teaching but from the depth of His experience. We believe that He Himself knew what it was to be importunate and persistent in prayer. Probably there were hundreds of times when the Saviour went alone and spent nights with His Father. What was He doing? Didn't He have prayers we know nothing about? He had a Commission to put through, a ministry to fulfil. You might think the Saviour could have chosen twelve disciples without prayer and communion with His Father, but He spent the whole night in prayer (Luke 6:12-16)."

Samuel stressed in his ministry this intense and powerful awareness of the need for importunate prayer to soak into every fibre of his life and into the lives of all those concerned for, and committed to seeing the Kingdom of God penetrate the far corners of the earth in his generation.

In College life, everything was to become subservient to the particular prayers given by the Holy Spirit, just as it had been under Rees Howells' ministry. For many who did not fully appreciate the need for such a focused prayer ministry, and failed to recognise the thread of intercession throughout the Scriptures, this became a stumbling block as Samuel developed the ministry. He had promised his father not to deviate from this pathway and he remained true to his word. On more than one occasion he stated very clearly:

"If intercession is neglected in the College for anything else, then the Lord will bring it to an end."

Chapter Five

The Silver Thread

To fully appreciate the depth and far-reaching effects of the next fifty years of Samuel's hidden ministry, it is important to have a clear understanding of the legacy of ministry that had been revealed through his father, Rees Howells.

The main elements of truth that constitute a silver thread running through the ministry emphasised by Samuel, are as follows:

- The cross stands central in history. The vicarious death of Christ to atone for mankind's sin was complete. Christ rose triumphantly from the grave and returned to His Father in Heaven (1 Corinthians 15:3-8 and Acts 1:9-11).
- It is essential for the new birth to be established in the life of an individual before God takes him any further into a true personal walk with Himself. To be born of God is a wonderful miracle, not just a hackneyed phrase. So many disappointments in so called Christian lives are the result of neglecting this initial step into the Kingdom of God (John 3:3-8).
- God's Holy Spirit will then seek to lead the individual to the point of being totally yielded to His leading and direction. It is then possible for the Holy Spirit to endue that individual with Divine power and authority and use him as a clear witness of His character.
- There are only two Intercessors. The first is Jesus Christ who, as our great High Priest, is interceding for the Church. The second is

- the Holy Spirit on earth, commissioned to complete God's purposes in the world (Hebrews 7:24-27 and John 16:7-14).
- The Holy Spirit on earth must have 'bodies' through whom He can intercede in the world. He uses the bodies of believers cleansed through the application of the blood of Christ (Hebrews 9:14).
- As the cross stands central in history, the Holy Spirit has always been able to minister the cleansing power of the blood of Christ to prepare His channels. In the Old Testament this process was used retrospectively in the lives of certain individuals raised up for specific ministries, i.e. the Patriarchs and Prophets (Hebrews 11).
- Today the means of grace are available for all believers. All can be totally cleansed to become temples for God to live in (1 Corinthians 3:16-17 and 1 Corinthians 6:19-20). The NCV rendering of James 4:5 expresses this truth clearly.

Do you think the Scripture means nothing that says that the Spirit whom God made to live in us wants us for Himself alone?

The expression *'possessed by the Holy Spirit,'* often used in the early translations of the Bible (e.g. the AV) has prompted many debates among the scholars. The root word for complete possession (as in Judges 6:34, 1 Chronicles 12:18 and 2 Chronicles 24:20) means 'the Spirit clothed Himself with the individual,' later repeated in the lives of the Apostles on the Day of Pentecost (Acts 2:4). Then the blessing was extended to the Gentiles at the house of Cornelius (Acts 10:44).

- The Apostles were the selected few in their day who turned the world upside down, because they were totally filled with the Holy Spirit and made pliable for service (Acts 1:8).
- In these last days the Great Commission,

with the total fulfilment of Joel's prophecy, will only be completed through channels of this calibre, able to deal effectively with the spiritual powers of darkness that rule the world.

Even on My servants, both men and women, I will pour out My Spirit in those days. Joel 2:29.

God has always used these means. There is no other way (Acts 2:17-21 and Ephesians 6:12).

- The eleven disciples were stripped of their confidence and were truly baptised into the death of Christ before He met them on the resurrection side and later revealed their position in glory to them. Any individual aspiring to these spiritual heights will be asked to pay a great price. The illustration of purchasing a chocolate bar from a machine on a railway station was often used. You must pay the full price before the machine will release the chocolate. So it is in spiritual matters. There are no short cuts, no easy roads. Resurrection life is only obtained when the old nature is completely put to death in any given part in our lives. The Holy Spirit deals systematically with our old nature. Some of what we hear today, even in conservative, evangelical and charismatic circles, is a religious counterfeit which carries no authority in Christ.

- Intercessory prayer means becoming responsible for a particular situation, individual or group of individuals, as the Holy Spirit gives a burden, and continuing to carry that burden until it is lifted (having 'prayed through'). Christ's teaching on the need for importunate prayer is in the parables of The Friend at Midnight (Luke 11:5-10) and The Importunate Widow (Luke 18:1-8).

You can trace this silver thread weaving its way through every stage, as Samuel's ministry unfolds through the years. To complete it in triumph, Samuel would be torn to shreds by metaphorical lions, hardly able to take a further step at times. Any victories would be totally those of the Holy Spirit.

Some of the new buildings built on the three estates of Glynderwen, Derwen Fawr and Sketty Isaf as seen in the *Every Creature Conference* booklet of 1936.

Chapter Six

Progress on Every Front

Those years of intense spiritual training under his father's ministry would now need to be applied moment-by-moment if the work was to develop. It had been such logical and common sense teaching, and familiar phrases often flashed back into Samuel's own mind as he considered his own daily challenges. To quote some:
- There is no satisfaction nor conviction in anything, unless it has been given by a revelation, otherwise it is only mental assent.
- Have you overcome the temptations of the world? Is the Saviour in you greater than them? Will He live anything in you differently from the Sermon on the Mount?
- It is evident that we are not born again by merely saying we are.
- Would the Saviour in you, live with sin after He has conquered and destroyed it?
- A statement can never be a fact until it is proved.
- Teaching will never change your position.
- Words and phrases do not convey anything.
- The Holy Spirit will never come out of the Kingdom to live with a corrupt nature.
- When the Holy Spirit comes in, man must go out. Two persons can never live in the same body.
- He will put the old nature to death and it will be a complete and total death.
- Has the Holy Spirit been revealed to you? Have you seen Him? If He has not, then why not?

- If you lived at the time of the Saviour you would have to judge Him from what you could see and not from the historical standpoint of today.
- Jesus fed five thousand men, plus women and children. Moses fed two million people, so God must have been dwelling in him. If God is in you, what have you done?
- A man is a fool if he attacks anything he cannot prove himself.
- In every promise, there is a condition.
- The life of faith is most intelligent because God is in it. Faith must become substance before it becomes evidence.
- God does not exaggerate in what He says.
- You may preach anything and everything without proving anything, which is nothing but spectacular theory!
- The Holy Spirit is THE authority on telling the future. He is God and He has foretold everything accurately till the end of time.
- Unless you can prove God to answer in an emergency and in a test case, it is nothing but talk in a very big way. The 'old man' can sound very convincing but he does not see his folly. You can never exercise real faith for £100 ($160) unless you've had £50 ($80), nor for £50 unless you've proved God for £20 ($32), nor for £10 ($16) unless you've proved God for £5 ($8). You only give mental assent and imagine these things, unless you have had an experience with God in the impossible. Man's extremity is God's opportunity.

In the course of his ministry, Samuel regularly included and stressed the importance of each facet of this very personal teaching.

One of Samuel's responsibilities was the Bible College School which was renamed Emmanuel Grammar School and Emmanuel Preparatory School in 1955. Dr. Kingsley Priddy was appointed as headmaster[1] of the Grammar

School, supported by Doris Ruscoe as headmistress, whilst Kristine H. Jones (the author's future wife) was the headmistress of the Preparatory School. Both schools had a team of dedicated teachers. The Boarding Home for missionaries' children was under the care of Matron Gwen Roderick assisted by another team. The School had received a favourable report following His Majesty's Inspection in May 1948, and was growing steadily, with its two hundred and fifty-five pupils in the Secondary Department and one hundred and twenty-five in its Preparatory Department, making a significant contribution to the educational provision of Swansea and its neighbourhood. One quiet dedicated teacher in particular, in the Grammar School, who was to give stalwart support to staff and pupils throughout her active career till she finally retired at the age of eighty, was Mrs Winifred Jones (mother of Gweno and Kristine). So remarkable were her contributions in Mathematics that she received special mention in HM Inspectors' reports in the 1948 and 1966 visits (the latter when she was aged 66).

She is a graduate who joined the Community and School in 1936 after three years teaching in maintained grammar schools. She does her work with remarkable vitality and competence. It was a pleasure to observe her lessons and see how her insistence on hard and careful work by the pupils was combined with sympathetic attention to their difficulties. The very good quality of her teaching is confirmed by the good examination results achieved.

At the same time she gave her full support to Samuel's ministry and took part in all the prayers for different world situations.

Samuel also gave his full support to those directly responsible for the training of students in the Bible College, which was just finding its feet again (having been closed for six years because of WWII), preparing men and women for the mission field.[2] His personal contributions as a lecturer were much appreciated. Ieuan Jones, Dr. Kenneth Symonds and Brash Bonsell had met together in Aberystwyth after the war to design a suitable course for students and had agreed on main ideas. Brash Bonsell favoured a more Evangelistic outreach which led to his forming the Birmingham Bible Institute, whilst Ieuan Jones and Kenneth Symonds wished to follow the pattern established by Rees Howells with a greater prayer emphasis.

Ieuan Jones as a student at the Bible College of Wales in 1924. He would become an anointed lecturer at BCW

Samuel had approved of this approach and the course had developed along these lines. It was particularly helpful for students wishing to learn the 'life of faith' since they had no fixed visible means of support but had a desire to serve the Lord. The lessons of faith were hard to learn but enabled students to face the problems and difficulties of the mission field with a confidence in the faithfulness of God to remain true to His promises. So many Christians today, exercising fruitful ministries around the world, will remember the anointed teaching ministry of Ieuan Jones and the later 'whistle-stop' weekly contributions on evangelism from David Shepherd. There were also lectures by Arthur Lewis and Arthur Neil, and the Thursday afternoon ministry on Ephesians from Glyn Morris, in the 1950s to 1980s. Kenneth Symonds himself was a father to the students and would never go on holiday until all of his 'boys' were through with their fees (all paid!).

David Davies, Samuel Howells and Arthur Neil, 1980s

These were days of strict discipline when, at times, there seemed to be more chiefs than Indians around the College. Prolonged fraternisation between male and female students was discouraged, but the final word rested with Dr. Joan Davies (lady students) and Norman Madoc (men students), whose ability to live with very little sleep was amazing.

But there were other burdens that Samuel was carrying in order to develop the ministry overseas as his father had wished. Central to Rees Howells' vision during the final years of his ministry was the establishment of Christian centres in the Middle East Bible Lands in order to stimulate believing prayer for their blessing.

Samuel could vividly remember a prayer meeting at the Bible College on 8th September 1949, when Rees Howells had declared,

"I have looked forward for ten years to the day I

would recover all, and this is the day. There is not a penny owing on one of the properties. I took £20,000 ($32,000) liability[3] in the bank for Penllergaer, our fourth property, to take in the Jewish children and the Lord said then, 'You will recover all,' and this is the day. Tonight I begin to pray for the establishment of Christian centres for the Bible Lands in earnest – I step on it now."

The Howells family, (left to right), Samuel, Lizzie and Rees next to the "Faith Is Substance" plinth in the grounds of Derwen Fawr, during WWII. The other side of the plinth says "Jehovah Jireh" (God will provide / the Lord my provider).

At this early stage in our narrative, it is important to clarify one issue which may be raised in the reader's mind and for which both Rees Howells and Samuel Howells have been wrongly accused. It would appear from the records that they both had a preference for the Jewish nation, particularly as it was through a Jew, Maurice Reuben, that the Lord convicted Rees Howells, leading to his subsequent conversion in the USA. This was far from the truth. The atoning work of Jesus, the eternal Son of God, was for the whole of mankind, and neither was it a limited atonement only for a certain few chosen people. Samuel had many dear friends from all nations, including those from the Arab nations in the Middle East, and endeavoured to stand behind hundreds in prayer and practical support. However, he had learnt always to respond to the prayers that the Holy Spirit gave, which were inevitably those involving the outworking of God's covenant purposes in the world. Obviously, when the Lord gave a particular prayer involving a Middle East situation, then everyone's attention was focused on Israel and, of course, the Jewish people, and those who were seeking to be a means of blessing and practical support to that nation were always welcomed at the College, as were people from every other nation.

Mrs Lizzie Howells in the Holy Land 1937. She travelled with Mrs Charles Cowman of the Oriental Missionary Society, whose vision was also for 'all nations' and 'every creature.'

Samuel was taking up this prayer so, through contacts already made by Lizzie Howells in a previous visit to Israel, planned a visit to the Middle East with a view to setting up a Christian centre near Jerusalem. He wrote to the Honourable District Officer of Ramallah, Jordan, to inform him that he (Samuel) had been appointed and authorised by the Bible College Trust, Swansea, Great Britain, to establish an elementary school for girls and boys in Ramallah, with the hope of enlarging it into a secondary school. He also enclosed copies of 'the bye-laws of the Society which is to administer the school.' A bold step to take in present day thinking!

Preparations complete, Samuel commenced his first of several missionary journeys to the Middle East in May 1951, calling first to encourage the members of the College family, Frank Nixon, Fred Ridgers, Vreni Rossler, Paula Ort and Mair Davies, who had previously established a centre in Bois de Boulogne, Paris, France, called Maison de l'Evangile (The Gospel House).

The Paris Team before departing to France after WWII (with the Howells family) at Derwen Fawr. Back row (from left to right) Paula Ort, Vreni Rossler, (Samuel), Mair Davies and Glyn James. Front row (from left to right) Frank Nixon, (Lizzie and Rees), Mrs Elizabeth James and Fred Ridgers.

From Marseilles the journey was by sea, travelling on board the *Champollion*, calling in at Alexandria on the way. On 10th May 1951, Samuel wrote to his loyal friend Tommy Howells (no relation), who had stood with Rees Howells

- 79 -

throughout his ministry from the early days in Brynaman where they were both coal miners:

My dear Tommy,

I'm sure you will be glad to have another word from your old friend who is now travelling on the high seas in the Lord's service. Tomorrow we are due at Haifa at six o' clock in the morning and as the ship doesn't leave for Alexandria until late in the afternoon I hope to spend some hours ashore. It is a thrill to think that we are now so near to Israel. I can imagine how you will feel when you will arrive in the Holy Land. I am sure a big shout will ascend to Heaven that day. (Tommy was always shouting his praises to the Lord in the College services). For some hours yesterday afternoon we sailed within sight of the Island of Crete. I thought of the great Apostle Paul who laboured there and suffered so much for the Gospel. Paul has been much in my thoughts during the last day or two because he sailed this part of the Mediterranean in his days. It is a great inspiration to think that we are now allowed to follow in his footsteps. I am looking forward very much also to visiting these sacred places such as Bethlehem, Nazareth, Bethany and Jerusalem, which were so dear to our Master when He was on earth. I shall especially remember you when I get to the top of Mt. Carmel and stand on the spot where Elijah challenged the prophets of Baal and called down fire from Heaven. Pray that the Lord will fulfil all His purposes regarding Lebanon and Israel. Surely He will, after all the travail and intercession of the Director. As the Holy Spirit has prospered the work in Swansea He will do the same in the Bible Lands again.

Tommy was to remain a loyal and trusted friend to Samuel until his death on 22nd March 1973. Such friends are rarely to be found and are greatly missed when they are eventually promoted to glory.

The important discussions went well in Jordan and resulted in Bible College staff members Ceturah Morgan (better known as Kitty) and Gwladys Thomas sailing out in March 1954 to establish a Home and School for girls in Ramallah (meaning Hill of God), north of Jerusalem. Bob Grupp was an American missionary who ran a boys' home nearby and he arranged for them to stay with his sister, Mary Jean and her friend before they moved to a house rented for them by Samuel. Mary Jean was helping in the boys' home for a year, and was burdened with the need for a girls' home and school. Mary, Kitty and Gwladys became a team with the same vision, and Emmanuel Home and School opened in October 1954, with ten girls in the Home and twenty-two pupils on the School register. By 1955, Gweno H. Jones, Doris Leafe and Winifred Morgan (Kitty's sister), all from the Bible College, had augmented the ranks. The work was hard at first, with few funds coming in to support it, but as with Joseph, the Word of the Lord tried them (Psalm 105:19, AV) and a solid foundation was laid. Samuel kept in touch but communications generally were not to be compared with our modern satellite links, just postage, but via the Throne there were never any problems!

The Middle East Team c.1954, (schools in Ramallah and Beirut). Back row (from left to right), Dora Holder, Gwladys Thomas and Eva Rose. Front row (from left to right), Kitty Morgan, Dr. Hughes, Jean Holder and Mary Jean Grupp.

Samuel remained acutely aware of these single ladies who had gone out to pioneer a new work in a land where women played a different role in society, than in the West. He was therefore thrilled to receive a letter from Kitty, at long last, and read it out in the Tuesday evening service on 16th August 1955.

"We can again raise our Ebenezer and tell you of two wonderful answers to prayer."

Ebenezer was a Hebrew word meaning 'a stone of the help received.' It was an old custom to set up a large stone when and where they received some miraculous help from God. It is used in the Bible in 1 Samuel 7:12 when the prophet Samuel received help from God to defeat the Philistine army as it threatened to annihilate the defenceless Israelites at Mizpeh in 1142 BC. Nowadays, Christians use the expression to show their joy when God has brought them safely through potentially difficult circumstances. Samuel continued reading the letter,

"Our rent was due on Sunday. We had paid all our current accounts, also bought tables for children and had £137 ($219) to find. We received £67 ($107) by Saturday. When the landlady called for the rent we told her it was not due till Sunday and we did not transact business on Sundays, so would she please come on Monday at 3pm. We went back to the Lord as the lady was a Muslim and we had testified to her. She could neither read nor write but always knew when money was due!

"On Sunday the Lord gave us assurance and told us to rejoice, and we did. On Monday, we received a cheque for £30 ($48) and we reminded the Lord that another £30 was due. We had a busy morning in school and after dinner, Jean and Dora went to the post office. The mail was not sorted – please call in half an hour. It is necessary to have a national to witness transactions like these and we usually ask Jedd the chemist. Jean was tested now. Was she really sure of the deliverance? Could she ask Jedd to be at the home at 3pm? She went to ask him and then to the post office – one letter – £30 ($48) – and arrived home at 2:50pm. The landlady arrived at five minutes to three and there was great joy!"

Samuel was always pleased to hear testimonies like this of the Lord's deliverance in answer to prayer as it enhanced the life which the Founder had introduced into the lifestyle of the College. Samuel wished these principles to be retained in the training programme, lessons which could not be learnt in the classroom, only in the school of life in fellowship with the Lord. Samuel continued the service by reading the second answer to prayer from Kitty's letter, and then explained that he had been hindered from sending them money but the Lord had intervened Himself,

"The needs here are great but God has supplied," he said. "We have spent much time in prayer and that is the only way, wrestling through like the Director (Rees Howells) and George Müller. We could easily slacken but what would God say? He would say, 'You are a hireling and not the shepherd.' The world is heavy upon us and we do not know what God is going to do; we are waiting upon Him. What a wonderful letter from Kitty. God will never let His children down," Samuel concluded.

The work in Ramallah was further tested in 1957 during the Suez Crisis when the staff were repatriated for a few months. On returning, it only became possible to continue by registering under the banner of the Arab Evangelical Episcopal (AEE) Church Council as the Evangelical Home and School for Girls, which commenced in 1962. In 1966, a new building project was planned for a home on land donated by the AEE Church, to accommodate ninety-six girls and a school for three hundred students. A crisis point was reached in 1967 during the Six-Day War when the home was shelled, two of their beloved girls Dina and Lucy were killed and five staff injured, some severely. Samuel arranged for their return to the UK where they were nursed in the College Hospital. Arising from the ashes, as God's work invariably does, emerged substantial new modern buildings, erected through generous funding from the USA and churches in Germany, with the former founding staff able to lead and administer the work and to share the Gospel with the children. Vreni Wittwer from Switzerland became the Director of the work from 1962 and Najah Rantisi, a former pupil of the School and also a BCW student, took responsibility in the Home. They worked in close fellowship with Audeh Rantisi, at one time Deputy Mayor of Ramallah, and his wife Pat, both former Bible College students, who ran a similar Home for Boys. The combined work has grown since and is highly respected in its local territory, with six hundred children, boys and girls, on the school register, although there is no legal link with the College now.

Returning now to his first Middle East visit in 1951, Samuel was very pleased with the outcome of his talks and travelled then to Beirut, Lebanon, probably by taxi, to meet Vartan Atchinak, owner of the Atchinak School in Rue Sioufi, Ashrafia.

Samuel Howells in Beirut, Lebanon, June 1951

For some while, Samuel had been impressed by the testimony of faith that had been raised at Sweifat in Lebanon, amidst hostile opposition during the early twentieth century by two single young ladies. Amelia and Asma were daughters of the Hon. Faris Bey Trad, member of an old and noble family of Syria, and were raised in the strict traditions of the Syrian Greek Orthodox religion. But when their hearts were both touched in a deep way by the Lord they became deeply burdened for the salvation of their own countrymen. They earnestly sought God for guidance and through reading the biography of George Müller of Bristol, England, they were led to start a school for girls and boys in 1907. For two young ladies to take such a unique and bold step of faith in such a culture, with no promised support at all, trusting solely on the promises of a faithful God and much prayer, is a challenge for all today seeking to embark on a ministry. The first year the Lord sent fifty children to the school.

It was to this school that Vartan Atchinak, a Christian colporteur with the British and Foreign Bible Society arrived in 1909. Born in Tarsus, Vartan witnessed atrocities against the Armenians by the Turks, so later became an active member of a socialist revolutionary organisation resulting in his having to leave Constantinople for Romania to escape arrest. In order to discover inconsistencies in the Bible to discredit Christianity he read it very carefully and in a wonderful way God revealed His salvation through its passages and Vartan's life was transformed. So now, in the course of a very extensive tour of many Middle Eastern countries distributing hundreds of Scripture portions and Bibles in twelve languages, he arrived at the Bible School on Gazelia Street, just off Rue Sioufi, Ashrafia in Beirut. He was so moved by what he heard and saw that from then on, whenever possible, he visited the two sisters and was later asked to lead the Sunday services. He married Asma in 1913. The work passed through deep trials and persecutions during two World Wars, when Vartan was treated harshly in prison by the Turks, on two occasions, for refusing to close the School and cease preaching and teaching the Gospel. Eventually the Ottoman Government gave special permission for the School to continue and teach the Bible.

As the work prospered under God's hand, the Bible Lands Gospel Mission was founded and a separate High School for boys opened, under the direction of Madam Melvina Trad Hunaykaty, sister of Mrs Atchinak and Amelia.

Gradually the work grew with the addition of a large building in the city centre.

Mr Vartan Atchinak (left) and Samuel Howells in Beirut, 1962

Samuel considered it a great privilege to meet this brave servant of God, Vartan Atchinak, and later invited him to the College to share his experiences with the staff and students. As a result, two former Bible College staff, Eva Rose (Preparatory School head teacher) and Jean Holder went to teach in this School, joined later by Dr. Hughes, a trained medical doctor and Dora Holder (sister of Jean). Eva Rose was later appointed as head teacher of Atchinak's School. It was hoped that this School would also become a Bible Lands centre for prayer.

The School in Lebanon was subsequently blessed through the persistent prayers of the staff, as a letter dated 29th March 1954 from Eva Rose, prior to Samuel's second trip to the Middle East, indicates:

> You will have heard how the Lord was in the school convicting and converting. Last week was a week of preparation and we saw many children coming through for salvation. The Xth

class was really facing surrendering their lives to the Lord. Previously there had been much weeping and brokenness but when I went into the room the presence of God was so real that I hardly dared step forward. Each head was down on the desk. When challenged that if they were ready to give their lives completely into the hands of God the whole class, as if some invisible hand were lifting them, rose – en bloc – without a sound. One by one, in a little room alone, they dedicated their lives to God; what a solemn time it was! I do wish you could have heard the testimony meeting on Friday.

Emerging from that blessing in Lebanon was a student at the Bible College, Fouzi Ayoub who for many years, along with his faithful wife Wendy, exercised a very fruitful postal ministry throughout the Arab world from his base in Wolverhampton, until his death in a tragic road accident in Mali on 22nd March 2000. Samuel always welcomed Fouzi to the College for an annual weekend ministry visit. His warm, provocative personality won the affections of many staff and students through the years and he stood loyally with Samuel during difficult times. He was a true friend.

Some of the men students and staff in November 1963
1. Samuel, 2. R. Maton, 3. Dr. Symonds, 4. Fouzi Ayoub

Chapter Seven

The College Stirs Again

While Samuel was away from the College (May 1951), without the luxury of emails and mobile phones that we have today, he received regular reports waiting for him at every port of call, posted by staff members, including a weekly encouragement from his mother, Lizzie Howells. Many were in Welsh, of course, his first language, and affectionately signed 'Cofion gorau, Nana.' Any correspondence received from Rees Howells, when Samuel was a young man, had been signed from 'The Director,' as Moses Rees had fathered him during his early years.

From left to right, Samuel Rees Howells with Miss Alice Townsend and his foster parents Elizabeth and Moses Rees, c.1922. In later years, Alice lived in Sketty Isaf for a time.

There was certainly much stirring in the College and at the School. The new students were on the beach at 8pm, holding their first real open-air meeting in Swansea since the war years, and they preached to a crowd of forty interested folk. Preparations were already in hand for the Every Creature Conference (the second, under Samuel's leadership) to become a well-attended annual event for the following thirteen years (ending in 1964), during the last week of July prior to the August Bank Holiday. Missionaries from across the world, many former students, would share their news, and present students would testify of God's call upon their lives, and sing as a choir under Olive Raven's training. Then followed challenging ministry from prominent figures in the evangelical world including Cyril Francis (China), Len Moules (WEC), Leonard Harris Unevangelised Fields Mission (UFM), Percy Hassam, Dr. Charles Stern, Major Alistair Smith (from the Salvation Army in South Africa) and Charlton Smith.

Duncan Campbell in the grounds of Derwen Fawr c.1955

Duncan Campbell was to make significant contributions in these conferences, following his experience in the Hebridean Revival of 1949 to 1952. While he was preaching in 1955, the presence of the Holy Spirit was so manifest that the strong stone walls of the Conference Hall trembled!

Dr. Priddy wrote to Samuel about developments in Emmanuel School:

> There has been such a burden for the School and now He has begun to do a new thing. He has given us the key to leading the children into a keen life of practical walking in the light with the Saviour, and that in a way which will not be a 'flash in the pan' revival, but will do what we have prayed much for, to raise the normal level of their Christian living to one of fullness of victory and joy in the Saviour. Without excitement and emotion He has broken right through in the lives of many of the boarders and some day children, and they are quite transformed. He is beginning to revive the fellowship groups throughout the School, which meet in Wednesday dinner hour. There has been a marvellous move among the home staff too, many barriers swept away, many reconciliations and much brokenness before the Lord.

God was really at work in the College.

You can imagine the warm reception Samuel would have received when he finally returned to Swansea. As Dr. Priddy expressed in his last letter to Samuel:

> It will be grand to have you back again – it has been long without you. We are longing to hear more fully of St. Samuel's First Missionary Journey!
>
> With much love. Ever your brother in Christ,
> Prid.

Each department of the College rose to the challenge, taking financial responsibility for some of the needs. In the office Eva Stewart did this, acting as Samuel's personal secretary and leading the ladies in their Monday evening prayer meetings. In the garden, David Rees took over from Ernie Allen, later to become the Founder of 'Every Home Crusade' which has produced and distributed thousands of tons of Scriptures across the world. Both were former students. David worked tirelessly to provide fresh vegetables for the kitchen, and Archie Jones assisted with producing an annual display of geraniums. Elsie Payne and May Pearce took over in the kitchen when Kitty Morgan went to Ramallah, and they made sure that the weekly dinner of fish and chips and daily breakfast porridge continued throughout the years! Doctors Cecil and Maule Brien, Dr. Kenneth Symonds and Dr. Joan Davies took charge of the College 'Hospital' (sick bay) assisted by nurses Judy Judkins and Catherine Orsman. Lizzie Howells kept a watchful eye on the house (Derwen Fawr building – the administrative centre of the College) ably supported by Margaret Williams (Aunty Peg to her niece Ruth; Ruth later became Samuel's personal secretary). Margaret had been one of the original College students in 1924. Ethel Dinmore and Alice Dawson, both brilliant organisers, added their expertise to the smooth running of the domestic side of College life. For a while, Leslie Taylor and his team ran the College bakehouse, providing a full supply of fresh bread and delicious confectionery. When Les left to join the Manchester City Mission, William Rowlands stepped in and, through the years, also taught many men students the art of pounding the dough. Even though William was up at 4am every working morning he often remarked about the lights already on in staff rooms, as folk were having their morning Quiet Times.

One such early bird was Joan Rush, art teacher, who was led to write out the whole Bible seven times by hand. She found this morning exercise helped her to focus her attention on each page of Scripture, and she even received free supplies of biros from a manufacturer, wishing to have their products tested!

Building up the library was another challenge, which successive generations of staff and students engaged in, to bring it to the excellent standard it reached finally. In those days Nancy Halcrow kept it in good order (in tandem with running the College laundry) until too many donations of books overcrowded it. On several occasions, it experienced a 'thinning out,' once when six and a half thousand books were sent to African colleges, where books were desperately needed.

How many will remember the massive belt-driven, industrial washing machines rattling away in the laundry on a Monday morning, and Maggie Brown keeping a watchful eye out for any intruders into what she considered to be her territory! The coal-fired stoves in the ironing room kept the supply of cast-iron flat irons hot enough for constant ironing, while the revolving machine rolled out the sheets and linen tablecloths. Samuel's shirt collars were starched to pristine condition!

Samuel Howells with Tobias 'Toby' Bergin, c. late 1980s

On the men's side, Tobias Paiton Bergin, disowned by an aristocratic Irish Protestant family for turning his back on the riches of family home to follow the Lord, took charge of the garage. He kept the wheels running for succeeding generations, making sure that there was always a 'truck' available for collecting the weekly supply of coal from the docks, and distributing it around the College. It was certainly a matter of keeping the home fires burning throughout the winter months, and students often found themselves immersed in smoke and ashes, as they wrestled to keep everyone happy! Yes, it was post-war College life in the raw, an excellent environment for developing a close walk with the Lord, and first class GMT (good missionary training).

All the time great strides were being made to improve the facilities, to renovate buildings and introduce electric power lines, and to update ancient central heating systems. Controlling all these projects was Norman Madoc, whose organising and practical skills ensured that jobs were completed to a high standard. He was backed up by decorators Arthur Ewing, who had worked in the Belfast Shipyard and gentle giant Ernie Dent, who was an all-rounder and a Methodist preacher trained at Cliff College. When they were not teaching in Emmanuel School both Norman Brend and Leslie Lee, who originally cycled to College together from London when they came as students, were top class decorators too. Samuel was certainly blessed with a versatile, willing and skilful team of dedicated workers whom he loved very much in the Lord. He constantly urged them forward and encouraged their every contribution, and prayed much for each one.

Students regularly preached in local churches on Sundays, and many were their testimonies of trusting God to supply bus or train fares in order to 'get to the church on time.' Some forty local churches and chapels were served in this way, and later teams gave a week of their holidays to arrange missions and children's programmes.

One special event was the Coronation of Queen Elizabeth II on 2nd June 1953, when the whole College and School were given the day off to watch the service on a large television (black and white of course!), hired for the day and erected in the Conference Hall. Watched by over twenty million people around the world, the Queen made her solemn vows before God. She has sought to keep through many trials for six decades now, as Dr. Fisher, the then Archbishop of Canterbury, placed the diamond-studded crown on her head. The symbolism of crowning a monarch stirred the College audience into a familiar chorus 'and crown Him, crown Him, crown Him Lord of all.' Floodlights illuminated Derwen Fawr House to mark the memorable occasion. Samuel prayed often for her Majesty, Queen Elizabeth II, and encouraged others to do so also, knowing that she too fully appreciated and accepted the great God-given responsibility she was carrying to represent the nation.

The College year was divided into three roughly equal terms of ten weeks, although the spring and summer terms often varied considerably because of the moveable date for Easter. During the holidays, for the most part staff remained on site, as this was their home, but students, once they had paid all their fees to date, departed for a well earned break. It was a normal working week for anyone staying at the College and there was much to do for everyone, staff and students but gradually the tempo of life lessened and a lovely atmosphere prevailed around the grounds. Samuel usually restricted College services to one weekday evening meeting and two services on Sunday. He revelled in the many long uninterrupted hours he could spend alone in God's presence particularly during the ten week summer break, following the student graduation service. For many years, he saw each student personally in his room before they left, and was pleased to hear their testimonies. He would follow the progress of many in prayer and practical support in ensuing years.

During the warm summer months, Samuel walked around the College grounds and talked to the various staff and students painting, gardening or cleaning – whatever their task was for the day, to encourage them with, "Come and see me upstairs after dinner. Wait on the landing." That would often herald instructions to preach on Sunday in his place, or chauffeur the College car for him for an afternoon run or even to give an envelope with a £10 ($16) note (bill) in it, as a gift. Who knows? If it was to preach there was no gift – that came the following week if Samuel felt that the preacher was carrying an anointing, proving that he was following the prayers the Lord was giving at the time.

Yes, life at the College was certainly on the move and a vibrant atmosphere prevailed – even when folk were tired and often weary in the spiritual battle which continued.

By now, Samuel, having experienced God's mantle of spiritual authority coming upon him in 1950, had settled into his pulpit ministry. Ending a long exposition from Luke 2 on 9th October 1954, he said,

> "This is the realm where God is. We are praying for the closing of the dispensation. Let Him find us in the right relationship with Himself, humble and at His feet. As we seek His Kingdom He will answer other needs. This week we have spent about £500 ($800) (about £11,000 / $17,600 in 2012 currency) but the Lord is very gracious. This week also we have received sums to cover – £100 ($160), £250 ($400) and another £100. Surely He will deliver what is required. Do not neglect this life of faith. If you have not been delivered spend the weekend in prayer. It is a hard school, but a glorious school. We know God is real. He answers prayer every day."

The 1950s were to be the prelude to many glorious victories in the decades that lay ahead, and some fierce conflicts, but God was on the move.

The College was certainly a-stir once more!

Aerial view of Derwen Fawr Estate. D. F. House (back left), Men's Hostel (middle back) Hospital (right) & Italian Gardens

Chapter Eight

The School of Faith

Ever since God had met with Rees Howells on the Boxing Day morning of 1934, and placed a special responsibility upon him to see the fulfilment of the Great Commission of Matthew 28:18-20 and Mark 16:15, there was a deep desire in him to see new countries reached with the Gospel. So, from its earliest years, young men and women had already left the College and pioneered new work. Cyril Francis and Ieuan Jones had gone to China. Jack Lenny, along with several other WEC missionaries, had been landed on the beach of Liberia with their baggage to develop a work there. The two brothers, David and Ivor Davies, spent the war years deep in the forests of the Belgian Congo. Bessie Fricker (later to become Bessie Brierley) sailed alone into Portuguese Guinea to commence the work there. Jack and Rose Robertson paid a heavy price to see a Church finally planted in Upper Volta. Roland Williams, the strong Welsh farmer, made his way to Calcutta where he poured out his life in ministry to the beggars there. Annie Duffy maintained a constant witness in Malawi and, when she died, received posthumous recognition for her service by the President himself. And John Roderick Davies had opened work in Brazil. There were many others too who entered strategic ministries throughout the world and became cogs in God's machinery during those pioneering days under Rees Howells.

The process of seeding the nations was renewed and encouraged again under Samuel's ministry. Jean Henderson joined CLC in Italy, George Oakes joined John Roderick Davies in Brazil and Kathy Cowan sailed to Japan and later, Korea. So the stream continued throughout his years as Director. To augment this, it now became possible for candidates from abroad to train in the UK, so the

College was able to welcome students of all nationalities, even those without financial support, very difficult today. An essential aspect of the College training was to encourage the students to learn the life of faith, which included trusting God when resources were not available, as preparation for pioneering situations that would be encountered in the Lord's service anywhere in the world. Under the ministry of Rees Howells, staff and students had been schooled very thoroughly in this area of Christian experience.

"If you fail to move God for yourself in the basic areas of living you are not going to move Him for another person, and it is doubtful if a person knows the Holy Spirit if he can't trust God. You will certainly be building on sand," he would say.

He impressed upon everyone that you couldn't pray for other people to give you money if you had money in your pocket. It always needed to be a full surrender first: use your own resources, then God's unlimited supplies will become available. People soon learned how difficult it was to part with their own money!

The Howells family – Faith Is Substance plinth c.1930

These, of course, were the initial stages towards living in constant fellowship with God, through the Holy Spirit, to such a degree that the *greater works* referred to by Jesus in John 14:12 (AV) would be demonstrated through every Spirit-filled believer. The Founder had always raised the standard of discipleship for effective ministry, and pointed out that the seventy disciples empowered and sent out by Jesus (Luke 10:1) returned with glowing reports but failed to keep their instructions and lost the power. No doubt they learned their lesson and, when the Holy Spirit was given after Pentecost, were able to become part of the early Church. The life of faith was such a vital area of experience for every new student at the College to learn, and Samuel was determined to encourage them during their initial steps. Soon a stream of students from all parts of the world were experiencing their first culture shocks of College life as it was in that post-war era, and finding their lives radically changed.

In many countries today there are Christian leaders who passed through the 'school of faith' and are now exercising, or have exercised, fruitful ministries.

Such names as: Tom Lewis (BEE), Henk Binnadek, Rudolf van Leusen and Jim and Janet Heinigen (Netherlands), Reinhard Bonnke (Christ For All Nations), Robert Hyslop (Nigeria), Paul and Kate Jinadu, Colin Lamb (New Tribes Mission), Roy Davey, Peter Wilson (Japan), Cyril and Barbara Davies (Thailand), Paul Olise (BCM), Alan and Betty Scotland (Lifelink), John Rocha (Israel), Brian and Stella Halliwell (CLC), Jill Priddy (France), John Premkumar (India), Richard and Carolyn Davey (WEC), Peter and Eileen Lofthouse (CLC Rome), Chong Yang Kim (Malawi), Billy and Hazel Glover (WEC), Samson Rajkumah (Vietnam), Julie Cox (Central Asia), Mary Pritchard, Bryn (now with the Lord) and Edna Jones, and his brother Ceri (Covenant Ministries), Marleen Muire (Gospel Recordings), Janny van der Klis (Kenya), Janny Riemersma (Netherlands), Graham Brown (CLC) and a host of other unsung heroes have been used by God in their varied ministries.

Samuel prayed for them all and made it his responsibility, in the Lord, to correspond with, and send gifts to, all those whom the Holy Spirit laid on his heart. Many former students would later testify of timely gifts received from Samuel. He was certainly always pleased when they called in to the College to say "Hello" and some to minister to the College. Knowing that the Charity Scheme of Administration had as one of its objects, 'to maintain a Home of Rest for Christian missionaries of all denominations where both board and residence are provided for them either free or for less than actual cost.' Samuel would invariably assure visitors engaged in the work of the Gospel that 'this is your home as much as it is ours,' and went out of his way to make them feel that it really was. In actual fact, it was difficult for anyone during those days to really rest as the staff were already at full stretch, but the former students usually 'pitched in' with everyone and their support was much appreciated.

It was certainly Samuel's intention that the seeding of the nations must continue as before, and along the same lines as in the foundation years of the College.

In an early College pamphlet, it had been written:

> The great object of the College is to prove that the work of God can be carried on by trust in God, and that faith and prayer are efficient agents. If this principle is a Scriptural one, God can make it a success in the hands of any of His servants, to whom He gives grace, to have faith and trust in Him. The Apostles acted on this principle:
>
> *Be careful for nothing; but in everything by prayer and supplication with thanksgiving let your requests be made known unto God.*
>
> *But my God shall supply all your need according to His riches in glory by Christ Jesus.*
>
> *Because that for His name's sake they went forth, taking nothing of the Gentiles.*
>
> Philippians 4:6, 19 (AV) and 3 John 7 (AV).

The College pamphlet continued:

> These principles are not held in living faith by the Church, and every great truth which has been lost through unbelief and carelessness must be regained through deep travail and suffering, and often through great persecution. But the Word the Lord gave to the Apostles is true for us:

My grace is sufficient for thee.... Therefore I take pleasure in infirmities, in reproaches, in necessities, in persecutions, in distresses for Christ's sake. 2 Corinthians 12:9-10 (AV).

Our desire is to give the very best tuition to young men and women, and also to encourage them to enter the School of Faith. And that all the students who graduate from the College will be able, not only to expound the Word of God, but to give practical demonstrations of it in the same literal sense in which the words, *Give us this day our daily bread*, are so often proved in the provision of the temporal needs of the College from day-to-day. We are not aiming to make a new sect, nor to train men and women for any particular denomination, but to give free tuition to men of all denominations who have been called to the home ministry, and to those who are called to be missionaries who are not able to afford university training.

Moses Rees and Samuel Howells in his Oxford days c.1935

The need of trained ministers was great even in Wales (the land of revivals), and this was the burden which made the Founder (Rees Howells) pray for a strong interdenominational college in Wales that would give a full theological course, and without added expense to the denominations, faith was to provide the money for free tuition.

Rees Howells had never presented the life of faith as an easy exercise and stressed that the entrance fee for the life of faith is a full and complete surrender (1 Kings 19:19-21).

If you want to know what a full surrender is, it is this. You have made a surrender the same as Elisha. Only one thing you know; God has told you to do it, and He will inspire you, and will inspire faith in you. Faith works when you are in a test by choice, not when you cannot get out of it. Exodus 4.

With regard to accepting help from home, Rees Howells' approach was:
- Never let your parents know your need.
- Do not refuse family gifts unless specifically guided to do so. God will supply your personal needs but He will never deliver you while you are not abiding. He will deliver you every time you are abiding.
- You may think you would learn the life and get it to work at once, a thousand times. No. You must start at the bottom. If you need 7s. 6d. (35p / 56¢), get 7s. 6d, not 10 shillings (50p / 80¢). Anything more is a gift and not your gained position of faith. If ever I needed £5 ($8), God would not give me £10 ($16). If you need £10 ($16) and receive £2 ($3.20), you only need to pray for £8 ($12.80).
- You may study many things in the Bible but be unable to live a life of faith.

A learned professor was once being rowed across a lake by a boatman and a conversation ensued:
Professor: "Have you studied philosophy?"

Boatman: "No, sir."
Professor: "Then you have lost a third of your life. Have you studied psychology?"
Boatman: "No, sir."
Professor: "Then you have lost another third of your life."
Suddenly the boat shudders and begins to fill up with water.
Boatman: "Sir, can you swim?"
Professor: "No."
Boatman: "Then you have lost all your life!"

There were then presented several laws in the life of faith which are well worth noting:
- No needs are to be made known. No debt.
- Do not question a deliverance if you have not attempted to influence the donor and have not made the need known.
- Natural deliverance before extraordinary, miraculous deliverance.
- First need, first claim. You use the resources you have to pay all immediate expenses.
- When essential needs and non-essential needs come at the same time – use any money for the essentials first.
- You cannot claim deliverance until you have gone to your extremity and used all your own resources.
- Claim on your abiding. When you are living in obedience to all God has shown you then you can ask God to fulfil His promise of John 15:7.
- Claim your wages from God.
- Whatever God asks you to do, you can go back to Him and ask Him to pay for it.
- You must have victory in private before you are tested in the open. Victory is when a particular personal sin no longer has control over your mind or life.
- Do not run on the spoil. Do not use finance

> or materials available for corporate needs (e.g. in the office) for your own personal needs.

Samuel certainly agreed with all these statements, but it was quite another story to put it into practice in an age which is not an age of faith. Fees were introduced but set at a minimum so that students would not be overwhelmed as they themselves entered the School of Faith, with all its lessons to be experienced and learned.

George Müller established and ran a home for orphans in Bristol beginning in 1835, then much larger homes were built during the nineteenth century entirely on the principle of faith and without ever making any appeals for finance. He once commented on the many trials and difficulties that were met by the way:

> In one thousand trials it is not five hundred of them that are to work for the believer's good, but nine hundred and ninety nine of them, and one beside.

The seeding process remained clear in Samuel's mind and on his heart right through to the end of his life, but he recognised that an essential ingredient in the training of students for God's purpose to be fulfilled, was the exercise of faith.

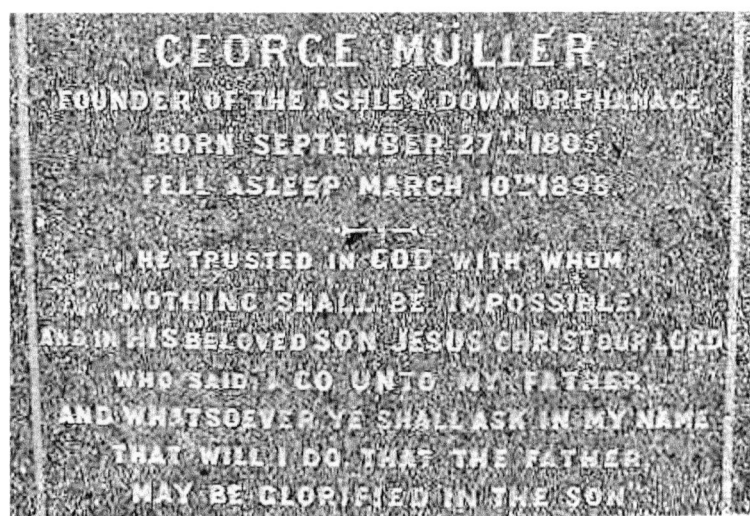

Top section of George Müller's gravestone

Chapter Nine

Challenges At Home

Shortly after Rees Howells' death Samuel received a letter from Norman Grubb, then in South Africa, dated 14th February 1950, expressing his deep sympathy to Samuel, his mother and all the friends at the College. He fully appreciated what it meant to them, as C. T. Studd, the WEC founder and leader of his mission, had died previously.

Mrs. Rees Howells & Samuel Howells
desire sincerely to thank all friends for their kind expressions of sympathy in their bereavement.

" He staggered not at the promise of God through unbelief; but was strong in faith, giving glory to God "—
ROMANS 4, 20.

THE BIBLE COLLEGE OF WALES,
DERWEN FAWR,
SWANSEA.   FEBRUARY, 1950.

Mrs Rees Howells' and Samuel Howells' thank you card

A week later on 21st February 1950, Norman wrote offering his services and expertise to write a book documenting the life of the Founder:

> I do most keenly hope that God will guide you about putting Mr Rees Howells' life story in print. Actually, for years I have wished that I could do it! I have felt so strongly that these marvellous stories of God's dealings with him through the years are just full of the teaching which the Church needs. I would suggest that

this is deeply important while the details are all fresh. The Church of Christ needs it all.... I shall never be able to thank God sufficiently for all the light He poured into me as I drank in the inner teaching in all those experiences.... I would gladly lay the time aside for such a great work.... I thought I would mention it as it is so much on my heart, and that the glorious opportunity of giving the world some of the 'deep and sacred things' He taught Mr Howells may not be missed. I am at the service of the Lord and you in this thing.

This was followed by another letter on 25th June, following his return to WEC headquarters at Upper Norwood in London. In it, he confirmed his offer to assist in writing a biography of Rees Howells. Samuel gave this generous proposal much prayer. In these important decisions he had learnt 'always to get counsel from God before you act,' one of Rees Howells' sayings. The people of the Spirit in the Scriptures had discernment and would pray only the prayers that the Holy Spirit gave. Each decision that Samuel would make in College affairs was only made after much waiting upon God.

There was more than adequate material to draw from and Samuel was able to produce the manuscript which Rees Howells had already written as a testimony of God's dealings in his own life. In addition, several staff had written copious notes of meetings during the six years of war and later until 1950. The outcome was very positive in this case, and the result was the first publication of *Rees Howells Intercessor* which came off the Lutterworth Press in 1952. Later editions were to be printed in the USA, with Lutterworth's approval, by CLC Press in 1980. Worldwide circulation of the book has proved great ever since, with lives being challenged and dramatically changed, through the deep experiences of the Holy Spirit recorded with such clarity. A more recent DVD is also now having a wide circulation around the world.

To safeguard his position as Honorary Director, and that of the whole College and its ministry at home and abroad, Samuel commenced the process of securing full charitable status, yet preserving the spiritual nature of the work. This was a very difficult period requiring much courage and wisdom in the face of stiff opposition. A Declaration of Trust only, had previously been made in 1940 with five trustees, but now a carefully worded Charitable Trust Deed, according to guidelines of Charitable Trusts Acts between 1853 and 1939, was approved of by Mr Justice Roxburgh at Chambers in the High Court of Justice, Chancery Division on Monday, 25th July 1955. The property, doctrinal basis and objects of the Charity were set out clearly, and the position of the Honorary Director and his trustees defined. No salaries were ever to be received by the trustees or resident staff of the College, and the Director would be personally responsible financially for the whole work, certainly a great liability to assume, but a test of the position of faith that Samuel was assuming. Samuel also had to deal with the future of the Penllergaer Estate.

During World War II, the fourth estate, Penllergaer was requisitioned by the government for military purposes. It was originally purchased by Rees Howells in November 1938 as part of his ambitious plan to provide a home for, and a place to educate, Jewish refugee children being sent to Britain from Europe. It was a beautiful mansion, six miles west of Swansea, with acres of woodland and a magnificent collection of rhododendrons surrounding two lakes fed by a cascading waterfall. Samuel had swallowed hard when his father had originally announced his intention to purchase this vast estate, but he followed every step closely.

On his first visit, they had been driven in the College car through the impressive gateway up the 1¼ mile drive, past Weaver's Lodge and the fields, then the Upper Lodge and quarry, winding their way through the breath-taking display of even more rhododendrons and azaleas to the Walled Gardens and Orchid House. Samuel later discovered that trees from all parts of Britain had been thoughtfully planted by its previous owners. In the distance, the constant play of the waterfall controlling the water level of the upper lake blended with the chorus of birds that revelled in the peaceful grounds.

Suddenly the mansion, affectionately known as the Big

House by the locals, had loomed into full view. Samuel could not believe his eyes. Was this to be their new home when the Bible College was relocated from Derwen Fawr, and refugee children were housed in purpose-built homes in the new estate grounds? The plan was for Derwen Fawr to become a secondary school for girls and Glynderwen a secondary school for boys. Sketty Isaf would be accommodation, and possibly Sketty Hall and Gwern Einon House, two other local mansions, would be rented for accommodation as well. Once provided with a good educational foundation, these children would have been taken to the Holy Land, where Rees Howells planned to purchase plots of land in the Middle East to establish centres. Samuel was to play a key role in this project.

Actually, Lady Molyneux who held the lease for Gwern Einon had not been willing to sublet, so approaches were made by Rees Howells to purchase another property, Summerlands, in Caswell, several miles away on the Gower Peninsula. That venture, although promising at first, proved not to be the Lord's provision. The outbreak of World War II and the British Government's decision to return fleeing Jewish refugees back into Europe had brought all these plans to an abrupt end, which left the Bible College as owners of the near 300-acre estate, with its 18-acre trout fishing lake. Home Farm and other cottages were sublet, the Forestry Commission took over the management of the woodland and the Big House was requisitioned to accommodate first British and then American soldiers, who soon undid the good work previously undertaken to restore the paintwork to its former glory in readiness for use.

Before his death, Rees Howells had asked Samuel to promise that he would become responsible to pray in the £100,000 ($160,000), which he had asked God for, as a seal on the veracity of the Vision he had to see the Gospel reaching the whole world in the last days. Samuel had agreed, but felt he could only manage it in 'small doses at a time!' Now, in 1950, this challenge was a reality. Samuel did not think it was right to ask God for money when you have assets that were surplus to need. One possible source of income was to sell Penllergaer Estate for housing development but the application for planning consent, submitted by Samuel on 17th July 1950, was refused on the grounds that the land was part of a Green Belt – land on the perimeter of a town or city reserved for 'open green spaces' only, so focused prayer was necessary for God to work. Could Samuel secure a good sale for the now redundant property? He also prayed much for the War Office compensation for the old house to be released.

The County Council did agree in 1950 to purchase the stately mansion[1] which had deteriorated considerably during the war years, and in 1961, an unsuccessful attempt by a demolition squad to blow it up was followed by determined efforts to bulldoze it down, wall by wall. In its place, administration buildings for the Glamorgan County Council were later erected. The lakes and the rhododendrons remained, along with acres of arable land worked from Home Farm, leased out with its cottages for an annual rent. It was a great sadness for Samuel to see the mansion, with all its special memories, go in such an ignominious way, and now he was unable to sell the valuable land for development. It would take many years of focused, costly prayer before that could begin.

Closer to home, Samuel rarely appeared at the meal table in the College, except when there were visiting guests, because of distracting conversations. Usually he remained in his room, often without taking food at all. His normal diet was simple and he was a vegetarian during his younger days. Lessons and stories he had heard from his father encouraged him in his present test to set himself to continue to pray through for the £100,000 ($160,000).

Although the staff, who had spent years with the Founder, fully understood and appreciated that Samuel needed to be alone in this way, and that he was by temperament a retiring person, it did present a problem for the new students each year. For many, after their home experience of lively charismatic pastors and preachers, here was a College apparently without a Director, just a solitary, lonely figure who appeared at the pulpit several times a week, then disappeared to be cosseted by a bevy of elderly ladies. It was difficult for these young men and women to understand what was actually going on behind the scenes and that Samuel was deliberately stepping out of the limelight to provide maximum space for those directly responsible for the welfare of the students to exercise their authority. He was able to concentrate on the major challenges which faced the development of the College ministry. Also, perhaps, he was quietly endeavouring to avoid the trap of becoming a popular figure. His father had been outgoing and forthright in his public statements and drew together a band of followers, not all of whom could appreciate the nature of his walk of faith. As with Jesus when He rode into Jerusalem on His final entry into the city on 'Palm Sunday' (as we call it today), the fickle crowd wanted a conquering hero. Samuel wanted none of that and he would not oblige.

One source of encouragement and challenge came through reading the account written by Norman Grubb in the freshly published book of the way the Holy Spirit led the Founder to open the College in the first place. Beside Norman Grubb's account, Samuel also had access to correspondence written at the time in 1923, all of which brought vivid personal memories back to him. Along with other leading Welsh ministers, Rees Howells had been exercised to open a College, either in Swansea or Cardiff, both strategic centres in South Wales, for the training of young men and women converted in the 1904 Welsh Revival. This was considered vital by the majority of ministers of the time. Strong differences of opinion about the possible location existed in South Wales so that when the Lord had eventually indicated a site in Blackpill, Swansea, Rees Howells met stiff opposition even from the ministerial fraternity. In Porth, near Cardiff, R. B. Jones was already nurturing a Training School, so another seemed unnecessary. It was then that Rees Howells had discovered the reason why the Lord had selected Glynderwen House for another College. The Roman Catholics too had made a strong bid, in their policy to locate colleges in Britain near to universities, and Swansea University was within walking distance along the Mumbles Road. Having experienced firsthand, the Roman Catholic persecution of evangelical Christians in Portuguese East Africa (present day Mozambique), when he was a missionary in Africa, Rees Howells saw this as a challenge of faith and even with only two shillings (10p / 16¢ in old English money) in his pocket had taken the plunge and approached Mr Edwards, the draper, owner of Glynderwen House about a sale. One letter, dated 4th September 1923, expresses a little of the situation that Rees Howells was facing as he shared his heart with a close friend. God had promised Rees Howells a talent of gold only (worth £6,150 / $9,840) and when told, Mr Edwards kindly lowered his asking price of £6,300 ($10,080) by £500 ($800). When all the bills were paid, including solicitor's charges, the total cost was the amount that the Lord had told Rees Howells! However, the pressure was on, especially when Rees received a letter dated 8th October 1923, from his solicitor, Arthur James, in Goat Street, Swansea:

> Dear Mr Howells,
> I had a phone call last week that Mr Edwards was coming in and held no hope for any extension of time for completion. At 4:45 Mr Edwards called me over to his solicitor and would have nothing but a signature there and then and completion on 1st November. I concluded that you would be flung up and he would sell to somebody else, so I signed and paid over the deposit. I hope you do not think I have overstepped the mark. If you cannot find the money, the bank will advance it on better terms than the vendor! I tried to get out of it but it was better to leave him alone now.
> Yr eiddoch,
> Arthur James.

Samuel was only eleven years of age at the time but somehow had been emotionally caught up with all that was happening. For his father, Rees Howells, the purchase of Glynderwen had been no stunt or ambitious step into the unknown. He was following the Holy Spirit's leading and this involved considerable financial liability. All along he had needed the Holy Spirit's confirmation.

Among the many personal treasures which Samuel always kept in the drawer of his room was a postcard of the largest liner of its time, RMS *Majestic*, the ship which was taking Rees and Hannah Howells to New York in 1922.

Rees and Samuel Howells with Miss Alice Townsend c.1921

The postcard carried news of his parents on their way to the meetings in the USA. They had received a remarkable last minute deliverance of £138 ($220) for the fare, a seal on God's will for them to embark on their work to open a College in South Wales. It reads:

> Here we are within a day's reach to New York. We have had a splendid voyage. We can truly say, 'Fy nhad sydd wrth y llyw.' (My Father's hand is on the rudder and in control). We only wish you were with us especially Uncle Joe, but he prefers running around Pentwyn. We are looking forward to be in New York tomorrow. We shall give Uncle Joe all the news again.

This was the beginning of an intense spiritual battle for them and Samuel, even as a young lad, was to feel the impact of it on his own life. However, his school studies did not suffer and he applied himself diligently, showing great promise for the future.

The Holy Spirit had already told Rees Howells that no appeals for money, as had previously been intended by the group of interested ministers, should be made. Instead, Rees had returned to his home town of Brynaman and spent the next ten months in God's presence, waiting for the word of assurance that the money would be forthcoming. That had been a fierce conflict for Rees and as he mused over these matters now Samuel took careful note as he re-read that paragraph in one of his father's earlier letters:

> I can assure you that I have been through testings of faith before, and have gone through darkness to gain the objectives, but it all seems to have been child's play to compare with this. It seemed that I was fighting with principalities and rulers of darkness, spiritual wickedness in high places. At times it was like Egyptian darkness or, as it was with Abram:
>
> *A horror of great darkness fell upon him.* Genesis 15:12 (AV).
>
> The battle was so desperate that I was willing to let everything go in order to win the victory over the enemy of souls.

Samuel could understand more now of what he himself was experiencing, and was encouraged to realise that the Holy Spirit had led through to complete victory during those early days.

Rees and Lizzie Howells in America with some friends in 1922. They spoke at the Moody Bible Institute in Chicago and the church in New York where revival broke out in 1857.

Samuel now held no illusions about what would be required of him in the 1950s, to pray through his present challenges of faith. This included the securing of charitable status in the 1950s for the College, much opposed by one particular individual with other ideas, and the selling of Penllergaer Estate to raise capital for the £100,000 ($160,000) he was praying for. It would require many hours spent in the Divine Presence. Sometimes he would make startling pronouncements in his pulpit ministry during the evening prayer meetings, as one student recalls, such as,

> "Don't think you can pray like Moses and see God's purposes fulfilled unless you spend the time Moses did in God's presence. If you think you can pray like him without spending the time he spent – you are shallow."

Little did staff and students know what he was really facing which produced such passionate words.

It was mainly through reading and meditating upon the Scriptures in the Lord's presence that Samuel now drew his real strength. Considering the Old Testament passages relating to the rebuilding of the Temple in Jerusalem, after the restoration of the Jews from seventy years of captivity in Babylon, through the intercessions of Ezekiel and Daniel, Samuel saw afresh, through reading Ezra 4:5, that the work was suddenly brought to a halt. These satanic onslaughts on God's work often bring progress to a standstill even today. However, as a result of the persistent, prevailing prayers of Haggai and Zechariah over a fourteen year period, the Holy Spirit came upon the prophets in a powerful way, enabling their work to proceed.

> *The prophets, Haggai and Zechariah prophesied to the Jews who were in Judah and Jerusalem in the name of the God of Israel...* Ezra 5:1 (NASB).

The prophecy of Zechariah brought great encouragement to Samuel.

> *This is the word of the Lord to Zerubbabel, saying, "Not by might nor by power, but by My Spirit," says the Lord of hosts. "What are you, O great mountain? Before Zerubbabel you will become a plain; and he will bring forth the top stone with shouts of grace, grace to it!" Also the*

word of the Lord came to me saying, "The hands of Zerubbabel have laid the foundation of this house and his hands will finish it. Then you will know that the Lord of hosts has sent me to you. For who has despised the day of small things? But these seven will be glad when they see the plumb line in the hand of Zerubbabel – these are the eyes of the Lord which range to and fro throughout the earth." Zechariah 4:6-10 (NASB).

The Lord brought great relief to the situation and led eventually to his main prayer objects, already referred to, being achieved. The Holy Spirit was teaching Samuel the vital place of prevailing prayer in the progress and development of God's work in the world. He was proving the truth of the Lord's promise in John 15:7.

If you remain in Me and My words remain in you, ask whatever you wish and it will be given you.

He knew that remaining in Christ every moment of every day was the key.

Samuel loved his daily constitutional walk after dinner, and would stride at an amazing speed which even the fittest visitor to the College, accompanying him on occasion, found it difficult to maintain. A regular half hour walk was to Sketty Green and back, a good mile each way, which kept him fit. Although he had a small appetite he consumed regular supplies of fresh fruit and dates, and would be considered in today's gastronomical climate as a healthy eater. However, when the smell of chips being fried in the kitchen wafted up to his landing, it was not uncommon for him to succumb to the temptation and request that a 'sample plate of fresh chips' be delivered to his room! Instructions in the kitchen were for a maximum of eight chips only, but we have it on record that the cooks ensured that the longest chips were selected, counted out and arranged suitably on a warm plate!

Chapter Ten

Kingdom Prayers

Samuel loved the beautiful College grounds especially during the summer, with their flowerbeds, rhododendrons and Italian Gardens of Derwen Fawr, a special feature bordered by a moat. Sadly, the moat, which fed its water into a deep well, proved too dangerous for mischievous cats or rummaging hedgehogs so had to be drained. Young fox cubs would play on the lawn early in the mornings as Samuel enjoyed magnificent sunrises over Swansea Bay, visible from the veranda of Derwen Fawr House, a view so familiar in photographs. Across the Bay, white clouds rose from the Port Talbot Steel Company of Wales' cooling towers and the occasional ore carrier sailed in from Nigeria. By then, most coal mines in South Wales were closing as it became cheaper to import from Boston, USA. The Bay was quite busy with shipping until the nearby BP Oil Refinery closed at Llandarcy. Still, the 9pm ferry to Cork in the Republic of Ireland was always a sight to see, fully illuminated and sliding gracefully past the Mumbles lighthouse into the deeper waters of the Bristol Channel.

Derwen Fawr became Samuel's home and it was his responsibility to preserve its sanctity, for visitors invariably remarked about the sense of God's presence that pervaded its grounds. Because of its transformation from once being a working farm into a private residence and then into a Bible College, buildings had been erected in varying period styles, with seemingly little planning, and were linked by a series of paths. Lower ground had been sold by Rees Howells to Swansea Corporation for playing fields and Samuel himself sold adjacent fields for housing development, rendering the grounds manageable yet still very spacious. In the days when gardeners abounded and student labour was at hand, the flowerbeds were tended regularly, producing a beautiful annual display of colour.

The rhododendrons and azaleas were managed well and grass lawns mowed with precision. Photographs show the half-acre kitchen garden with its parallel rows of lush vegetables and a row of fruit trees and bushes beyond, a credit to David Rees and later to Stan Teed, the head gardeners. Sadly, weeds began to win the battle in some flowerbeds, as gardeners were fewer during the long summer breaks, but Michael Williams and Ivy Impey worked tirelessly to provide a constant splash of colour around the house, and to crop the lawns.

Kitchen garden 1970s, situated behind the Hospital

Samuel knew every inch of the buildings from the bungalow to the left of the stone-pillared entrance, to the Men's Hostel (for students and then staff) on the right, where he had once lived when responsible for the male students. The main drive from the entrance forked to the left and right, each direction opening up new vistas of the grounds. He could remember when the footings were laid, during his father's day, for the new hospital / residential block to the left, and the narrow path round to the Conference Hall, obviously once part of the old farm complex. At one end of this low solid stone edifice, pebble-dashed and whitewashed to keep it dry, was the cottage. Mr Crane made use of the lower floor for his on-site printing, while up the rickety wooden stairs was useful storage space. For many years the unsurfaced dirt paths and square outside the Conference Hall became mud tracks during the wet seasons, presenting a constant headache for the cleaning teams designated to prepare the hall for Sunday services, which were held there. Eventually, not without a little persuasion, Samuel agreed for tarmacadam to replace the dirt surfaces.

The Conference Hall was not exactly ideal for speakers who, standing on a stage type platform with a curtained rail around it, found the congregation peering up while sitting on not always too comfortable wooden chairs which stretched back along the narrow building in front of them. With its red corrugated roof and plywood ceiling acoustics were not first class, and it took many years before a suitable PA system was finally found to meet all the criteria for good listening. Lighting, too, had presented a problem and the eventual solution of powerful lamps inset into the ceiling, generated heat too and needed replacing often – an expensive method! Samuel was never fond of speaking there! However, the war years had taught everyone that ideal conditions were not always possible and they had learnt to praise the Lord for all things at all times.

Samuel had often stopped by the Conference Hall to admire the splendid copper beech tree that rained down its nuts and leaves in the autumn, many on to the roof of the Chapel, a taller stone building, originally used for services until it became too small. It then served a multitude of purposes for Emmanuel Preparatory School, from morning assemblies to school dinners, gym classes, music, drama and art lessons. Until a suitable oil fired central heating system was installed, Samuel remembered stories of how its large round coal-burning stove had belched out clouds of smoke when first lit. Gradually the Lord had answered prayers and the facilities and general comfort of the Conference Hall had been greatly improved.

Beyond the Chapel were the student lecture rooms, two in one wooden building, familiar to all as a one-time army barrack, which had been purchased at the end of the war for a reasonable price and erected on a concrete pad. With a regularly maintained roof and an annual coat of creosote, the lecture rooms served well in this cosy corner of the estate for many years. From one end, students could view the beautiful Italian Gardens, landscaped by its previous owner at great expense, and were able to enjoy the shade of a magnificent elm tree for afternoon lectures in the summer. Sadly, with the advent of Dutch elm disease throughout the UK this beautiful tree was felled (in the 1970s) and its timber used to fuel the College boilers. The most difficult challenge was to dig up the extensive root system and stump, and this took the students over a year to complete in their morning work sessions. The garden was a much loved trysting place for Samuel, who slipped out from Derwen Fawr House when the sun was warm, although very rarely was he ever seen relaxing in a chair outside – perhaps too shy! We do have a record of at least one occasion, however, when he was recuperating from an attack of influenza.

Samuel Howells recuperating outside Derwen Fawr House

Returning to the main entrance of the College and following the right fork along the drive, a visitor passed the fragile glass green house used extensively to propagate plants for the garden and also to nurture a bumper crop of juicy tomatoes for the College each year. The cooks were often stretched to invent new ways of serving them, but blanched, peeled and stuffed tomatoes were always Samuel's favourite. The drive opened up to the front of the main house where hundreds of smiling people have stood to have their photographs taken through the years. The other favourite place was in front of the large white stone with 'Jehovah Jireh' (The Lord will provide) embedded in marble on the side (see pages 89 and 97). This stone represented a spiritual landmark for future generations to be reminded that God always fulfils His promises, and that the faith of God had been gained, not just for a college, but for the fulfilment of the Vision.

Courtyard of Derwen Fawr. Ladies' Staff Hostel on left, Men's Hostel (front) and old Bakehouse (right)

Visitors were usually spotted from the library windows in the Ladies' Staff Hostel. The library was a focal point for College life, where folk could call in and browse around at leisure, catching a glimpse of the missionary pamphlets on display. As these had increased in number they were later transferred to a table in the dining room and became a constant source of up-to-date information on God's work around the world, through dozens of different missionary agencies. Despite his love of reading, Samuel rarely ventured into the library except when the College was quiet, but preferred to call for the resident librarian if ever he needed a particular book. It was this shyness which dictated much of his activities, even around the College, so that the grass quadrangle outside the library and in front of the Men's Hostel, a romping ground (to play boisterously, in a carefree manner) for men students during the warmer days, would be a deterrent to Samuel. Walking towards the library a visitor was always impressed by a verse from

Scripture in Welsh, inscribed in white letters above the Ladies' Staff Hostel door. A surge of Welsh pride always welled up inside him as Samuel would read and translate, *Ti yw'r Crist, Mab y Duw byw. Thou art the Christ, the Son of the living God.* Matthew 16:16 (AV). (As just visible on the top left of photo on page 119).

Inside the courtyard of Derwen Fawr (opposite the Bakehouse). Toby Bergin (back) with students c. early 1980s. On the reverse of "Ebenezer" (visible from the street of Derwen Fawr Road) was: Bible College of Wales – Have Faith in God.

Most of the Derwen Fawr Estate was enclosed by a high stone wall erected by the previous owners, acting as added security from the very busy road outside. Passengers upstairs on the red double-decker buses which jostled their way past each other every fifteen minutes on the narrow road, were easily able to view activities that went on 'over the wall.'

Yes, this was Samuel's much loved home and he never failed to appreciate how kind the Lord had been in allowing him, and his staff, to be responsible for it in His name.

**Italian Gardens in the grounds of Derwen Fawr
(The drained moat is in the middle)**

On one occasion when he was preaching Samuel referred to the 'ball of fire' rising slowly over the Bay, early one morning. It had struck him quite forcibly that the One who had created that magnificent sunrise was the One who had died for him and for all mankind, on the cross. How could he not but worship such a wonderful Person and live for Him alone.

From this vantage point on the veranda, Samuel would often catch a passer-by and arrange a visit to his room, or feed the rich variety of frequent bird visitors. Or folk would just hear him pacing up and down for long periods, locked in prayer. The front lawn was sacrosanct in those days, out of bounds to anyone, staff and students, without the nod of approval being given. It was reserved for the Director, Samuel, bowed in prayer, 'watching on the walls,' occasionally pausing to admire the goldfish in the circular pond at one end. Inevitably these goldfish became prey for local herons from nearby Singleton Park, or even for the curiosity of the white College cat, Snowy, so William

Rowlands, the baker, whose job it was to feed them regularly, suggested that replenishing the stock was proving too expensive an exercise. William had originally responded to God's call to surrender his whole life for service when he was trapped for several hours in the darkness of the coal face, in a mining accident at the colliery in Cwmllynfell during the war years. He had never baked before but stepped into the gap when the need arose.

Already we have mentioned some of the burdens that demanded Samuel's focused attention: the development of both the College and Emmanuel School, the very kind offer from Norman Grubb to document the life and ministry of Rees Howells, the need to produce a watertight document to register the whole ministry for charitable status, the tying up of loose ends regarding Penllergaer, and praying in the finances required to maintain the work, and also to secure the £100,000 ($160,000) which he had promised his father, as a seal on the veracity of the Vision. £100,000 in 1950 (when Rees Howells died) would be the equivalent of £2.7 million ($4.32 million) in 2012. Very heavy burdens to carry for Samuel, then in his early forties.

By temperament, Samuel was always very quiet and extremely sensitive, particularly in spiritual matters. Before ever he preached, many hours would be spent in the Lord's presence. Once in the pulpit, with exceptional discernment, he would know exactly where members of the congregation stood in their relationship with the Lord, and would sometimes speak about these issues to staff members responsible for students. In private conversations, Samuel would usually know beforehand about the particular burdens the individual was carrying, and many a Christian leader wept in his presence.

It was this sensitivity and close walk with the Lord which also enabled him to discern what he termed the 'prayers of the Kingdom.' These were special burdens that the Holy Spirit gave for national and international situations, particularly where satanic forces were seeking to disrupt God's purposes for the advance of the Gospel.

At 4am on 25th January 1950, the army of the Democratic People's Republic of Korea opened fire on all fronts, on the South Korean positions south of the 39th Parallel. By 11am, North Korea had officially declared war on its southern neighbour. In a land where revival fires had swept and blessed whole communities, this was an attempt to engulf the whole peninsula in virtual slavery to a godless ideology. Fighting was vicious, often hand-to-hand, and the defending U.S. forces, later backed by other UN countries, gave way. The conflict continued until 27th July 1953 when an Armistice was agreed, but not before battles for Bunker Hill, T-bone Hill, Spud Hill and Old Baldy had found their place into the history books. Very little is written of the burden Samuel and those closest to him were carrying in those days, as they stood alongside the dear Korean people engulfed in the conflict and who suffered terribly.

Samuel continued praying for the Korean people, particularly those suffering under the oppressive North Korean regime, right till the end of his life. Following the devastating war, his response was to ask the Lord to restore the land and bless the people spiritually. In a prayer meeting on 27th September 1954, his inner feelings burst through in an impassioned declaration,

"God is opening up the world – He has men in all the countries – I have told the Lord that I will go to Korea. I am exercised about it. There are things I have to finish here now. If someone could go, tens of thousands could be reached with the Gospel. Are we alive to these things? Korea is ready and God is going to give the offer of the Gospel to them. There are key people there and we would like to help them, whether financially or spiritually."

God answered these prayers in an abundant way and the Church in South Korea grew and now sends out, and supports, missionaries in many countries in the world.

Another brief upsurge of persecution occurred in 1955 against the Kikuyu Christians in Kenya. Through visits from Ken Terhoven, the College was given reports of the testimonies of those who had courageously survived the fanatical (demonically inspired) Mau Mau attacks, and of the sound of Christians returning home through the bush singing 'Onward Christian soldiers' gradually growing less and less, as one by one, they were slaughtered. Those dear martyrs paid the supreme price for freedom and blessing. It was never a case of taking sides in these prayers. People of every nationality and persuasion are all very precious to the Lord, whose atoning death was for all of mankind. However, the Mau Mau had taken demonic oaths, calling upon ancient spirits to possess them to fight against the British and the Christian God – they did not represent the true Kenyans desire for a peaceful transition.[1] As the Holy Spirit was establishing Christ's Kingdom in Kenya, so Satan would stir hatred into human hearts and conflicts erupted. Again the College had the privilege of remembering them and the whole nation, and having a small part in a Kingdom prayer.

Samuel's leadership and personal involvement in these world situations was already evident in his pulpit ministry at the time, as he drew strength from the life of Elisha. Quoting from a Saturday evening service we find him at full stretch,

> "Elisha and the prophets didn't do these things in their stride. He had entered into the realm of God. In the case of Dothan (2 Kings 6:8-18) was he perturbed? Not in the least, but his servant was. This realm is so delicate. One man was living in the spiritual realm and the other in the natural realm. A life of faith has a very sobering effect, it is a real gauge of our spiritual life. Unless we are in victory here we are not going to be in victory in these greater prayers. There is no confusion with God. His dealings and guidance are all orderly. When the eyes of the young man were opened he saw the hosts of God and then he was as strong as the prophet. God has visited us. His presence can be felt brooding over the whole place. These revelations are given to us so that we can be more effective in our service and believing prayer. Forget everything else now and concentrate on these battles. It may not be our work but the Holy Spirit is so keen. If I had not prayed that prayer for Korea last night I

would not have been able to go to bed. There would have been a cross-examination with the Holy Spirit. I know these searchings well. He would ask, 'Don't you live for the Kingdom?' We are dealing with a Divine Person who knows everything within us. But I can say I have prayed for these people with the same feeling as if they were our people. He tries to get us to be as concerned about other people's work as with our own."

The world was brought to the verge of a nuclear holocaust in October 1962 when a United States U2 spy plane reported a build up of Russian SAM missiles sites in Cuba (with a range of 2,000 miles / 3,200 kilometres) and aimed towards the United States. The situation prompted a red alert with 125,000 U.S. troops being marshalled ready for an invasion of Cuba. Two weeks passed and the first Soviet nuclear missiles went operational on the 20th October. President Kennedy held emergency meetings to decide on which of six options to take. Immediate action to invade Cuba was likely, as additional spy planes reported Russian ships carrying more nuclear missiles on deck, halfway on their journey across the Atlantic. The situation was serious. Samuel sensed the urgency and once more resorted to prayer. The Lord led him to consider the life and ministry of Elisha and how the prophet had learnt the secrets of prayer. In 2 Kings 7 the story of the siege of Samaria is told. If he could, Elisha would have prevented it, but he couldn't. He knew he had to wait for the word of the Lord to be given. Samuel also knew that the nuclear crisis could only be prevented when the word of the Lord was given. The situation was entirely in God's hands. The word of the Lord only came at the last minute, in Elisha's case, just as his servants were holding the door against the King of Israel's henchmen sent to kill. The immortal words,

Hear ye the word of the Lord. 2 Kings 7:1 (AV),
reversed the situation in a flash. The College meeting went well into the night but the word came from the Lord:

Tomorrow about this time…
The Russian Missile ships stopped their onward voyage

and returned home, and the crisis was averted. God had worked. Samuel was proving his willingness to assume responsibility through these Kingdom prayers.

Samuel Howells in the early 1960s

Chapter Eleven

Easter and Whitsun

Continuing in the custom passed on to the College family through the Founder, both Easter and Whitsun (Pentecost) remained very special times for Samuel who wished these monumental landmarks in the history of mankind to be remembered too. Although no religious fasting period was declared throughout the weeks of Lent (the six week period preceding the Easter weekend), Samuel prepared himself prayerfully and his pulpit ministry usually took the form of an intense study of the final weeks of Jesus' public ministry.

During that period, he would suggest that the staff and students should ask the Lord to point out any particular areas in their lives that did not please Him, and seek cleansing and forgiveness. He would exhort his congregation to spend as much time as possible in the Lord's presence. Good Friday was set aside entirely for the Lord as a quietness rested over the College. Everyone gathered in the prayer room at 10:30am and Samuel would minister from the Scriptures, usually for about one and a half hours, following carefully chosen Easter hymns from the *Golden Bells* hymnal, and several of the congregation were asked to lead in prayer. Drawing from his vast knowledge of the Scriptures, Samuel's style was to provide an overall background to the passage of Scripture he was reading, and then to develop the story, linking it with many other passages connected with his main theme. There were times when he seemed to be labouring in the ministry, but there always came a moment when the spiritual atmosphere in the room was strangely charged with a Presence and, as Samuel continued, those present felt transported in time and became part of the action. Every word spoken by the Saviour became personal and the emotional experience very intense. This was particularly so during the reading of the Passion Week events and the Passover.

Samuel preaching in the prayer room of Derwen Fawr House with world map behind him – Every Creature c. late 1980s

On one occasion, when Samuel read the narrative of the Passover Meal in the Upper Room, a stunned silence swept through the prayer room as Matthew 26:20-22 (AV) was read.

> *Now when the even was come He sat down with the twelve. And as they did eat He said, "Verily I*

> *say unto you that one of you shall betray Me."*
> *And they were exceeding sorrowful, and began everyone of them to say unto Him, "Lord, is it I?"*

Such was the power of Samuel's ministry when under the anointing that a wave of conviction would touch the hearts of all present, for reasons known only to themselves that day.

The Saviour's inner conflict in Gethsemane, the betrayal, the trial, scourging and crucifixion scenes, all were graphically portrayed as the Holy Spirit revealed afresh the agony of those fateful hours in the Saviour's life. Throughout these times, Samuel's command of English, his second language was masterly,

> "His life and ministry had exposed their hypocrisy. Have you paused to consider what the impeccable Son of God has done for you? Have you? The physical suffering was terrible but it was the dereliction He could not face. Yet He was willing to accept it for you and me. That bitter cry of desolation as Christ plumbed the depths and was accursed by God the heart of our redemption. Aren't you profoundly affected today? Then spend time low at His feet."

There was always a poignant pause whenever Samuel read Matthew 27:36 (AV).

> *And sitting down they watched –* (pause) *Him –* (pause) *there.*

On another occasion, Samuel examined in-depth the seven sayings of Jesus uttered from the cross, including the assurance given to the penitent thief enduring the same fate as Himself.

> *Today shalt thou be with Me in paradise.* Luke 23:43 (AV).

What a powerful Gospel this is! No waiting period necessary even for the worst of sinners who truly repents and believes.

Again, in another service Samuel revealed just how much every verse of Scripture was being considered prayerfully in God's presence.

> *Behold, the veil of the Temple was rent in twain from the top to the bottom; and the earth did*

> *quake...and the graves were opened.* Matthew 27:51-52 (AV).
>
> "I have been dwelling on that verse for the past few days – all barriers between us and God have been broken; death can hold us no longer."

Samuel's Good Friday expositions of chapters 52 and 53 of the prophet Isaiah were always inspired and deeply charged with emotion. Chapter 52 begins with a wakeup call for Jerusalem, assuring them that a day would come when all its shackles would be removed and it would become a city where only the righteous would enter. Before introducing the manner by which this purging would become possible through the suffering Servant of Jehovah, God reminds His people of previous miraculous deliverances they had experienced from the hands of Pharaoh in Egypt and then, much later, through Isaiah's own ministry, from the Assyrian monarchs. Samuel would remind his listeners that God Himself had raised up those pagan overlords in order to demonstrate for all the world to see, that by simply stretching forth His hand, they were utterly destroyed. This is exactly the same today with respect to all the current world powers and religious systems and will be in the future, even when the anti-Christ is manifest. However, in each case, God must have a pure channel, as with Moses and Isaiah, through whom the Holy Spirit can exercise the commensurate Divine faith. Then again, the deliverance from Egypt through Moses led Samuel to refer to the power of the blood of the Passover Lamb to protect the children of Israel from the Angel of Death, as it stalked through Egypt on that fateful night and touched all the firstborn of men and beast.

Samuel treated Isaiah's graphic descriptions of the suffering Servant with great reverence and respect as a holy hush descended on the prayer room. It was obvious that each verse touched his tender spirit, drawing from him such phrases as,

> "We shall never know what it meant for Him to become incarnate. These words haunt one (referring to himself); we don't know what to do, it is all beyond our comprehension. We are not heavy or sleepy today, are we? There is

something radically wrong with you if you are. We shall never be able to discharge our debt; all other things pale into insignificance. The prophet was completely taken out of himself and saw the suffering Christ."

One very interesting observation made by Samuel, obviously gained through much reflection, was that death itself was a terrifying prospect to those living in the Old Testament days. Psalm 55:4 speaks of the terrors of death troubling David, and Hezekiah's prayer in Isaiah 38 reveals his inner concerns about it. It was only the Holy Spirit who could minister hope to those Old Testament saints as in Job 19:25-26 (AV).

I know that my Redeemer lives…yet in my flesh I will see God.

Isaiah 53 was inexhaustible to Samuel, whose spirit searched for every depth that it held. Jesus' personal response to those prophetic chapters during His final years and months of seclusion in Nazareth before being thrust out into the limelight of His public ministry, must have affected Him in every way, and this produced fresh revelation for Samuel.

Every step was clearly marked out and Jesus had to give assent to each one. How did He read that it would please the Father to bruise Him?

Yet it pleased the Lord to bruise Him; He hath put Him to grief. Isaiah 53:10 (AV).

What depths did He see in Psalm 22:1 (AV)?

My God, My God, why have You forsaken Me?

The only person with whom He could have a measure of fellowship was His mother, Mary, over whom the aged Simeon had prophesied – when her young child, Jesus, was presented in the Temple – that He was destined to cause the falling and rising of many in Israel, and a sword would pierce Mary's own soul too (Luke 2:35). It was only by grace that Jesus ever left Nazareth to proceed to the Jordan, where He identified Himself with sinful men in the waters of baptism.

During these sacred Good Friday sessions, time seemed to stand still. For some moments Samuel's voice was reduced to barely a whisper. At others, his pitch was raised as the Holy Spirit empowered him. So often, passages from the book of Hebrews filled his thoughts, particularly the priestly office of the Saviour, High Priest after the order of Melchizedek (Hebrews 5). This remarkable figure who blessed Abram (Genesis 14:18-20) was the facsimile of the One to come, Jesus Christ the reality.

"Now we can boldly" (emphasised by Samuel with a firm thump on the pulpit!) "enter the Inner Sanctuary of God's presence, previously only permitted once a year following the most stringent preparations, to the Throne of Grace.

"We have had many totally impossible prayers recently, almost absurd to pray, but the Holy Spirit has enabled us to present them before that Throne and the Father has answered them all. That's God!" Samuel exclaimed. "We must thank Him as we have never done before, and believe Him in ways we have found difficult before...I don't think it is worth prolonging this session any further – we will close now."

These were not sermons that Samuel was preaching, but everyone knew that it was his life that was being poured into each session and the physical exhaustion, felt later that weekend, would be very real. Easter Sunday morning was always a time of worship and praise as some of the traditional resurrection hymns were sung to familiar tunes. Problems did occur in later years, as the senior staff members found it increasingly more difficult to reach the higher notes in many of those old tunes, so the choice became more restricted!

Samuel usually felt it most appropriate to include the Communion into the Easter morning service, after a long ministry session from relevant Scriptures. Although he had no mystical views about the service or its elements, Communion was always considered a very special sacrament. It was clear to Samuel that the Saviour had changed the nature of the Passover Meal with its backward remembrance of an earthly deliverance of the nation from Egypt, and the establishment of an Old Covenant, to the institution of a New Covenant sealed with His own blood. Such a costly sacrifice, he felt, should never be treated lightly by believers in any generation.

The preceding ministry on Easter Sunday followed closely from Samuel's Good Friday meditations and showed so clearly just how much time he must have spent in God's presence beforehand. Every section of the resurrection narrative received his typically thorough attention, interspersed with impassioned declarations,

> "Despite all the efforts of the Saviour not one of the disciples could understand the resurrection. Neither will we. These truths must be revealed to us – that is the need of the hour.... The danger is that we consider these lovely meetings but we are not changed.... I have been praying through the night that the Lord will meet us as He did these early believers.... How important is Divine revelation. We cannot deal with these matters with our own understanding ...I do trust that a large portion of the night was spent at the open sepulchre. You haven't spent all night in sleep, have you?"

The powerful chapter 15 of Paul's first letter to the Corinthian Church provided ample material for inspired ministry with its undisputed evidence of resurrection appearances to Peter, a number of women (see the Gospels) the disciples, a gathering of more than five hundred people at one time, James, all the Apostles and finally, Paul (1 Cor. 15:3-9). The transformation in the lives of these individuals, once Jesus had breathed the Holy Spirit into their lives, was remarkable.

With the clock hands moving forward steadily, unnoticed, and the sun shining through one window, then the next, and a curtain being quietly drawn to shield Samuel's eyes from the glare, he would draw the ministry to its close.

> "I feel the Lord is speaking to us...to deny the resurrection is to be equalled to the sin of blasphemy...spend these hours very carefully.
> It would be a tragedy if you spoke about other things today."

As years passed, Samuel was not always able to sustain such an intense ministry and would ask senior staff members to take the Easter morning service. But if he felt well enough he would love to play his part, spending a longer time reading the Scriptures, and providing more space for prayer and the singing of Easter hymns.

Forty days following the resurrection came the glorious ascension, when Jesus returned Home after spending the time with the newly born Apostles.

Blessed be the God and Father of our Lord Jesus Christ, which according to His abundant mercy hath begotten us again unto a lively hope by the resurrection of Jesus Christ from the dead. 1 Peter 1:3 (AV).

This must have been an intense time of teaching and preparation before they were instructed to remain in Jerusalem and wait for the promised Holy Spirit. Ascension Day never went unnoticed by Samuel, who pondered deeply on its truths and its promises of the King's return to the mountain top of Olives to establish His Millennial reign on earth. No doubt, these will be troublesome days, particularly in the Middle East, but ones of hope and deliverance for God's people everywhere, as they anticipate His return.

Mr and Mrs Howells amidst a crowd at the Llandrindod Wells Convention, Wales, c.1930

Then, ten days later, came Pentecost or Whitsun as it is

also known in Britain, because of the white garments that were once traditionally worn on that day. Whitsun, during the Founder's days in the College, was always a great occasion when he spoke of his own remarkable encounter with the Holy Spirit at Llandrindod Wells, and all that had transpired in his life since.

The outpouring of the Holy Spirit on the early believers on the Day of Pentecost in Jerusalem had birthed the Church, and only He is totally responsible and able to oversee these end times. The promise of the outpouring of the Holy Spirit on all flesh in Acts 2:17-21 would be a worldwide demonstration of the power of the atonement, completely orchestrated by the Third Person of the Godhead Himself. Whitsun (Pentecost) was always celebrated at the College by an Open Day when crowds came from the locality to attend the meetings and enjoy refreshments. Samuel was never one for large crowds and public meetings but he continued the remembrance of the Whitsun weekends.

Mrs Lizzie Hannah Howells, Samuel Rees Howells and Miss Alice Townsend c.1921

Sometimes Samuel would share in private some of his

earliest recollections of these annual Christian festivals as they were celebrated in the Amman Valley. Good Friday was always a solemn occasion of thoughtful meditation and discussion in the home, centred on the crucifixion of Christ. Joyful celebrations characterised Easter Sunday, the girls parading their beautiful homemade dresses with new bonnets, while the boys sported their fashionable waistcoats and caps.

It had been a long week since Palm Sunday when every grave in the cemetery would be lovingly decorated with fresh daffodils. Now the chapels and churches were packed as practically one hundred percent of the population, young and old, rejoiced together, and preachers were at their best.

1939-Whitsun (Pentecost) Meeting. The fifteenth anniversary of the Bible College of Wales with the banner The GOSPEL to EVERY CREATURE. Rees Howells is preaching. Mrs Howells is on the front row (to the right of Rees wearing a hat). To the right of Mrs Howells is Dr. K. Priddy. Samuel Howells (age 27) is partially obscured by a man's arm (right of photo).

On Easter Mondays, crowds from across the valley descended upon Moriah Chapel, Brynaman for a Gymanfa Ganu (a singing festival). Actually, local chapels hosted the festival in rotation but Moriah seems to have claimed the honours. This was Welsh singing at its best, as the crowds sang praises to God throughout the day. No wonder Samuel never really warmed to the modern brand of singing.

Annual-Whitsun (Pentecost) meeting showing a section of the congregation from the edge of the platform 7 June 1938

Whitsun (Pentecost) too drew packed congregations in their finery to hear fervent preaching and fill the air with praise, but Whit-Monday was very different. As if drawn by some invisible magnet, all the youth throughout the Amman Valley voluntarily set out across the hills to Carreg Cennen Castle, each armed with a packed lunch and bottle of water. Some tramped for miles, finally coming upon this magnificent stone castle perched on the edge of a steep rocky cliff, near the village of Trapp. Then came the final climb to the top and the reward of the breathtaking panoramic views across the lush green fields of the valley. All the adventurous youth were tempted further along to the sloping, often muddy, escape tunnel leading to the field below. Its final destination was unclear, perhaps leading up again to the nearest high vantage point or further, only imagination could tell. Not Samuel's 'cup of tea!' Some went further to the wishing well below, where dreams and ambitions were rehearsed alone.

Samuel's ministry on the Whit-Sunday was, as usual, very powerful, once he found liberty. Often he would take time to trace the activities of the Holy Spirit in the Old Testament, as He took possession of individuals for specific ministries. Now, however, the promise is to all men, for all whom the Lord calls to Himself.

> *For the promise is unto you, and to your children, and to all that are afar off, even as many as the Lord our God shall call.* Acts 2:39 (AV).

Sometimes he would read letters and articles illustrating just how powerfully the Holy Spirit was at work throughout the world, particularly in China and Eastern Europe. Whitsun was always a time of great rejoicing at the coming of the Holy Spirit, and also an opportunity for personal challenge to go further with God.

These significant events in the life of Jesus are sometimes shrouded by different local presentations and have almost been forgotten by some religious groups. Perhaps if they were more closely linked to their original biblical feasts of Passover and Pentecost, which portray their true meaning, there would be greater understanding for younger believers.

The College Vision.

GO YE INTO ALL THE WORLD

AND PREACH THE GOSPEL TO

Every Creature.

The College Motto (Mark 16:15) from the front cover of the Bible College of Wales prospectus 1935

Chapter Twelve

New Faces

The 1950s had seen the addition of new staff to take on roles of responsibility in various departments of the College and School. Dr. Kingsley Priddy himself was comparatively new as Headmaster in Emmanuel Grammar School, after having played such an important role in developing the medical side of the College, and lecturing the students in theological and medical subjects. Now he was learning the art of discipline and produced an excellent list of suggestions for teachers finding problems with controlling a class. Audrey Potter and Valerie Sherwood, who had both dedicated their lives to serve the Lord while pupils in the School, had worked late and hard during the war years to study for their degrees, and were now teaching English, Latin, History and Scripture in the School. Kristine Hunton Jones who had originally come to the College with her sister, Gweno, when their parents joined the teaching staff before the war, joined the staff of the Preparatory School. Her life was dramatically changed when asked to take on the headship of the School in 1954, after Eva Rose left for Beirut. In 1957, the Boarding School saw several additions when Norman and Nollie Brend, both former students in the 1935/37 era[1] returned to the work after several years away in Southend. Norman would eventually become an excellent woodwork master, working in his spare time and during the school holidays to improve the facilities for the boarding children in Glynderwen House, while Nollie would become House Mother to the boarder girls when Gwen Roderick and Doreen Thomas died. On the boarder boys' side, Leslie Warren joined the staff as House Father, following years of experience in Barnardo's Homes.

Richard Maton, converted under the ministry of Dr. Martin Lloyd-Jones, also joined the Preparatory School in 1957, having met the Lord in a deep way through the ministry of Leonard Ravenhill in the 1956 Every Creature College Conference. This had followed his personal call at Keswick in 1955 to serve the Lord, and a clear call to 'sell all and follow Me' and 'The just shall live by faith.' Mary Tennekoon (Maud to the staff) also returned to the College, having been touched afresh by the Lord in 1956. She was a former student and now was to prove a skilful staff member, able to turn her hand to most practical jobs.

Some staff members of the Bible College of Wales late 1950s

Samuel welcomed his new team and prayed for them constantly, appreciating that to integrate new with old is not a straightforward process. Always one to encourage, he would either see an individual personally, or send a message indirectly, to say how he was deeply blessed by their efforts and would continue to pray for them. If the Welsh 'bach' (a term of endearment meaning 'dear') was included, then that really did indicate a sign of approval. Although he left the running of the School to its head teachers and staff, Samuel liked to attend the public performances which they arranged, usually at Christmas time. Grammar School carol services of a high standard were held in Mount Pleasant Baptist Church, through the kindness of its Church officials. The Preparatory School used the College Conference Hall, alternating each year with a Carol Service or a concert that always finished with a nativity play. Harvest Festival was another Preparatory School annual event, when children brought gifts of vegetables, fruit and preserves to be distributed to the elderly and to others in local nursing homes. When Lizzie

Howells was in her eighties and confined to bed, Samuel was always deeply touched when a gift of fruit for her was delivered to the College by two of the senior pupils in the Preparatory School, and he would remark how polite and friendly they were. Samuel particularly loved the younger groups, and made a point of seeing the girls dressed in their colourful Welsh costumes on 1st March, St. David's Day, while the boys nibbled away at large leeks (a Welsh emblem!) pinned to their blue school blazers. St. David's Day was also celebrated with a half-day holiday, a tradition no longer kept in schools.

Samuel himself was not a practical person, so had to rely on the advice given by the 'experts,' although the experts themselves often had differing views on how jobs should be done! This sometimes resulted in what appeared to be a U-turn in the way the work proceeded, which enabled the Holy Spirit to exercise His ministries of grace in the lives of individuals, in order to preserve the unity of the Spirit so necessary in the prayers the Lord was giving at the time. Samuel always endeavoured to pour oil on troubled waters in his desire to maintain this unity.

Music in the College was under the supervision of Olive Raven LRAM who played the piano and organ and trained a student choir each year. All students were in the choir, the good singers nearest the microphone and the not so good on the far left or right! It was a struggle at times but on the 'day' – in a Conference or on Graduation Sunday – it usually went well, especially as the ladies wore blouses and skirts made by themselves as practical training in dressmaking! Men students had been taught to darn socks as part of their training!

Having a good Welsh Chapel background, Samuel appreciated and recognised musical ability. Occasionally a talented soloist would emerge from among the students, such as Dawn Mellon, Miriam Davies (daughter of former student Ivor Davies of WEC) and the 'silver tenor voice' of Ivor Hopkins, later to become a senior lecturer in the College. The Russian students sang well, and the Koreans who all seemed to have beautiful voices, and both formed their own most talented groups. Then there were the accomplished pianists such as Sharon Baker (now with

Revival Fires Ministry), Erik Dewhurst, Delmy Choi and Mike Brown (also to become a senior lecturer), who were given permission to lead in the College services, and later Terry Woodward, who played solos on his saxophone.[2]

Guitars and drums did not register much with Samuel. He himself played the piano and was known to sit down at the piano in the drawing room downstairs (in Derwen Fawr House) and play, or slip quietly into the room if someone was practising there, to encourage them in his gentle way. Although reluctant to do so at first, Pearl Temple played the piano and organ very competently for many years, always encouraged to overcome her fears by Samuel. His piano lessons as a child must have been very unexciting, as he never really enjoyed playing himself – just listening. Commenting on musical contributions from students, Samuel always saw the life behind the individuals or groups, and measured what came from the heart. With a wry smile he would remember the 'early days' when Elaine Bodley, an elderly, very accomplished cellist and violinist, arranged monthly musical appreciation sessions on Saturday afternoons for staff and students. Budding musicians treated everyone to selected excerpts from the classics, the first steps in introducing the 'arts' into the College programme. Those who were involved then have clear recollections of those creative sessions together.

Throughout this period, Samuel remained diligent in his care of those who had not received the rich ministry which had steered his generation through such troublesome years. Besides his evening ministry for many years, he also took the morning devotion on a Monday; these devotions (mini-services) were held every weekday and Saturday before lectures or other programmed activities. They were shorter sessions when, invariably, Samuel worked consecutively through the Gospels. In reminiscing about College days, one former student's comments were that Mr Samuel spoke about the life of the Lord Jesus on earth; speaking of Him in such a way that Jesus lived to her as never before, and touched her life and spirit in a profound way which she has never forgotten.

In his teaching, Samuel always treated the men and women of the Bible with great respect. Leaning over the podium and pointing his slender index finger in everyone's direction he would challenge them by saying, "Could you do what Abraham, Isaac, Jacob, Moses and Daniel did? And if you can't do it, then be careful what you say about these men." Sound advice for budding preachers! It was these men and women who had preserved the whole thread of salvation through the Scriptures by their faith. This emphasised the essential need to cultivate true faith and believing in our Christian walk with God.

Samuel was always conscious of traumas that faced true preachers of the Word, and knowing that human eloquence and confidence are not everyone's strong points, he was eager to encourage whenever possible. One former student tells of the time he was asked to preach on a Sunday evening – and Elijah was his subject. After the service his conversation with another student was interrupted when Samuel came over and whispered in his ear, "That was a great word!" "What could I ask more in this old world of ours?" comments the student.

It was by these personal touches of encouragement that so many people have remembered Samuel, from the new cooks working in the kitchen who, when everything was quiet, received an unexpected visitor from upstairs to tell them how much they were appreciated, to young drivers asked to take Samuel into town. One had just passed his driving test and remembers how overawed he felt to be chosen to take the 'Director' for a hospital appointment. He waited patiently in the car for two hours reading and, on returning, Samuel asked him what he was reading. "*Savonarola*" came the reply.[3] "A good man," said Samuel, nodding gently, and waited for his seat belt to be fastened. This was usually the driver's job!

On another occasion during the long summer break, a young staff member was involved in his first car crash, always an unnerving experience. The following week Samuel asked the young man to take him for a drive into the country in his own car, a real sign of confidence – and a long drive too. Contrary to so many observations levelled against him for his remoteness, Samuel was a very caring person, ever sensitive to the true needs of individuals, and preferred to give time to all those who were genuine.

Chapter Thirteen

Give Ye Them To Eat

The intensity of the first ten years in the driving seat was having its effect upon Samuel's physical frame, and he began to experience what is recognised today as 'burn out.' Writing to his dear friend and confidant, Dr. Gordon Thomas, of Messrs, Gordon Thomas and Pickard, Lower Union Street, Swansea, on 3rd February 1960 he shared a little of the intensity of those experiences:

Dear Dr. Thomas,

It had recently been my intention to see you at the beginning of this week, but as I had taken up much of your precious time on Saturday morning I felt rather diffident to do so. In spite of all the great pressures under which you often work, you have always received one with such kindness and consideration.

As I intimated to you, it will be a great relief to mother and myself when these current matters are finally cleared up. The burden and tension lately have been well nigh insufferable, and if things continue I am afraid one would experience a complete physical breakdown. Sleep seems to have departed, and all one can do at present is to spend most of the nights in prayer and intercession.

Incidentally, there are now just ten years since father was called home. That was an awful test, and the pressing needs of the work at that time, together with the great liability, seemed insurmountable. But God gave us the grace and strength to get through with everything. And you were a tower of strength to us then.

The one desire father had before he passed

on was to gather enough means to help needy missionaries who are labouring for God in the different parts of the world. Mother and I have now assumed this responsibility, and we hope to give thousands of pounds away in the near future, for the help and support of these Christian workers. To be quite frank we have no other aim in life and I believe the Lord will enable us to fulfil this great task.... Samuel Howells.

Not for the last time would Samuel feel so weak as he pursued this very costly intercessory path.

Hudson Taylor, founder of the China Inland Mission, certainly refers to it in his lifetime, and Christian leaders around the world would understand its true meaning. As one observer has noted:

I remember Samuel as having a global interest in the work of God; his outlook was not parochial so much as international, neither confined to the past but with interest in the future.

Samuel carried the burden for world blessing. Coupled with this were the domestic issues, dealt with through prayer, one by one. The sale of land at Penllergaer still presented a challenge, after the initial refusal by the Council of the planning application for development, on the grounds that it was part of a Green Belt. Finally, restrictions were lifted but Satan was not prepared to let this proceed easily. There followed an unpleasant period of legal wrangling concerning the tenancies of Home Farm, but finally the obstacles were removed and a prospective buyer, the owner of Hendrefoilan Estate in Swansea, was found. On 30th June 1962, the trustees proposed a sale of 236 acres to the prospective buyer for £10,600 ($17,000) – a good price for those far-off days (equivalent to £166,400 / $266,240 in 2012). At that point, it was realised that the original purchase of the Penllergaer Estate from Sir Michael D. V. Llewellyn in 1938 was on condition that, in the event of the property ever being offered for sale up till twenty-one years after the death of Rees Howells, the offer must first be made to the Baronetcy of Dillwyn Venables

Llewellyn – who would then have one month to consider the offer. Here was a further blow impacting upon the already burdened Samuel. He spent many more nights in waiting upon God for guidance. With these deep experiences in mind he once counselled his congregation never to sing lightly the words of John Bunyan's hymn, *He who would valiant be 'gainst all disaster*. He was referring particularly to the phrase, 'I'll fear not what men say, I'll labour night and day to be a pilgrim.'

"How many are really prepared to follow like that?" was his challenge.

'But God,' was a familiar expression in Paul's writings, and Samuel's indomitable spirit enabled him to 'lay hold on God' once more. Strengthened by the book of Daniel; as was George Müller, who raised up orphanages in Bristol by faith in the nineteenth century – Samuel always drew strength through prolonged meditation on passages of Scripture. It became clear again that this great Old Testament prophet was similarly tested, and there were times when he was exhausted (Daniel 8:27), but God touched him and strengthened him.

Llewellyn Family and Staff at Penllergaer c.1915

Similarly, the Lord drew near during the night hours, while Samuel meditated quietly in his room, and he was enabled to proceed. Sir Michael Llewellyn did accept the opportunity to buy back the once named Llewellyn Estate for the agreed price and Samuel knew that money would finally be released for the Vision.

It was like refreshing springs of water welling up inside him in praise to God when he read the brief letter dated 24th October 1962 from his solicitors:

>Reverend Sir
>Penllergaer Estate
>
>I am very glad to be able to tell you that at long last I have been able to complete the sale of Penllergaer to Brigadier Sir C.M.D. Venables Llewellyn.
>
>I enclose herewith my firm's cheque made payable to the trustees of the Bible College of Wales for £10,600 ($17,000) being the amount of the purchase money.

There was a concluding paragraph mentioning the usual additional expenses incurred in these transactions and the letter was signed off with a signature of some distinction.

Those months and years of agonising persistent prayer had finally produced the tangible answer and a valuable token released towards the £100,000 ($160,000) that Samuel had committed himself to pray through for.

It was during this period in the early 1960s that the Lord spoke to Samuel in a very personal way concerning his involvement in supporting the worldwide missionary endeavours, and to share with individuals news that he was receiving through his own correspondence. The release of finance through the eventual sale of Penllergaer would contribute significantly to a new development in his ministry. He referred to this as a 'new thrust forward' in response to the Holy Spirit's instructions, *'Give ye them to eat.'* These were words that Jesus Himself spoke to His disciples, as recorded in Luke 9:13 (AV), when they asked Him to send the crowd of five thousand men, plus women and children, back home empty-handed at the end of a long day with Him on the hills. It is interesting to note entries from Samuel's personal diary in 1962:

>Monday 1st January, Watch Night Service
>   Spoke on *'My presence shall go with thee,*

and I will give thee rest.'
Exodus 33:14 (AV).
New Year's Day
The faith of Caleb and Joshua. Numbers 13-14.

The omnipotence of faith. Matthew 17:20 and Mark 9:23.

Wednesday 3rd January
Opened the Foreign Missionary Fund in the National Bank.

Friday 12th January
Read more letters from abroad.

Further comments on *When He saw their faith...* Matthew 9:2.

Great liberty in prayer regarding the new commission.

Monday 15th January
Drew out a list of societies and individuals to be assisted by the Missionary Fund. About 25 countries included and a sum of over £1,000 ($1,600) involved. This is only the initial list – more will be added in the course of the next weeks.

Wednesday 17th January
Received from M and J a gift of £2,000 ($3,200). This is a real seal on the new step and very timely, especially after the meeting last evening.

Tuesday 13th February
Spoke on the preparation of Joshua. Special prayer for Portugal, Lebanon and Algiers. Good liberty. Paid out £1,000 ($1,600) in gifts and transferred another £1,000 ($1,600) to NBCA.

Wednesday 14th February
We are desirous of doing everything possible to place the Word of God in the homes of the people.

Wednesday 21st February
Received from DR. a gift of £1,000 ($1,600). Another sacred token and a further

confirmation to proceed with the new ministry.
Monday 12th March
Received £100 ($160) from Miss B. A lovely token.
Wednesday 21st March
Received a cheque in settlement of the Carmarthen Estate.

(Samuel and Mrs Elizabeth Rees of Carmarthen had been beneficiaries of Miss Alice Townsend's will. Mrs Rees, who became Samuel's foster mother, was by then deceased so Samuel received the estate. As with further estates from which he benefited personally, the money was always placed entirely on the altar and used for the Vision).

Monday 2nd April
Received a packet containing £250 ($400) from an anonymous donor.
Monday 7th May
Left the College at 12:15pm on the start of the long journey to the Continent and the Middle East.

(This, the second of Samuel's missionary journeys, will be mentioned in the next chapter).

Tuesday 3rd July
Prayed for the 900,000,000 (900 million) under Communism.

(This was the beginning of another burden that the Lord was laying upon Samuel's shoulders and would last until 1987 and is covered in two subsequent chapters).

Thursday 12th July
Conversion of Saul. One of the greatest miracles recorded in the New Testament. Related to the prayer for the Communist countries.
Sunday 12th August, 9:45am meeting
'Feeding the 5,000' Matthew 14:15-21.
Sunday 19th August
Matthew 14-15. Great liberty in prayer for the distribution of the Word.
Sunday 26th August, 9:45am meeting
'The keys of the Kingdom of Heaven'

Matthew 16:13-19.
The fulfilment – Pentecost: Cornelius. Acts 2 and 10.

Sunday 2nd September, 9:45am meeting
'The manna and water' Exodus 15-16. The Lord can again provide.

Tuesday 25th September
'Branches in the Vine' John 13-15. A very sacred meeting.

Friday 5th October, second meeting
Special prayer for Italy.

Tuesday 9th October
Read reports from the different countries. Then a long session of prayer for Beirut, Katerina and Turkey.

The first Sunday morning service from 9:45 to 11am was always given to prayer, following an initial period of preparation, when hymns were sung from *Golden Bells* hymn book, various folk were asked to open in prayer and Scriptures were read.

Sunday 4th November, 9:45am meeting
Daniel 4. Prayer for Jordan, India, Cuba, South Africa, Angolan refugees.

Thursday 8th November
1 Kings 20. Special prayer for Jordan in view of the acute situation arising there.

Tuesday 13th November
Read letters from different countries. Much prayer for India, Jordan and Turkey.

Thursday 15th November
Daniel 6. Continued prayer for India, Jordan and Macedonia.

Tuesday 20th November, 7:30pm meeting
1 Kings 21-22. Special prayer for India in her hour of crisis.[1]

10:30pm meeting
2 Kings 6, 7. Assured that God was intervening in the situation.

Thursday 22nd November
Received a gift of £1,000 ($1,600) from Miss B. A wonderful token.

Friday 30th November
> Brother Andrew from the Netherlands gave a wonderful account of the activities of God's servants behind the Iron Curtain.

Tuesday 25th December 10am meeting
> Luke 1. The wonder of the Incarnation. Special prayer for the Russian evangelical preachers, that they each might soon have a copy of the Word of God.

Wednesday 26th December
> It has been a lovely Christmastide. Everybody seems to have enjoyed it and we have been deeply blessed. The dining room was full and the carols went well.

It was the custom for many staff to remain at the College for the Christmas services and to celebrate the giving of the Vision on Boxing Day. The dining table was full and the evening meal was concluded by singing carols together. Samuel always enjoyed a particular brand's box of chocolates too!

Friday 28th December
> Prepared the last number of letters for this year with relief to missionaries abroad. It has proved to be a wonderful year in giving to others.

Saturday 29th December
> Had a telephone conversation with RS re: the large deliverance that will be forthcoming in about a week. It will be one of the most sacred tokens received to date. Another great confirmation in the ministry of giving the Word to the people in the world.

In glancing through Samuel's 1962 diary, it names over thirty countries being prayed for, and some of the organisations. Over £10,000 ($16,000) was received that year in gifts committed for the ministry alone (this is worth £166,400 / $266,200 in 2012). The strategy was for the Lord to link Samuel with an individual or agency working in as many countries of the world as possible, preferably nationals. These would become 'points of intercession' representing the nation. Samuel was to pray for, and provide practical support to each one in the name of the Lord. The Vision was for the world and everyone should have the Bread of Life.

Later diaries were less informative but the ministry intensified as the years unfolded.

When all was quiet, and staff and students had settled in their rooms at the end of the day, Samuel was at his best. He would tour the building making sure that all windows had been secured, outside doors locked and lights put out. The night was young – time to reflect on the challenges of the day and to rejoice at the blessings, then further hours to be spent reading passages of Scripture and praying through them, until he had the assurance that God would meet the need. This spiritual exercise of 'touching the Throne in prayer' was one Samuel felt strongly was missing in the Church, and it was his desire that all the students passing through the College should learn. First of all it would commence with praying for practical needs, from a tube of toothpaste to fees for the term, but then it would progress to larger issues in the Church or nation, and eventually would lead to participation in world challenges involving God's Kingdom. There were a hundred and one particular needs in the work, and people struggling in their walk with God, and Samuel sought answers for everyone before he finally switched off his bedside lamp in the early hours of the morning, although when talking to visitors or staff about sleep, he was always concerned that they should get a good night's rest!

Chapter Fourteen

Second Missionary Journey

Although Samuel turned his hand to driving earlier in his life under the able tuition of Toby Bergin, an unfortunate accident (the facts are unknown) brought the venture to an end. He did not however, lose his love for the open road and travelled extensively throughout Britain, Europe, Scandinavia, USA and South Africa. During his lifetime, he visited most parts of Wales, Scotland, England and Northern Ireland, either by car or on summer coach trips.

He occasionally stayed with friends in Godalming or Bournemouth. Then there were longer journeys with Toby Bergin, his driver, for formal visits to a College Trustee, Miss Effie Bentham at the Gaines, a spacious country house in Scarborough, Yorkshire. Beneath her stern Victorian presence lay a magnanimous heart of love, particularly for children whom she generously cared for through Dr. Barnardo's Homes. During her visits to the Bible College, she taught the Fellowship to sing the following prayer before every midday meal,

"Our Father, in the name of Jesus,
Speak to every child in Asia,
Africa, America, Australia, Europe,
And all Thy world."[1]

Samuel's favourite runs were into the hills of South Wales, which he knew well, sighting lone kestrels hovering against blue summer skies, and listening to those familiar skylark songs and the rhythm of munching sheep, and to the Usk and Llyn Brianne Reservoirs. Samuel envied the tenants of solitary stone cottages clinging to brackened slopes, and welcomed the shade from clumps of conifers along the way. For one who would totally concur with the actress, Penelope Williams, when she said, "I don't make much of being private. That's just how I am," the prospect was idyllic. For midweek breaks, they would drive further afield to Snowdonia and Anglesey, staying overnight at Betws y Coed. As with many others, Stan Teed, another driver and Welsh-speaking himself, found Samuel to be a great encourager with a wonderful sense of humour.

Several times Samuel rented a self-catering holiday cottage near Snowdon in North Wales, for himself, a driver, and staff members to manage the cooking and packed lunches. Another adventure was to Pendine Sands, once made famous by Malcolm Campbell as his chosen track for an attempt on the land speed record in Bluebird in 1927. As they dropped down the steep road past Laugharne (pronounce Larn) the little coastal village which had inspired Dylan Thomas to write *Under Milk Wood*, the expanse of Carmarthen Bay lay before them. And then Pendine itself, nestled by the sea, birthing miles of clean smooth sand stretching east to the mouth of the River Towy, where the ancient skill of coracle fishing still remained. Here was another place for contemplation, prayer and memories, as Samuel could gaze across on a clear day towards Cefn Bryn on the Gower, seventeen miles away and perhaps with a good stretch of the imagination, even seeing the Worm's Head and Caldey Island to the southeast. Newquay and Tenby were specials too, while Stan recalls how they would drive for hours in silence enjoying God's presence.

Perhaps the most frequented trip for Samuel was to the 'bridge,' crossing a stream in the Black Mountains where his father had once held his hand up to the Lord and promised, "I shall not take a thread to a shoe latchet from any person unless the Lord tells me. I do believe You are able to keep me better than the Mining Company." That solemn transaction with God had been a foundation stone in the Founder's life and in the beginning of the College, and Samuel drew strength from every visit. As a boy he had often tramped that way with a packet of sandwiches and a bottle of water. Sadly, that old footbridge was recently removed and a substantial, but small road bridge placed over the ford, but its memories linger on.[2]

For many years a special treat on those mountain runs, was to visit his four cousins, Mary, Lucy, Maggie and Bertha, who lived at Twyn y Mynydd, the beautiful Welsh bungalow originally built for Samuel, overlooking Glanaman, almost opposite to Pentwyn where Uncle Dick lived. Uncle Dick had been miraculously healed during the Founder's ministry. The cousins fêted Samuel as he relaxed in the armchair in front of a coal fire, treating him to some of his favourite dishes. Pancakes and Welsh cakes were always on the menu, and the best china cups and saucers were out for the meal. Weak tea was preferred! Welsh was always spoken in those parts, and the traditional values of respect and warmth prevailed. It was home-from-home for Samuel.

Samuel Howells on the Black Mountain, near Glanaman

As the winter snows on the Black Mountains gave way

to warmer days, and the daffodils bowed their heads to welcome the spring, preparations began for a second missionary journey to the Middle East, this time by road. Toby was over the moon with a gift of a large green, gas-guzzling Armstrong Siddley car capable of managing the roads across Europe and beyond, and stops were planned with friends, mostly former students, at convenient distances.

Monday 7th May 1962, was bright and sunny as the College folk waved the travellers off from the front of the house at 12:15pm on their epic journey. Samuel's diary records 'Believing for great blessing in the different places.' Stopping for the night first with Toby's stepmother in Liss, Hampshire, they eventually arrived in Bois-de-Boulogne, Paris at 7pm next evening. Fred Ridgers guided them out of Paris next morning, enabling them to make good progress to Switzerland for the next stop with Christian Keller, an assistant pastor with the Swiss National Church. Margo Fisher (former student) and her fellow workers of the European Christian Mission welcomed them next evening in Salzburg, Mozart's city in Austria, where they picked up their post. It was an impressive city with its magnificent buildings and square. There was time to visit Salzburg Castle where many were tortured during the Counter Reformation. There were opportunities to minister in Austria before the breathtaking drive up through the Austrian Alps and crossing into Yugoslavia to stay with Dr. Horak. Samuel was the navigator on this trip and carried with him a small black booklet compiled by Eva Stuart in the College office before their departure. In it were precise details for each stage of their journey, with contact addresses. Arriving as strangers from the West in a Communist country, it was important now that they made no mistakes, so Samuel read through the directions carefully.

> On coming into Zagreb ask for Ilica-Ulica (Ilista Street) leading off Trg. Republique (Republic Square). A turning off this street will lead you into Kordunska 4/111 doe, Dr. Horak's flat.
> Please = Molin. Thank you = Hvala.
> Ask Dr. Horak for any landmarks leading into

Belgrade. Otherwise follow map from bridge over the Sava on to Bulevar Revoluceje 264 which is a very wide road going gradually uphill. When you pass the market on the left, look out for a block of flats on the right. Past this, after a few steps, the Baptist Church, no. 264, lies back on the right.

If you are afraid to drink the water, ask for Cheya, or mineral water (pronounced caj) mint tea. You can get information from Putnik, also change your money here almost any time of day, although banks give better exchange. Always English speaking clerks here.

Samuel and Toby arrived safely and spoke in Dr. Horak's Church in Zagreb, now the capital of Croatia, where the hall was packed with people. The great respect for God's Word was shown by the congregation standing for the reading of the Scriptures.

This was now Communist territory, yet the hunger for the Gospel was very evident. There were further opportunities for Samuel to minister in Belgrade and in Sophia, Bulgaria where Khrushchev was visiting. Red flags were flying everywhere.

The Armstrong Siddley was coping well on the Eastern European roads and they made good progress to Ediner, for a night stop just inside the Turkish border and finally to historic Istanbul, where they met a dear friend, Thomas Cosmedes and his wife. They had arranged a rally, so Toby and Samuel shared the platform with Dennis Clarke, the Director of Youth For Christ, a unique meeting for Turkey.

From Istanbul, after their 2,400 miles (3,840 kilometres) road journey they flew to Beirut, where they encouraged the friends there, and then proceeded by air to Jordan where they stayed at Ramallah for a week. Samuel loved the children there. Besides attending to official business he was able to visit the biblical sites of Jerusalem and was deeply impressed by the Garden of Gethsemane.

The return run from Istanbul was via Greece, staying at Philippi, Amphipolis, Thessalonica, Berea and Katerini with opportunities to encourage the brethren – following in Paul's footsteps.

Samuel Howells with Toby Bergin and Deborah and Heather Cosmedes in Istanbul, Turkey, 1962

At each planned stop Samuel had a congregation waiting for ministry from the Word, and the anointing of God was on him. The journey followed the River Varder into landlocked Macedonia, stopping at Skopji, then the capital, Belgrade, Zagreb, Villach (home of Wasyl and Joy Boltwin, both former students who had joined the Slavic Gospel Association) and then Munich in Germany. Although still in the process of being rebuilt after the devastation of bombing, Munich with its Marienplatz still commanded their attention.

Samuel Howells at Dachau Concentration Camp 1962

Their visit to Dachau Concentration Camp was a solemn occasion. They stayed with Ernie Palnock and his wife, both former students, in Eastern France, before crossing the Rhine at Strasbourg and driving through the rich French countryside to meet with Fred Ridgers again in Paris, where Samuel spoke to the Russian believers there and also visited the Bible Institute at Lamorlaye. Another former student, Bob Munn, had pioneered this work but the financial drain to comply with Health and Safety and EU regulations eventually forced it to close in the 1990s.

Samuel Howells in 1951 at an unknown location

On Thursday, 28th June 1962, they arrived back in Swansea about 8pm to a very warm welcome indeed. The second missionary journey was complete and the Lord had blessed all the way. Samuel loved travelling. As a footnote, the Armstrong Siddley did prove an expensive vehicle to run, especially locally. On a journey to Yorkshire it was rammed from behind at a railway crossing near Barnsley on 3rd December and severely damaged. Toby and Samuel were able to reach their destination safely. On 5th December, it is recorded: 'Through the kindness of X we were able to purchase another car, a Ford Anglia Saloon (1961) in perfect condition.' The Lord had supplied again!

Chapter Fifteen

The Congo Crisis

The conflicts of the Korean War of the 1950s, attacks against the Kikuyu Christians in Kenya in 1955 and the Cuban Missile Crisis of 1962 were to prepare Samuel for deeper intercessory involvements to follow. During 1953, the Belgian Congo had experienced a powerful spiritual revival, as recorded in *This is That* (1954) edited by Norman Grubb, whilst a new edition is called *The Spirit of Revival* (2000).[1] Two former College students, Ivor and David Davies from Gowerton near Swansea, were Worldwide Evangelisation Crusade (WEC) Field Leaders at the time, so gave graphic accounts of their experiences and the dramatic effects on the Church in Congo when they spoke in services on their return.

Satan did not let this sudden growth in the Church in Africa go unnoticed and he replied in 1960-66 with infighting, civil war and the Simba persecution of Christians and all things colonial. Politically, the whole country was in turmoil as Patrice Lumumba, founder of the National Congo Movement and newly elected Prime Minister, called for sweeping social changes and independence, which it gained in 1960. Two years later, Dag Hammarskjold, the UN negotiator was killed in an air crash and Seseseko Mobutu succeeded Patrice Lumumba as leader.

The years 1964-65 saw a vicious wave of persecution, known as the 'Simba Uprising' (also known as the Simba Rising and Simba Rebellion) directed against the native Christians and the supporting missionaries: Unevangelised Fields Mission, Pentecostal, Brethren, WEC and others. Drug crazed gangs of Simbas swept through the villages and mission stations, rooting out any semblance of colonialism and subjected their victims to horrific tortures and deaths. The heroic tales of those twentieth century martyrs are well catalogued[2] in Church History literature, as a permanent tribute to their devotion to Christ. Samuel set everything to one side and called the College back to prayer, with each morning and evening session in the prayer room being devoted to the subject, particularly as three of the College family were there: David Davies whose son Glyn, was a boarder in the School, and Brian Cripps, who had only recently joined the WEC missionary force in Congo, following his father's footsteps as a printer. Also Jack Scholes, whose children had been through the Boarding School, was working there. In these Kingdom prayers an amazing unity pervaded the College meetings, which included extra voluntary sessions from 10pm to midnight, and sometimes another till 2am. It was a real life training ground for the students, as they experienced the Spirit's ways in these conflicts.

The strength of the prayer lay in the believing, or faith, that the Spirit was able to generate through the anointed reading and exposition of the Scriptures. Samuel would be led to read from certain passages which threw particular light on the current problems. One such passage was in Acts 8, when the Jerusalem Church experienced its first wave of intense persecution and was scattered abroad. This seeming tragedy resulted in the expansion of the Church and the fulfilment of the Lord's words that they would be witnesses in Judea, Samaria and to the uttermost parts of the world (Acts 1:8).

The prayer continued for weeks, and heightened when news reached the College that David Davies and Brian Cripps were in rebel hands. News of their whereabouts was scant and the College was tempted to fear the worst. The ordeal continued for nine long weeks. At one point, held captive in one room with other hostages, they watched each day as one was taken to the next room and hacked to pieces, and their numbers decreased. As David later testified, it was not the fear of death that troubled him but the fear of pain. A Scripture calendar verse on the wall, reminding him of all the Saviour had endured for him, brought peace and calm. This was an evidence of the power of the Word of God to heal a troubled soul.

It was then that the Lord told Dr. Kenneth Symonds, following a night of prayer, and despite other reports to the contrary, that Brian Cripps was alive and there was a shout of praise in the College, especially among the students. Later the BBC news confirmed what the Lord had already revealed.

> **WOMAN BEATEN**
> **"Mercenaries cried"**
>
> This was at noon, and the rebels told her she would be executed at 2 p.m. and the others at 3 p.m. "Just before 2 p.m. we heard intensive firing in the distance. When the mercenaries came near all the Simbas ran away."

British newspaper clipping – November 1964

David and Anne Davies by then were back on their Mission Station in Nala. Simbas had a system of telling their next victims the exact time when they would arrive to massacre. David and Anne received their notice and waited. The Lord brought them into a position of peace knowing that the perfect will of God for their lives was the pathway of joy. Quoting from David and Anne's own description of their situation:

> Nala Mission compound, where we were stationed, is a cul-de-sac two hundred yards off a secondary road. At the entrance to the Mission there was a large metal sign, painted white with black letters 'Mission Protestante, HAM Nala.' No one could miss seeing the sign. The rebels passed along that road almost every day, and often several times a day. For three and a half months we were moment-by-moment in danger. You can imagine the tension. The Africans brought us news of the slaughter and torturing of blacks and whites. We looked death in the face and gave

ourselves over to the will of God, happy to die for Him if He wished it. But each time we returned to prayer (and we had several sessions of prayer each day) we were led to pray for deliverance. Oh the preciousness of the Word of God! Oh what a wonderful Book! What great assurance and strength we gained from such verses as: *Call upon Me in the day of trouble. I will deliver thee and thou shalt glorify Me.* Psalm 50:15 (AV).

Our African Christians were wonderful, the Lord bless them. They travelled distances to see if we were safe. Their care for us was touching. They brought food which they could ill afford to spare as the rebels were stealing so much, leaving the village folk in a state of almost famine. In the prayer meetings, we saw fruits of the deep work of the Spirit in their lives. Each day, at 2pm we joined them for a special period of prayer. They knew our danger. Often during the prayers we could hear the rebels pass the entrance; we would sometimes stop, thinking the cars were coming in. Their prayers were intelligent. How they marshalled their arguments before God. 'O Lord, You put a hedge round about Job; now put a hedge around the Mission, then the rebels will not be able to come in.' A great challenge when we were only two hundred yards away and the rebels could see some of our houses from the entrance. The Africans reminded the Lord of the cherubims with the flaming sword keeping the way to the Garden of Eden; of the enemies of Lot who were struck blind and could not find the door of the house; of the Israelites in Egypt who had light in all their dwellings whereas the Egyptians were in darkness, and so on and on. They argued: *Jesus Christ is the same yesterday, today and forever.* Hebrews 13:8 (NCV). And God marvellously answered prayer. When one morning the planes carrying Belgian paratroopers came over we were thrilled to think of the rescue of the European hostages. But we wondered if they would come as far as Nala for us.

In an amazingly courageous last minute rescue run, twenty-five mercenaries (who flew into Stanleyville in September 1964), guided by Colin Buckley from the Assemblies of God Mission at Paulis nine miles away, fought their way through to Nala. It hurt David and Anne to bid farewell to their African Christian friends before being whisked off to fight their way back to safety, and then via Leopoldville with other missionaries to the UK. Among the group was Brian Cripps who had similarly witnessed and experienced so much in his short missionary career. There was still one missionary being held by the Simbas, Winnie Davies, but she met her death just hours before her rescuers arrived.

At the College, Samuel brought the special services to a seemingly abrupt end. With a developing ministry, he was learning to discern the word of the Lord for a given situation. As with the true prophets in the Scriptures, there was always a personal involvement, a point of identification and responsibility, the hallmark of intercession.

Samuel ministered on the life of Jephthah (Judges 11) in one late meeting. Jephthah had vowed a very costly vow before the Lord that would unlock the situation before him. At this time, Samuel made a costly personal sacrifice though he never divulged the details of the vow. Ammon was soundly defeated but Jephthah had opened his mouth to the Lord and he could not go back on his vow. Similarly the Simba Uprising was subdued, the prayer was through, and Samuel continued his quiet walk with God alone.

CONGO 'DEAD' COME HOME TO BRITAIN

EIGHT more Congo survivors, including two who had been thought to be dead, arrived back in Britain yesterday after their rescue on Wednesday by mercenaries.

British Newspaper clipping – November 1964

Chapter Sixteen

The Spectre of Communism

Samuel's second missionary journey of seven and a half weeks from May to June 1962 had served to deepen a growing conviction that, in order to break the rapid spread of Communistic ideology which was gripping the world, intercessory prayer must be focused upon this need. He was under no illusions that if he responded to this new leading from the Holy Spirit, both he and the College would be plunged into an intense spiritual conflict resulting in misunderstandings and many 'casualties.' His personal reputation would be shattered and outwardly there would be the inevitable pathway of failure in the eyes of the world, even the Christian world.

He had seen these aspects of intercession enacted at a very deep level in his father's life when World War II had broken out in September 1939. Rees Howells had known the threats posed by Adolf Hitler and the Nazi Movement, but being fully convinced that the Holy Spirit had complete mastery over all powers of darkness in the world, he was totally confident in making a prediction that there would be no general war in Europe. This he made publicly, even writing to the Prime Minister, Mr Winston Churchill, and publishing a book, *God Challenges the Dictators* in December 1939, which was split into two parts. It was not a prophecy as such, but a declaration based upon the total believing the Holy Spirit was giving him for the demise of this evil system in Europe, a quality of faith that very few have exercised. Nothing would prevent the fulfilment of the Vision the Lord had given Rees Howells in December 1934; every knee would bow to the eternal Son of God. Of course, from this assurance he used, on several occasions, the Lord's Name which brought complete confusion and mistrust into the minds of people who had, up till then, become ardent followers of this 'Welsh prophet.'

Samuel remembered very vividly how that prediction, and all his father's plans to assist the Jewish refugees and eventually enable them to settle in land purchased in the Holy Land (modern day Israel), all publicised widely in local and national newspapers, had come crashing down. He had lived every minute of those dark days, when even his own personal faith was tested to the limit.

He had endeavoured, as best he could, to stand alongside his father and was inclined to agree that, had the whole nation turned to God for His help, the story might have been different. However, Rees Howells had not wavered in his total conviction that the doom of the Nazis would one day be realised throughout the world.

Derwen Fawr Road showing the end of Derwen Fawr House (right) and Skety Isaf Estate (left)

At the same time as these momentous events were taking place, Samuel had been personally touched as a graphic parable was enacted outside the College. Separating the two estates Derwen Fawr (Great Oak) and Sketty Isha (Lower Sketty) ran the Derwen Fawr Road, which wound its way past a line of tall and graceful trees.

With Samuel's love for nature, he always had time to appreciate the beauty which these lofty giants provided throughout the year, so it was with great sadness that he joined a small crowd of onlookers as the trees were felled. They had been in danger for years of crashing down in strong winds, so in the interests of public safety in October 1938 the woodcutters moved in. It was a slow painful process in those days, without chain saws, and as one newspaper wrote:

> The gathering watched the decapitation of the last big tree. The arboreal giant withstood the woodcutters' axes during a whole afternoon but eventually it fell with a mighty crash.

Little did Samuel realise then the spiritual parallel that he would experience, nor the spiritual truth encompassed in the final paragraph of the article:

> We are glad to say that the famous oak tree on the other side of the road, after which Derwen Fawr is named, will go on standing throughout the years. There is no danger of this landmark being removed.

Sadly, in the year 2010, that too has gone – another parable![1]

Derwen Fawr Road, Sketty Isaf (left), Derwen Fawr (right)
Some of the elderly lady intercessors lived in these rooms

The whole question of failure is one which every intercessor has to face at some point in his or her ministry and Samuel had faced it alongside his father in 1939. The war did proceed and the bitter struggle lasted for six years. So what Divine purposes was God planning in those dark days?

The Howells Family late 1940s

At that crucial point, the Lord had shown Rees Howells clearly that it was necessary that he should experience this failure in the world's eyes so that full focus and attention could be given to the spiritual conflicts which were to ensue. No explanation should be given by way of justification; death to reputation was an essential ingredient for the intercessions to follow. Russia, then under the heel of atheistic Communism since the Bolshevic Revolution of 1917, was to be opened up for the Gospel. God's far-reaching purposes for blessing across the vast expanses of Siberia were to be unfolded, but the spiritual conflicts would call for intercessory prayer at the deepest level. Besides the obvious reason that Russia's involvement in World War II would direct Adolf Hitler's attention away from his intentions for Western Europe and the Free World, the Holy Spirit revealed this greater plan and Rees Howells was a man thoroughly prepared for the hour. Samuel recalled the ignominy of those days when even the Christian world kept them at arm's length,[2] so he himself would not flinch when plunged into further depths to see the development of God's covenant plans for the blessing of the world in his day, and an outworking of that Divine plan for the USSR, as it was then called.

Now forty years later, Samuel was challenged by God, through looking at a photograph of five Russian pastors who were imprisoned for their faith, to intercede for them and others suffering under the brutal regimes of Joseph Stalin and Nikita Kruschev.

Immediately after World War II, the Soviet authorities imposed tight security on all borders between the Eastern European countries which they had occupied, and the West. Their aim was to make them satellite Communist states in which vibrant Christianity was marginalised and driven underground. The Bible was outlawed and influencing children on Christian truths forbidden.

Even Berlin itself, which was isolated in the Eastern section of Germany, was zoned off between the four major Allied nations to oversee. The Potsdam Agreement, signed in 1945, had seen to that. To prevent too many defections into West Berlin from the East, the Russians tightened their grip and prevented vital daily supplies, even of water, reaching the West, forcing the Allies to launch the famous 'Berlin Airlift' from June 1948 to May 1949. A continuous convoy of planes ferried in everything required by the beleaguered population.

Changing tactics, the Russians created the German Democratic Republic (GDR) of East Germany with its one candidate voting system, strongly supported and controlled by its 'mother state' with its much-feared Stasi (GDR Security Police) arresting any suspected dissenters. The situation intensified when a complex barbed wire barricade between East and West was erected in 1961. By 1969, the infamous concrete Berlin Wall completely isolated the inhabitants of West Berlin until 1989.

The 'Cold War' between East and West was truly established, a bleak era especially for the Christians, so many of whom were transferred to slave in the harsh corrective camps known as 'gulags' in the frozen wastes of Siberia. Tens of thousands were to die there.[3]

In one evening meeting, holding up the photograph of the imprisoned pastors, Samuel explained to the congregation its special significance for him. The Lord had spoken to him asking if he would intercede for these pastors. Fully understanding the cost of intercession, Samuel did not give an immediate response, but in the Lord's presence there was no other response he could make than bow his head and say in the words of Jesus, "*Not My will, but Thine, be done.*" Luke 22:42 (AV). The intercession was to grip Samuel and the College for the next twenty-five years and proved to be very costly indeed.

One of the chief ingredients of intercession is identification with the situation or people being prayed for, with the Holy Spirit exercising His right to baptise the individual into death. It is always important to understand fully that death and resurrection are one process. As death to the old nature operates in the life of the intercessor, so the resurrection life of Christ can be appropriated. Paul sums the process up in the words of 2 Corinthians 4:10-12 (NASB).

> *Always carrying about in the body the dying of Jesus, so that the life of Jesus also may be manifested in our body. For we who live are constantly being delivered over to death for Jesus' sake, so that the life of Jesus also may be manifested in our mortal flesh. So death works in us, but life in you.*

The importance of baptism and its accompanying teaching in the lives of young believers cannot be stressed enough today. It is an essential ingredient in the new birth process linked with repentance,[4] believing and the subsequent experiences with the Holy Spirit, and enables Christians to understand some of the strange paths the Lord leads them into.

There is often a misconception conveyed in Christian teaching that there is a good side to our nature and a bad and that only the bad needs to change. That is far from the truth. Being baptised into the death of Christ, means that all of our self-life, the good things and the bad, will be subject to the same process of death if the Holy Spirit is to have room in our lives to express the true nature of Christ.

> *The heart is deceitful above all things, and desperately wicked: who can know it?* Jeremiah 17:9 (AV).

This principle would therefore take place in different ways and be at work in the College as identification with the Russian believers. But for the believers in the Eastern bloc countries, it would mean life and true spiritual growth. Deep friendships were forged with men like Earl Poysti, a regular College visitor and responsible for Russian Radio Broadcasts from Monte Carlo into Russia for decades. Using powerful transmitters originally commissioned by Adolf Hitler for the propagation of his ideology, Scriptures were read out at dictation speed, to be copied out by hand by the Russian and Ukranian believers in the Underground Church. Earl's brother, Daniel, also visited the College as a representative of the Pocket Testament League and enthralled us with the miraculous ways God worked to ensure that Bibles and New Testaments were taken safely through the border checkpoints to the believers.

Both Earl and Daniel had grown up in Siberia, sons of a godly father who would pace the bare floors of their home during the long night hours, pouring out his heart to God for revival throughout the Soviet Union, a heart cry which was to determine his sons' ministries. In broadcasting to the Russian people during those days of persecution to the Underground Church, Earl is said to have led over a million people to Christ. Throughout those years, the College was privileged to train several Russian born Christians, some with German origins. Victor Haam, son of Gerhart Haam the Russian evangelist, spent his childhood in Vorkuta, the heart of Siberia's gulag, and described the conditions at the College, when he came as a student with two friends as 'like living in a palace.' Having spent their three years of compulsory military service as Christians in the Soviet Army, there really was not much that the College could teach these young men. Artur Schmit had been a choir leader among the Christian youth of Russia, so soon organised a group and, complemented by several young Russian Christian ladies during the summer vacation, they formed a very talented choir. Earl Poysti once said that if the College were to have saunas, they would attract many more students from Russia! Quite a thought!

As the intercession continued, there were many visiting speakers to the College, all involved in varying ministries into the Communist world. Some showed slides and films. On several occasions, nationals themselves, who had spent terms of imprisonment under terrible conditions, shared their testimonies of how God had revealed Himself to them and delivered them. Samuel was always visibly moved through hearing the testimonies of visiting speakers from the Communist world, each one helping him in the intercession he was carrying and in his resolve to see it through to the end. One young believer spoke of his years in a Communist prison as his 'honeymoon with the Lord,' such was his deep experience of God's presence with him every day. A similar moving testimony was from Pastor Popov from Bulgaria, who was dropped into a covered pit with a crowd of other prisoners for many long days without food or water. He was one of the very few who survived. When he shared these moving experiences in an evening service in the College the experience of Communist occupation became very real. The whole story is told in his biography written by Keith Johnson. In 2008, the College links with Bulgaria deepened through its first Bulgarian student and his family, preparing to serve the Lord in his country once more.

Samuel considered it a great joy to have Pavel Vagala from Tito's Yugoslavia, not quite such an extreme Communist state as some others, staying at the College for the summer to learn English. His testimony as he worked as a skilled car mechanic was highly respected by the Communists and he is now a pastor in Serbia.

Albania too, the last bastion of Communism in Eastern Europe, experiences the Lord's blessing now. Another former student and now a senior College lecturer, Mike Brown, had responded to a burden placed on him by the Holy Spirit for Albania, even before coming to the College, and was instrumental with others in pioneering churches there as soon as the country opened up for visitors from outside. Albania too has sent the College her first student.

The spirit of Communism was spreading. In 1964, Mao Zedong, who had become President of China in 1949, commenced his open criticism of the intellectuals though he had been preaching Communism since the early 1920s.

It is interesting to note that, for several weeks during the 1960-61 period, former students can vividly recall the spirit of prayer for China that came upon Samuel with the College staff and whole student body. Even before the full extent of the disastrous events that were to follow, the Holy Spirit was revealing where the spiritual battle lay and the final victory that would be realised.

By 1966, Mao had organised his Red Guards and launched the Cultural Revolution at a Plenium of the Central Committee, organising his own Revolutionary Committee. *The Little Red Book* became the handbook for its adherents who memorised its slogans from cover to cover. Quoting from *The Role of the Chinese Communist Party in the National War. Volume 2* we read:

> Complacency is the enemy of study. We cannot really learn anything until we rid ourselves of complacency. Our attitude towards ourselves should be 'to be insatiable in learning' and towards others 'to be tireless in teaching.'

This was a philosophy, which would shake China to the core.

The Great Cultural Revolution soon gained momentum, with terrible consequences for any semblance of the old colonialism including all forms of religion. The horrific reports – of children betraying parents and witnessing their barbaric executions, of Church leaders being publicly humiliated, of intense daily indoctrination classes for the people, and of families being separated for life – shocked the College family (staff and students) who resorted to prolonged periods of prayer under Samuel's direction. Missionaries were expelled and evacuated from China (largely during the years 1949-53) and their fine buildings confiscated for official government purposes. This would actually affect Samuel's general feeling about buildings considerably and determined his apparent reluctance to invest too heavily in a building programme at the College, often rousing the passions of many. He felt it a wiser policy to invest in providing the Scriptures, knowing that these would touch lives, while buildings would crumble or fall into the wrong hands. The situation seemed to strike a deathblow for the Church in China, which had experienced growth through turbulent times since its foundation days when Hudson Taylor and other great men of God, through missionary agencies such as the China Inland Mission and the Overseas Missionary Fellowship, had seen significant growth. How could it survive under such savage mauling?

It was during the darkest of days for China that Samuel welcomed Gladys Aylward, the then-famous missionary, who visited the College and preached in the Conference Hall. Gladys Aylward had commenced her missionary career in Swansea at the Gospel Mission in 1930 and two years later made her own way across Siberia to China after being declared unsuitable for mission work by a society. Now this diminutive figure, her face barely visible above the lectern of the platform of the College Conference Hall, pronounced with a resounding declaration of faith, "China WILL open again."

Gladys Aylward newspaper caricature 1950s

Little did people realise then how Mao's determined efforts to create one common language for the people throughout China, to improve the communications system between north and south, east and west, and to drive the true Church underground, would one day turn for the furtherance of the Gospel within that awakening giant. Samuel continued in his intercessory ministry for China, and constantly brought the land before his congregation in prayer meetings. Correspondence also confirms how he sought to support financially agencies and individuals who were engaged in providing Bibles and New Testaments for the oppressed, but still growing, company of believers.

The results today are a vibrant expanding Church of millions, still experiencing persecution in many provinces, with evidence of the power of the resurrection and the reality of Christ living among His people. In every area of China today there is testimony of a Christian witness. Prayer and the Word of God are prominent, signs following the preaching of the Word are common, and a strong and healthy missionary zeal to share Christ with the world exists.[5] The thousands of Chinese Christians who paid the ultimate price (martyrdom), or who spent long years of imprisonment for their faith, were true seeds sown into the ground, and through that process once more resurrection life has been poured out. The intercessory prayers of those days were contributing to the overall plan for the blessing of China.

Those early lessons of intercession, learnt thoroughly during the World War II conflict, now enabled Samuel to persevere through twenty-five difficult years. Later on the joy and glory that flooded his spirit were beyond measure, however, as he witnessed the dramatic changes in the world being registered in every Communist country. Once more it was to prove that for the intercessor, apparent failure had not be the end but the beginning.

Chapter Seventeen

At the Helm

With so much happening in the world, Samuel kept in touch with every development through reading reports in magazines and personal correspondence from missionaries serving God in many countries. The daily newspaper, often tucked hurriedly by his chair when a visitor arrived at his door, was scanned regularly too and Samuel could discuss current topics knowledgeably. He always sought the Lord's mind when controversial laws were being debated in Parliament and, on one occasion, received a strong letter of disapproval from a well known Honorary Member who had heard that Samuel was praying for an election victory for the opposite party. However, Samuel's aim was always to pray for measures which promoted the liberty of the Gospel in the nations. He firmly believed that all governments were in the hands of a sovereign God who works all things according to His purposes, and he was certainly in touch with his God.

However, true to the promises he initially made to his father, Samuel was resolute in the course that he and the College should steer – the pathway of intercession. He had seen very clearly that, throughout the whole Bible, God's purposes were only moved forward through men and women who became clean, anointed channels for intercession. At the pulpit during long ministry sessions, when time seemed to disappear in the Lord's presence, the Patriarchs like Noah, Abraham, Isaac, Joseph, Moses and Joshua became living characters, something which many former students vividly remember. The long and painful periods of preparation in their lives over many years, became necessary as God emptied them to fill them with Himself.

Moses was convinced after forty years in Pharaoh's court that he was the deliverer for the Israelite slaves, since no doubt his mother had told him of his miraculous rescue by Pharaoh's daughter. Knowing that the four hundred years promised to Abraham were complete (Genesis 15:13), he came crashing down as a failure when he was discovered to have killed and buried an Egyptian, and he fled to Midian. After a further forty years of tending someone else's sheep in the backside of the desert, his attitude changed to, "Who am I?" when God met him at the burning bush. A somebody had to become a nobody before God could use him. Who could feel sufficient to deliver a whole nation from slavery? However, the burden for the emancipation of the Hebrew slaves had gripped Moses more and more during those silent years, knowing that it was within the covenant purposes of God. Most probably, it was during those years that the Lord revealed to him the story of creation and the development of the covenant through the lives of the Patriarchs, as recorded in Genesis. God had promised that He would come down to effect the deliverance, but Moses had relinquished all thoughts that he was to be used as the deliverer. At the burning bush, God took full possession of His emptied channel and the work of emancipation began.

Samuel looking out of his bedroom window at Derwen Fawr as he anticipates the glories ahead (veranda outside)

Every character in the developing story in the Scriptures was different, but in each case the principles remained the same. It was the spiritual calibre of these men that challenged Samuel, as he realised that in every corner of the world the Holy Spirit was looking for a similar response from His people in order to further God's purposes today.

That had been the reason why the Holy Spirit had brought Rees Howells back from a powerful revival ministry in Southern Africa, to be buried as a seed in Swansea, all those years previously. A single buried seed would one day produce a rich harvest in the lives of many young men and women in the last days. Samuel could see the principle very clearly.

The prophets, too, (divided into two categories, "Major and Minor, for some unknown reason," as Samuel often remarked)[1] all exercised powerful ministries. With their fingers on the spiritual pulse of their day, they carried burdens for the nations around them, and were able to declare the Word of the Lord for each one. Yet they had that unique initial experience which lifted them into God's realm where they lived and saw Him at work. Ezekiel's experience as recorded in 2:2 (NASB) exemplifies the process that the Lord is seeking:

> As He spoke to me the Spirit entered me and set me on my feet...

In the New Testament the lives of the Apostles, including Paul the Apostle to the Gentiles, were studied carefully by Samuel under the searchlight of the Holy Spirit, as they touched the Jewish and Gentile world of their day. The Lord often led Samuel back to consider in-depth the life and ministry of the Saviour, and the sacred scenes of the trial, crucifixion and resurrection of the Lord came alive in the services. You could hear a pin drop, and folk just wanted to return to their own rooms quietly afterwards. Samuel always brought the presence of the Lord into the services. There was a quiet reverence and awe, with no cheap talk; how could there be when the Christians in the Soviet bloc and throughout China were experiencing such terrible suffering and when intercession was called for at a very deep level.

"Shall we let these passages touch us to the

depth of our souls?" he would say, and "In the light of these passages shall we tell the Lord again that we do not want to go part of the way, but all the way in our service for Him?"

"There is an ocean before us," he once declared, quietly closing his well-worn black leather Authorised Version of the Bible, filled with white slips of paper poking out from various pages for quick reference, "but we are still just paddling in the shallow waters."

Words spoken by his father in a meeting often echoed in Samuel's mind as he spent long hours alone considering these deep truths.

"Don't think you are ever going to be true leaders unless you are one hundred percent the Holy Spirit's."

The compass was set and the helmsman had a tight grip on the tiller as the vessel ploughed its way into deeper waters.

Tucked away in the top right drawer of Samuel's writing desk were verses of songs composed by Ardis Butterfield, the anointed singer and songwriter, whose ministry in the Spirit would lift the worship during the dark days of World War II. During the darkest hours, the theme had remained unchanged, and Samuel was strengthened through reading them often.

These intercessions will bear fruit one day
Completed Vision in unlimited way.
Great signs shall follow the Spirit's hosts
To earth's remotest ends and coasts.

Top section of the Italian Gardens at Derwen Fawr

Chapter Eighteen

The Stormy Sixties and Seventies

The growing momentum of the Communist threat around the world had stimulated much prayer which was heightened by events in Vietnam, as the Viet Cong threatened to swamp this beautiful country in South East Asia. The College had been deeply challenged through visits from Gordon Smith, working in alliance with WEC, whose slides of life among the Rhe people in the interior mountains had shocked everyone. Ritualistic drawing of blood from the oxen, and sawing the children's teeth to their gums had made everyone realise that there were still many unreached tribes needing the Gospel. Mary Henderson, Rees Howells' personal secretary, had responded to a call to join the Smiths and had even adopted a young boy, Fu, who was later educated at Emmanuel School. Now the Viet Cong threatened to bring all that to an end.

In 1964, President Kennedy initially sent in 21,000 U.S. troops and invested $2.4 billion in his attempt to stem the Viet Cong tide, however from 1965-1975, the U.S. spent $111 billion (£69.375 billion) on the war. In 1965, 200,000 U.S. troops were in Vietnam, which rose to half a million by 1967. There were fierce battles, but conventional warfare did not succeed against an enemy who lived in underground hideouts and fought with great tenacity. At the College, a Vietnamese student, Nguyen-Van Do, who was loved by all for his gracious manner, poured out his heart to God in prayer for his nation in the many long prayer sessions which Samuel convened. When he left the College, Do returned to his wife and four sons in Vietnam and worked with the Christian Youth Social Service in Da Nang. He worked tirelessly with others for eighteen hours a day among the millions of refugees fleeing from the Viet Cong. Again, God worked in His own way, with a long-term view in His heart, and following a concerted Tet offensive in 1968, Da Nang fell, a strategic city indicating that a military victory was now unlikely. Peace talks began and were agreed by President Nixon resulting in a total U.S. withdrawal from the country in 1975. Thousands of the Vietnamese refugees escaped, some crammed into small or larger craft and others by helicopter, fearing cruel reprisals from their new overlords.

However, God was at work, and in the midst of all the carnage He found His channel and met him. Samuel took particular note of one Vietnamese Pastor, Doan Van Mieng, and it was obvious that he was giving much time to praying for him. Here was another facet in the Holy Spirit's strategy in leading an individual to intercede for a nation. He will single out one individual, a representative of that nation, so that prayer can be focused and personal. In his own words, Doan Van Mieng told the story in an article he wrote concerning Abraham's experiences and the promises given to him:

> Now these promises are very large. Outside of God there isn't anyone who can fulfil them.... Because of faith Abraham dared to take his only child and offer him on an altar to God. When Abraham dared to believe like that, God could not do anything but honour His promises. Then I took these promises for myself. I said, "Lord, will You please apply these promises to me. As You promised the land of Canaan to Abraham I now ask You to give us the land of Vietnam, will You even open the doors of North Vietnam that we may be able to preach there also. I promise that we will not go out from this country. We will stand here. Please honour this promise to me even as You did to Abraham." Second, I thought how the Lord did a large thing for Abraham when He multiplied his descendants like the stars of the sky and the sand of the sea. So I knelt down and said, "Lord, please give us ten million converts in Vietnam." Third, I prayed, "Lord please allow Your children and Your Church here to be a

source of blessing for all the people around us." I asked the Lord to save me from unbelief. I asked Him to give me faith to be firm before Him because it is only by faith that I can praise Him. If I do not believe Him I will offend Him. I will show Him up as somebody who lies. I believe that God will fulfil these promises and I thank Him.

When the last U.S. helicopter loaded up its cargo of refugees at the airport, Doan Van Mieng was given the offer of joining them. He stood on the runway and waved them off to freedom. He chose to remain, a true intercessor. For many days he had prayed like this,

"Lord, in the past – way in the past – You considered 120,000 people in Nineveh and You did not destroy them. Now today, can't You love the 35 million Vietnamese – my 35 million people. In that number there are over 50,000 believers. Lord, give us the land of Vietnam. Allow us to stay here and worship and serve You. Give us 10 million converts."

The Holy Spirit had guided Samuel perfectly in his ministry.

Nguyen-Van Do, the Vietnamese student at the College did leave with the refugees later and took spiritual responsibility in the Lord for all the refugees airlifted to camps on the island of Guam in the Pacific Ocean, before their eventual settlement in countries around the world. The responsibility taken by these two individuals, and no doubt many others too, ensured the future blessing of Vietnam, irrespective of what the immediate picture then might have suggested. By 2007, reports from very reliable sources state that over 2,300 Vietnamese Church leaders were involved in a biblical training programme. Almost two hundred pastors had officially graduated having spent eight years to complete all seventeen courses of the curriculum. Despite continuing persecution, the Church in Vietnam grows and those believing prayers of the 1960s are bearing fruit.

While Yuri Gargarin, the Russian cosmonaut[1] on 12th April 1961 became the first of many to orbit the earth, and was alleged to have said that he couldn't see God anywhere, God was certainly at work on earth during that decade.

Billy Graham preaching at Wembley Stadium, London, England in May 1954 (120,000 were present on 23rd May)

A most memorable experience had touched Samuel deeply in 1966 when he was invited to attend the ten day World Congress on Evangelism hosted by Dr. Billy Graham between 25th October and 1st November in the Kongress Halle in West Berlin. At the Congress, the first of its kind since the Edinburgh World Missionary Conference of 1910, the theme of 1966 was 'One Race, One Gospel, One Task' and was chaired by Dr. Carl Henry. There were 1,200 invited guests from all over the world, quite a logistical exercise for those days. During the daily sessions, they considered biblical evangelism and its relevance to the modern world; the urgency of the message; new methods of witness in the developing technological world; and how to face the growing resistance to the proclamation of the

Gospel. Samuel had great fellowship and was deeply impressed as he heard about the ministries of candidates from so many overseas countries.

On one occasion Samuel was driven through the Friedrichstrasse Crossing (affectionately known as Checkpoint Charlie), one of the official crossings between East and West Berlin. The original crossing point still remains as an historic monument, part of The Allied Museum to preserve the memories. Samuel was able to meet several evangelical pastors, subject to constant harassment, and to tell them of his intercessory prayers on their behalf, with the assurance that their day of deliverance would come. He often spoke of those precious moments after his return.

The Congress confirmed to everyone how the Holy Spirit was at work all over the world, and the power of the Gospel to change lives was seen in the lives of the Auca Indian Christians who were there, and who had been responsible for the murder of five missionaries in Ecuador.

Reporting back to the staff and students at the Bible College, Samuel shared his thoughts about the final service. There was deep heart searching when Dr. Billy Graham spoke, entitling his sixty-one minute sermon, 'Stains on the Altar.' The large gathering of mature Christian leaders from so many countries fell on their faces before God. Many were broken and, with tears of repentance, rededicated their lives in a fresh way to work for the extension of the Gospel, particularly in areas where Christ was not known. Had the Congress continued for another week, Samuel felt, they were on the edge of a fresh spiritual awakening. But that was not to be.

In 1967, the medical world celebrated the first heart transplant through the skill of Dr. Barnard, but the New Covenant prophesied in Jeremiah 33, so many centuries before, promised heart transplants of greater significance. Samuel returned with a greater determination to pour out his life in the ministry God had given for a lost world. On 7th April 1968, he responded to a call for a Day of Prayer for Britain and another on Sunday, 20th October. Samuel was always concerned for the spiritual well-being of the nation and was reminded of his father's letter of 26th March 1942

to Winston Churchill:
> Since you became Prime Minister we have followed you daily with our prayers. We have always had prayer meetings each evening with about one hundred and fifty present. Since the war began we have had two prayer meetings each evening and, for over a year now, without a single break, we have had prayer meetings from 7pm till midnight. As you are the leader of the State, you have a special place in our prayers and what a hero you have been to these young students! They all say you are the only man who could have kept up the courage of the country to lead it to victory after the colossal disaster at Dunkirk. If the country will send a real cry up to God on the National Day of Prayer, we feel sure that the prayers will be answered.

Samuel wanted the College to respond in a similar way and called everyone to special sessions of corporate prayer following the reading of appropriate passages of Scripture around 2 Chronicles 7:14; 2 Chronicles 20:13-14 and Acts 4:23-33.[2]

On the morning of the 5th June 1967, events suddenly erupted in the Middle East in what was to be known as the Six-Day War or the June War. Threats to eradicate Israel, "annihilation," had been announced in May 1967 and Israel, in a pre-emptive strike, attacked preparing invasion forces from neighbouring countries.

The situation in the Middle East had actually been simmering since the Suez Crisis in 1956, when the United Nations were compelled to place an Emergency Force in nearby Sinai Peninsula to protect the Suez Canal from closure by Egypt. That same year, America gave Israel assurances that it recognised the Jewish State's right of access to the Strait of Tiran and in 1957, Article 17, passed by the UN, gave Israel maritime powers to transit the Straits which was confirmed by the Law of the Sea in 1958. In 1964, Israel's water was being diverted from the River Jordan to feed its Natural Water Corridor, so Syria and Jordan responded by constructing the Mukhaiba Dam for its Hardwater Diversion Plan, the following year. This would considerably restrict the flow of water from upstream into Israel along the River Jordan. Sporadic military skirmishes followed, leading to King Hussein of Jordan mobilising all his troops and Syria shelling Israeli settlements from the Golan Heights, encouraged by the USSR. Israel taunted Syria with armoured tractors ploughing no-man's land dangerously near the Syrian border, inciting air battles over the Golan Heights. Pressures were mounting and Samuel was deeply exercised in prayer, following every move very closely as it was released in the media.

By this time in 1967, President Nasser of Egypt, wanting to show strength among the Arab nations, knowing that he had Soviet support, expelled the UN Emergency Forces from the Sinai Peninsula. They were there to protect the Suez Canal. On 11th May 1967, a false report that Israeli troops were massing along the Syrian borders prompted the Syrian Defence Minister, Hafez-Al-Assad, to issue this inflammatory statement,

"I, as a military man, believe that the time has come to enter into a battle of annihilation."

Similarly President Nasser of Egypt confidently declared,

"The problem before the Arab countries is not whether the port of Eilat should be blockaded, or how to blockade it, but how to totally exterminate the State of Israel for all time."

The important Straits of Tiran were immediately closed to prevent assistance from outside nations to rescue tiny Israel, threatened by Syria in the north and Egypt in the south, with added support from Iraq, Saudi Arabia, Kuwait, Algeria and the USSR.

Israel's Prime Minister Rabin suffered a breakdown through exhaustion and was replaced by Moshe Dyan, who formed a National Unity Government in the crisis, and included opposition leader Menachen Begin. One military observer, Samuel Katz, wrote:

Never in human history can an aggressor have made his purpose known in advance so clearly and so widely. Certain of victory, both the Arab leaders and their people threw off all restraint.

People throughout the world watched and waited in growing anxiety, or in some cases in hopeful expectation, for the overwhelming forces of at least Egypt, Syria, Jordan and Iraq to bear down from three sides to crush tiny Israel and slaughter her people.

In the seclusion of his room in Derwen Fawr, Swansea, Samuel felt the burden and asked staff members to take the meetings until he found the mind of the Lord. One thing was clear. God was being challenged and He would certainly take up the fight.

For Samuel and senior staff colleagues at the College they immediately relived those days during World War II when the Holy Spirit led Rees Howells into the intercession of his life for the preservation of the Jews during the Holocaust and for the establishment of the State of Israel in 1948. In the longest closing section of his prophecy, which we now read as chapters 40:1 to 66:24, Isaiah deals in great detail with the redemption and restoration of Israel. To underpin and strengthen the prophecy concerning the final outcome of the Divine plans for the nation of Israel, specific details are provided of King Cyrus the Mede, instrumental in orchestrating the return of the Jewish captives to their land after seventy years in Babylon, all of which happened eighty years later (Isaiah 44:28 to 45:13). Such accurate prophecies cement into place the fortunes of Israel for the last times – waiting for someone to believe them. The ministry of Jehovah's Servant is unfolded. His sufferings and triumph described in poetic detail, offer the opportunity through grace, for all who wish to do so in the Gentile nations to embrace the blessings promised to Israel in chapters 49, 53, 55-58 and 60-64. All took on a fresh meaning in the College meetings, as the Holy Spirit shed His own light on familiar passages and enabled Rees Howells to believe for the impossible, the survival of the Jews in their darkest hour. It wasn't human eloquence and ideas which would cope with the satanic forces which gripped Europe, but the Holy Spirit applying the prophetic words of truth to inspire faith, as was originally intended.

Samuel would often share privately to close friends that the Holy Spirit shed exceptional light on those passages in

Isaiah, and Paul's exposition of the truths surrounding the restoration of the Jewish Nation in Romans 9-11, during the intercessions in the war and afterwards, the nature of which he had not experienced since. Those were monumental days in the College.

Now in the 1960s, Samuel put everything to one side once more and called for extra prayer meetings to be guided by the Holy Spirit. After 2,000 years, God had returned the Jews to their land, having preserved them through the most violent of persecutions, and they were not to be annihilated at this time. The prayer was intense, but Samuel found relief through returning to the book of Esther, a record of Satan's close attempt to destroy the Jewish people in the fifth century BC, during the reign of the Persian King Ahasuerus (Xerxes I).

As in the days of Esther, when Haman devised an evil plan to annihilate the Jewish nation, who are central to God's purposes of redemption in the world, so Samuel could see a modern day parallel. It reminded him of Hitler's evil intention when he implemented his "final solution," resulting in the Holocaust in World War II.

Mordecai had resorted to intercessory prayer. Esther's first attempt to speak to the king at the banquet failed. She was prevented by very powerful dark, spiritual forces at work in the unseen realm. Mordecai's intercession prevailed and that night the king could not sleep (Esther 6:1) until he had rewarded the person who had foiled an assassination attempt on his life. That person happened to be Mordecai, the Jew. At the second banquet, Esther found complete liberty of spirit to disclose Haman's evil plans, and the Jewish Nation was preserved. The power of intercessory prayer to break the spiritual forces of evil in the heavenly realms, referred to in Ephesians 6:12, is very potent and will prove again the only means by which the final phases of God's plan for this age will be determined. There had to be an Esther, willing to forfeit her life if need be, to seek audience with the king, but Mordecai told her that another would be found if she demurred. Mordecai was clearly the intercessor and he prevailed. History records the outcome. Samuel was strengthened as he listened closely to news reports of the new Middle East conflict.

Now, 1967, Israeli response was immediate, sending up all but twelve of their whole available aircraft at 7:14am on 5th June to destroy three hundred Egyptian planes on the ground as their crews had breakfast. Then a similar strike in the north crippled Syrian and Jordanian air capabilities. Israeli tanks rolled into the Sinai Peninsula and engaged Egyptian tank regiments in bitter tank battles in the scorching desert, finally pushing their way to the Egyptian border. On the Syrian front, bitter and costly fighting eventually secured the Golan Heights for Israel, and within six days the Shofar was once again sounded in Jerusalem. Despite efforts by the Israelis to prevent any fighting against Jordan, an agreement was broken when Israeli planes were mistakenly fired upon by Jordan. Israeli soldiers then stormed the West Bank gaining full control of their city, Jerusalem, including the Old City and the Wailing Wall, after thousands of years. Prophecies were being fulfilled before the eyes of the world and Samuel could see the hand of God at work in response to intercessory prayer. On 10th June, Israel and the Arab countries accepted UN Security Council cease-fire demands. Sinai was returned to Egypt years later between 1978 and 1982 and there followed a fragile Israeli / Egyptian Peace Treaty. History, of course, has continued to produce many developments in the Middle East, since it remains the focal point for the future, but through them all the Holy Spirit is ever seeking for a channel through whom He can intercede for the completion of the Divine plan.

In 1969 when Neil Armstrong was making his first tentative steps on the moon, Samuel was traversing the heavenly realms on a far more significant mission. Although Harold Wilson's government had abolished the death penalty in Britain there were killings on a broad scale going on all over the world and these were a concern to Samuel. The publication of Alexander Solzhenitsyn's book *Gulag Archipelago* (1973) revealed the extent of deaths in the correction (slave) camps of Siberia, and Communist takeovers in Chile and Cambodia did not bode well for Christians in those countries.

Letters continued to pour in from all corners of the world from missionaries and national workers with whom Samuel was in touch. The demand for Scriptures and Christian literature was so great. Samuel would read out in the meetings, quotes such as these:

    Thank you for your generous gift for Bibles. Men who are serving terms of imprisonment have sent letters beseeching us to send Bibles and books to them.

    This place is full of Tibetan refugees in Central Asia. Thank you once again for your timely gift.

    There are a great number of evangelical preachers in these countries without a single copy of the Bible.

    We had not had mail here in the Congo for four weeks. Thank you for your letter of 8th August and for the gift. A weekend meeting was arranged in a very backward area high up in the hills. Over a thousand men and women were present. They seemed to be there in their droves. (1968).

    What a great encouragement it was to receive another letter from you this week. Your generous gift has come as a real answer to prayer. (Kenya, 1972).

    This is my first few moments since the end of the campaign here in Jammu (North India). I came here from Kishtwar. We had about one thousand present and sixty-two responded to the altar call. Altogether one hundred and seventy-six came to the Lord. It was thrilling, especially for those who have worked for many years and have seen little fruit. (1972).

    I have received your letter and a sum of Vietnamese money equivalent to one hundred Pounds Sterling that you sent to help the work here recently. Thank you very much. (N.B. £100 / $160 was a large gift in 1973. In 2012, it is equal to £945 / $1,510).

    We would ask your prayers too, for the

Chinese workers without whom it would be impossible to carry on this work. (1973).

Thank you for your continued support. There is a spirit of revival amongst our young people here in Formosa, Argentina. (1973).

The Lord led us to move to a newly rising city (in Japan) where there is only one tiny church for 50,000 inhabitants. He also inspired us by the Spirit that we should not receive monthly support from any organisation. Thank you very much for your thoughtful gift and prayers. (1973).

> **Friday, August 12, 1966**
>
> # 'NO SNEERS' BIBLE IS BEST-SELLER
>
> Russians queued up in Moscow yesterday—to buy the Bible.

British newspaper clipping, August 1966. The first "Bible" printed within Russia without contemptuous scornful remarks since the Revolution of 1917. The State Publishing House issued 100,000 copies of the OT in simple Russian, which sold within minutes in bookshops across Moscow!

One special report concerned Ida, a very brave twenty-

seven year old young lady from the Russian Underground Church. Samuel had prayed for her. The KGB (secret police) finally caught up with her. She was put on trial for possessing and distributing Scriptures and was offered immediate parole on condition that she confessed her guilt and recent actions. She replied to the judge,
> "Freedom of course is a wonderful privilege and I long for it. But seek it I must not! The high cost will be too enormous to bear. I am constrained to esteem the value of my soul higher than your offer of a conditional freedom."

Ida was showered with flowers by the believers and sent to a labour camp by the authorities.

One very appreciative recipient of Samuel's ministry wrote:
> I am sending you some tea towels to hang on your wall as a decoration in your room. My mother got the idea.

Mmmm! This was such a thoughtful suggestion, but if he displayed one tea towel, Samuel imagined what his walls would look like in a year as others arrived. He decided against it, instead placing it under his tray when dining at his desk / table.

In 1973, there was another surprise attack on Israel from its neighbours, heavily armed with the latest military technology, on the holiest day of the Jewish calendar, Yom Kippur – the Day of Atonement – when the whole nation was in solemn contemplation. Again Samuel called the College back to prayer as the Holy Spirit led through another spiritual conflict characterised by many amazing miracles as individual testimonies later confirmed. One such testimony was from an Egyptian soldier who was converted on the battlefield, when the Israeli forces pushed to within fifty miles (eighty kilometres) of Cairo. This convert later became a student at the Bible College.

Since 1959, when Cyprus gained its independence, Samuel had been led to support Levon Yergatian and the work of the Christian Literature Crusade, in its drive to distribute evangelical literature throughout the Island. Archbishop Makarios, brought back from deportation by the

British, was now the popular elected President maintaining the strong Greek Orthodox tradition. The 1974 Turkish invasion threatened to engulf the whole island, so special prayer was again made in Swansea.

A deep impression was left on the College staff one Sunday morning in the 9:45 prayer meeting in the Conference Hall, when they heard Samuel pouring out his heart to the Lord for the dear people of Angola, who had gained independence in 1975. This had not produced stability but had plunged the country into a twenty-six year long civil war between the government forces and the Unita rebels. The work of the Gospel was disrupted and Samuel, ever sensitive to suffering and every move of the enemy of souls, was alert in the Spirit. There was a similar response to the upsurge of violence in Lebanon, when civil war broke out, particularly as Vartan Atchinak's school was there, with Eva Rose, Dora Holder and Dr. Hughes from the College. Often criticised for his, at times, frugal lifestyle, Samuel was a man whose companions in the Spirit were often the fifty-two members of the U.S. Embassy held as hostages for over a year in Teheran, or the hungry Africans experiencing the terrible drought of the Sahel.

Samuel always concluded his time of ministry and prayer by declaring a word of faith and confidence, no matter how dark and desperate the situation in question would seem to be. He was believing for blessing in every nation of the world and would round off his prayer with a quote from Isaiah 53:11 (AV).

He shall see of the travail of His soul, and shall be satisfied.

Christ's atoning death offered life for everyone in the world.

Chapter Nineteen

A Resolute Stand Amidst Gathering Clouds

The familiar figure of this upright, spectacled individual enjoying the fresh air of the sea front at Mumbles or the cliff path along the Gower coast, or speeding up Cherry Grove, a well-known road in a nearby upmarket residential estate, betrayed little of the conflicts and deep heart searching which were to sweep over him during the 1970s. Samuel was being gripped in very tangible ways by the truths of 2 Corinthians 11:28-31 (NASB):
> *Apart from such external things, there is the daily pressure on me of concern for all the churches. Who is weak without my being weak? Who is led into sin without my intense concern? If I have to boast, I will boast of what pertains to my weakness. The God and Father of the Lord Jesus, He who is blessed forever, knows that I am not lying.*

In 1969, his loyal friend Dr. Kenneth Symonds (who was in charge of the men students) fell ill and subsequent investigations revealed that a brain tumour was developing and required surgery. His recovery enabled him to return to his work and then to drive to Lichfield for Christmas. Samuel wrote to his dear friend:
> Dear Symbo, We were greatly relieved when we heard that you had reached your destination safely. We prayed continually for you all day when you were driving to your brother and felt assured that the Lord would be with you and give you a safe journey. The Lord has answered prayer and we are glad. We are delighted that you felt no ill effects after the journey and are quite well at present. It is wonderful how the Lord raised you up after that major operation and enabled you to do so much last term.

Then Samuel closes with these powerful words, from one who was personally passing through deep waters himself:

> One thing is certain that nothing is too hard for the Lord, nor is it ever too late for Him. As we look back upon His gracious deliverances during this year our hearts are full of praise and gratitude.

You can imagine the sorrow and grief that must have engulfed Samuel when 'Symbo' took a turn for the worse. Much prayer was made for his healing and recovery but he died in Singleton Hospital, Swansea, in September 1970. Tributes flowed in from all over the world. Len Moules, then Director of WEC wrote:

> We are all with you in a particular sense of real fellowship today. It is a day of triumph, for it always is when a fellow soldier marches through the gates into the audience of His Commander in Chief.

Other letters from the British Secretary for WEC, Robert Mackie, and another missionary, Charlton Smith, also expressed their sincere sympathy. Dr. Symonds was referred to as a man greatly beloved, and so he was.

It was during that period that a young, shy student Alan Scotland, destined to become the Director in the twenty-first century, joined the College family for the first time and later spent time on the staff while Betty, his future wife, completed her student apprenticeship.

In the College and Emmanuel School, the inevitable need for refurbishing, repairing and modernising existing facilities arose, especially after the war years. Samuel was often reluctant to finance the larger but necessary projects. He would take convincing before the 'go ahead' was given, but he was always pleased with the outcome. Perhaps some of his reluctance was tempered by the fact that he just did not like change, particularly if it involved the demolition of buildings or cutting down trees or bushes, so his caution did provide a buffer against the more ambitious members of the fellowship.

Samuel was carrying heavy burdens for situations around the world. The spiritual load was affecting his health, especially with his lack of sleep and it was suggested that he should share the responsibilities more with other members of staff.

Samuel in his bedroom, busy working at his desk. Notice the piles of mostly international airmail letters on his desk, the many pictures on the mantelpiece, alongside his leather AV Bible on chair (left) with dressing gown nearby.

One particular practical issue which the College medical team, including three doctors, seriously considered was the provision of suitable care for older staff members. This would include alterations in the existing hospital block to create nursing home care for the elderly, with the employment of paid local Christian nurses.

Samuel was never one to give a quick answer but listened carefully and promised to give the proposals his prayerful consideration. But to Samuel this was a radical idea, which ran contrary to the promise he had made to his father to continue the whole work in exactly the same way as at its inception. In addition to this, the general tenor of the proposals seemed to run contrary to the Charity Scheme of Administration, Number 212216, thrashed out earlier in the High Court of Justice. Although the Director could delegate his powers to any person(s) to any extent, it was he alone who must assume full personal financial responsibility for the work, (Schedule 3, Section 5). Also invested in him was his remarkable ability to have 'full power to spend, invest or otherwise dispose of or deal with any such property for the said objects or purposes...and no purchaser, lender or other person shall be concerned to enquire as to the expediency or propriety of the transaction,' (Schedule 3, Section 7). In no way did Samuel wish to jeopardise the ministry the Lord was giving him, nor did he wish to abuse it. He was always ready to hear people's ideas and opinions.

"Everyone is entitled to his or her opinion," he would say, "but the Lord never asks for our opinions but expects our obedience to Him."

The proposals were never implemented resulting in the older members of staff needing to be transferred to local nursing homes instead.

Dark clouds were gathering and Samuel resorted to prayer. God was taking him along the pathway that all true intercessors have trodden through the centuries, that of loneliness, misunderstanding and unpopularity and, for him, identification with those believers in Eastern Europe and the USSR whose burden he was sharing.

From his pulpit ministry he traced the development of God's work through the book of Acts and spoke of the Apostle Paul's decision to visit Jerusalem. In Acts 21:4 (NASB) it is recorded:

We stayed there (Tyre) *seven days; and they kept telling Paul through the Spirit not to set foot in Jerusalem.*

Yet Paul continued on his fateful journey. There were depths in his decision, based on the revelation Paul had received, which only the intercessor could appreciate. The Church today would be much the poorer without the valuable letters, familiar to us as the prison epistles, which were written as an outcome of Paul's decision then.

Samuel always stressed, as did Rees Howells, the importance of revelation in our dealings with God.

Samuel was experiencing for himself what it means for any real intercessor, as opposed to a prayer warrior, to contend with the powers of darkness in order to see God's covenant purposes established in the world. He knew that the *gates of hell* (Matthew 16:18) could not prevail against the Holy Spirit's intercession. However, in correspondence he did share with a close friend that the pathway was proving a deep and costly one. It was a matter of looking to the Lord for strength, not only for each day, but each hour. Samuel's sensitivity and determination to remain faithful to the ministry the Lord had given him were evident. For the casual observer, the crisis situation which Samuel faced was not apparent since he chose to carry the burdens alone. The loss of Dr. Symonds in 1970 and his own dear mother, on 9th August 1972 increased his grief. In correspondence, he wrote that events had proved a Gethsemane experience as he felt as though he was following the Saviour right to death. Every night was spent in agonising prayer and intercession, but the Holy Spirit was giving him strength to continue. Samuel realised that it was an essential part of the intercession. Despite the awful cost it was unquestionably a privilege to be identified with the Master in His death and to become a partaker of the Divine Nature (2 Peter 1:3-4). As far as he was personally concerned, Samuel did not wish to continue in the leadership of the work a day longer than it was the Lord's will for him to do so. How many critics realised that or had ever walked that way themselves?

Samuel was quickened and the work proceeded. Many improvements took place on the home front, and the support for individuals and agencies printing and distributing Scriptures overseas increased. Despite a further crippling blow when Eva Stewart died in 1974, Samuel remained resolute in his regular weekly pulpit ministry and he did so with much anointing. Privately he would confess that he hardly had enough strength to leave his room, descend the red-carpeted stairs and walk through the walnut-panelled dining room to the prayer room. Never a one to speak loudly, he now often began with a faint whisper and in fact a special microphone was installed to amplify his voice in the room. As the anointing gripped him, the Scriptures lived and, like David at Ziklag, Samuel encouraged himself in the Lord.

A welcome respite was provided through an unexpected source when members of Uncle Tom Jones' family, on

Samuel's mother's side and now living in Canada, arrived at the College on what was probably their one and only opportunity to meet Samuel in the flesh. Although reluctant to do so at first because of all the challenges he was facing, Samuel did finally accept their generous invitation to join them on a three-week cruise of the Scandinavian countries, a part of the world he had never visited. His weary frame badly needed that change, he thoroughly enjoyed it, and he returned to College in good form.

A fresh burden at that time came when dramatic changes took place in Portuguese East Africa in 1969, when leader Eduardo Mondlane was murdered and a Marxist regime, led by Samora Machel and the Frelimo party, gained power. The whole country from north to south turned into a bloodbath, when hundreds of thousands were exterminated and the brutal secret police (SNASPS) hunted down the Christians. Rees Howells had wanted to spend his days there as a missionary (he had made mission excursions into this country as had converts from Rusitu, Gazaland) and the Spirit in Samuel responded immediately to the holocaust. Graphic details were brought to the College by Gordon Legge, Director of the Africa Evangelical Fellowship (formerly SAGM, the mission which Samuel's parents joined in 1915) and his wife Katie (one of the first College students in 1924) who were now forcibly evicted from their work. Samuel assured them of his prayers and intercession, and told them that one day they would return, but it was to be a bitter struggle. Portuguese East Africa officially became independent in 1975 and became known as Mozambique. The day did come when Gordon and Katie returned to a royal welcome from the triumphant Church in Mozambique, which had survived such terrible persecutions.

By this time, intercession had burned its way into Samuel's life and it soon became obvious to his congregation, whenever he touched on the subject in ministry, that he was 'on the inside of it' and knew from experience what he was talking about. In April 1976 he spoke out strongly, quoting from an article he had read,

"You may be seeking some special gift, you may be looking for some special manifestation, it may be that some great emotional experience is your delight, but you look down upon those who have not received what you have received."

He looked up and added,

"What proud people those are. They are only sinners saved by grace. Why do we need to exalt man? Exalt the Saviour. There's nothing in man, nothing at all. It's all in the realm of the imagination, isn't it, not in the realm of reality."

The article continued,

"The highest form of Christian service is intercessory prayer. The high water mark of spiritual experience is an intercessory life. Unless you have attained to this you fall far short. I care not how emphatically you may boast of your spiritual experience and of the special gifts you have received, your ministry is void of power, valueless in the sight of God if you know not how to intercede on behalf of others. The Throne life is what counts with God."

To emphasise his point Samuel banged the wooden pulpit made specially for him by Norman Brend, the woodwork teacher, as he continued,

"Apart from intercession you couldn't carry this place on (referring to the College). That is what His servant (the Founder of the College) used to say and the work was far less complicated than it is today. I remember those last years of his life when he said that he used to get up in the morning feeling so physically weak and exhausted. He said that a man couldn't carry this place on for a day. Well, could a man carry it on today?" reasoned Samuel. "It is the Holy Spirit who is carrying the place but He is seeking for bodies. That is the price you have to pay. Think of the people whom we have helped. One (referring to himself) is going back to the Throne. You may think it good if you lose yourself in enthusiasm in prayer (and most of us are guilty of that, we must confess!). Are you sure you are touching the Throne? If you intercede you are touching the Throne each time. That is the need, and we heard it every day and every hour with the Founder. That was the revelation. I believe, you know, that the importance, the significance of intercession was revealed to him by the Holy Spirit just as salvation was revealed to the Apostle Paul in the deserts of Arabia. Galatians 1:15-17. That became His servant's ministry and it was on intercession that the Lord worked. And it is important to see that intercessions of the Holy Spirit are always made within the orbit – do you follow me – of the atoning work of our Lord, not outside of it, and it is by way of intercession that the Holy Spirit proves the fullness and completion of the atonement."

The deep truths which the older staff members had learnt, through bitter experience, during Rees Howells' ministry, particularly during the war years, needed to be revealed to the younger generation of Christians entering the final phases of the spiritual battles of the ages. There is no substitute.

Samuel knew that he needed to guard these deep truths well, without any distraction, no matter how legitimate those other causes seemed to be.

One regular and much loved visitor to the College was Michael Howard, founder of Kalibu Ministries in Malawi, With a burning heart for the continent of Africa, he had witnessed the power of intercessory prayer in Zimbabwe, Rwanda, Sudan, where peace was established after many years; Mozambique and more recently in establishing Kalibu Academy in Malawi. Notable of his fifteen books is *Tales of An African Intercessor* (1998) which speaks of his intercessions and a number of powerful revivals. Samuel had deep fellowship with this young firebrand who commands great respect throughout Africa.

Every Friday afternoon, Samuel's familiar figure, sometimes with a black umbrella over his arm, would be seen walking through Salubrious Passage in Swansea, a shortcut from the 'unknown-to-most' car park, to Wind

Street, then the business centre of town. He carried a bundle of letters containing encouragement and gifts, ready to be posted to nationals and Christian workers around the world. Samuel prayed over every letter before posting it. Both the Central Post Office and Westminster Bank were on hand, as was a small shop where he used to buy a large packet of favourite sweets for his mother. He always enjoyed a visit to this Dickensian haven of liquorice allsorts and barley sugar, or sent his driver in while he attended to more serious affairs. It is interesting to note that those visits continued even after the death of his mother!

In reply to his correspondence, letters of appreciation for prayer and practical support poured in from all parts of the world as the ministry grew. Many were from former students who were remembered constantly. Extracts from letters tell their own story as he encouraged others with news he received.

Reinhard Bonnke and others with Peggy Coulthard (holding his arm) in the grounds of Derwen Fawr late c.1970s. Peggy was converted in her home city of Liverpool during George Jeffreys' Healing and Revival Campaign of 1926 and later became a staff member of the Bible College of Wales. Peggy was one of the elderly intercessors who would have remembered Reinhard (and many other ministers) when they were young students learning the life of faith.

From Maseru in Lesotho, one former student wrote:
> Thank you very much for your wonderful and inspiring letter – your gift will help pay for a consignment of over five metric tons of paper for our Gospel Press. We shall print one million tracts to be dropped by aeroplane in April.... In our Conference at Maseru the power of God was mightily real among us. A totally blind man received his sight in front of all the people. In Pretoria, miracles happened by the score. I had never intended to pray for the sick – it was just the Spirit of God taking over. My prayer is that His Spirit shall be poured upon all flesh.
>
> Yours in His service, RWG Bonnke (Reinhard).

Reinhard had been a College student from 1959-1961.[1]

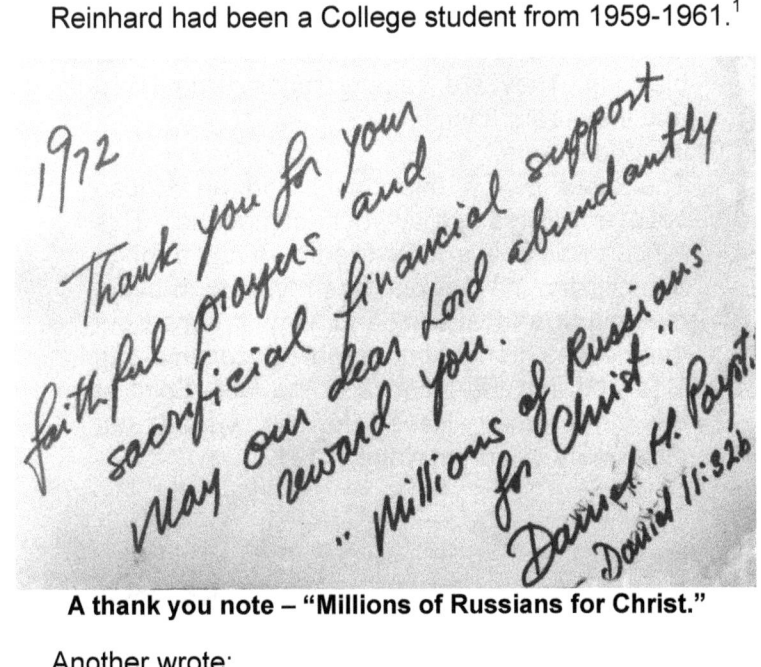

A thank you note – "Millions of Russians for Christ."

Another wrote:
> The Spirit is moving in many places, despite the relentless attacks from the evil one. There is much blessing here in Indonesia at this time. Hundreds are turning to the Lord. This is remarkable when you consider that just a while back the Communists made a determined attack to engulf the whole of this area of South

East Asia.

Again, another student wrote:

South America is undoubtedly a fruitful field these days. Hardly a week passes without many entering into the experience of salvation. It has not always been like this, for we have laboured for many years (actually about thirty years with only one furlough) with very few results. God has wonderfully fulfilled Psalm 126:6 to us. Now our principal work is to guide these new believers that by the power of the Holy Spirit they may become victorious and that their zeal may be guided into the right and most useful channels for Him. It is important to place the Word of God in the hands of these young converts and really that has been the secret of blessing. They are eagerly reading the Word and they really love it.

From Africa came:

The other day a missionary and an African believer visited us at our compound. This African was truly a Spirit-filled man and through his ministry, the Saviour was revealed in every meeting in a most wonderful way. It turned out that he was brought into a real relationship with God and into the fullness of the Holy Spirit at the time when Rees Howells visited our missionary station at Natal in 1917.

Rees Howells trekking in Zululand August 1917

In the face of mounting pressures in the home camp, and feeling his own physical weakness, Samuel fixed his spiritual eyes on Jesus in the intercessions God had laid upon him and pressed forward. In situations like this, his true spiritual stature shone through. With dogged determination (often misconstrued as stubbornness) his concentration and focus was in the prayer upon him, being fully persuaded that the Lord meant every promise that He uttered while He was on earth.

In concluding his letters, Samuel would often add:
> We are proving the reality of those words of the Lord,
> *Except a corn of wheat fall into the ground and die, it abideth alone: but if it die, it bringeth forth much fruit.* John 12:24 (AV).

Advance in Gazaland – The Continued Story of Revival by Bessie Porter Head, c.1920, tells the story of revival in Gazaland under Rees Howells and other missionaries. Found in Samuel Howells' Bible in Acts 2:38-39. *Repent and be baptised everyone of you in the name of Jesus Christ for the remission of sins and ye shall receive the gift of the Holy Ghost. For this promise is unto you...* **Acts 2:38b-39.**

Chapter Twenty

The Daily Walk

As the years unfolded, it was becoming increasingly difficult for newcomers to the College to feel that they could really get to know Samuel as a person. It was also possible to spend years at the College yet have only an occasional brief conversation with him in private, and many students felt this was wrong. As has been mentioned previously, here seemed to be an unapproachable leader, only occasionally seen at a distance unless he was in the pulpit.

One very sincere and much loved former student's experience would find a similar response from many others plunged into this most unusual spiritual community:

> Having been accepted at the Bible College of Wales at quite a tender age, I remember my first impressions of the College with its beautiful grounds and strange looking buildings. The first impression I had was of a very real sense of God when I walked through the gardens. One of the biggest issues for me, however, was to comprehend the ministry of Mr Samuel Howells. I was already familiar with the College and the Founder, Mr Rees Howells, but this seemed very different. I was encouraged by my grandmother to stay at the College despite any hard times that might arise, and they did. In my first year there arose a contention concerning the ministry of Mr Howells and I felt a slight rebellion arising. But my stance was that God called me to the College to learn something and not for me to teach the College a lesson or two. I felt God wanted me to come under the authority of Mr Howells and submit to what was expected of me. I thank God to this day for the stance I took then.

I soon realised that under the peaceful atmosphere that pervaded the College was a constantly raging spiritual battle.

For our struggle is not against flesh and blood, but against the authorities, against the powers of this dark world and against the spiritual forces of evil in the heavenly realms. Ephesians 6:12.

I never fully understood this but I did feel and see it, especially in the lives of Mr Howells and those who were close to him. I learnt that prayer was more than words – it was a life poured out.

And pray in the Spirit on all occasions with all kinds of prayers and requests. With this in mind, be alert and always keep on praying for all the saints. Ephesians 6:18.

I remember seeing the famous walk of Mr Howells on the veranda outside his room, where he would pace up and down, head bowed, in intercessory prayer. To me, this very misunderstood man of God became one whom I trusted and loved and had the privilege to get to know, and I feel, to understand in a small measure.

Samuel Howells on the veranda of Derwen Fawr[1] 1980s

Samuel's lecturing days decreased as he handed those responsibilities over to others, even his much loved Church History. Those lectures were given into the safe hands of Hanns Gross, one of the Jewish refugee children whom Rees Howells had rescued and provided a home for in the 1940s. Eventually, Hanns emigrated to the USA where he married Bonnie and took up several professorships in Chicago University. He died in 2006, a true Messianic believer.

Samuel really was a very shy person, as the embarrassing stammer during his early days showed. When asked for her immediate recollections of Samuel recently, one of the first boarders in the Bible College School replied after pausing for a few seconds, "Serious and shy." Once however, you were able to breakthrough this barrier of shy reserve, there was a gentle, refined, godly man, full of humour and always concerned for your personal welfare and the good of others. With his excellent navigational skills he was always a good companion in the car.

Samuel Howells having a picnic in the Welsh Countryside with Miss Ruth Williams (front) with a flask of tea c.1990

Pointing towards a lonely farmstead on one of his trips past Mynydd Trawsnant peak on the road to the Llyn Brianne Reservoir, Samuel once remarked with a broad grin, "What do you think; shall we buy a farm and come and live out here? But we won't keep pigs!" On numerous occasions when you would think the pressures of international affairs or College problems would be overwhelming him, he would mention that he had been all day in prayer for a struggling student, or for a prisoner in Swansea gaol (jail) who was facing the death sentence, or for the victims of a disaster reported over the radio. Eternity will record the number of people blessed through those prayers.

His daily walk with God was his priority and he fully understood that his entrance into the Divine Presence of the Inner Sanctuary of Hebrews 10:19-20 was conditional on passing *through the Veil, that is to say, His flesh* (AV). At that point, he would say, the enemy watches you and seeks to spoil the 'abiding.'

Quoting from several of his own expositions it can be seen how vital it was for Samuel to be living in the Lord's presence every day,

> "John 4:46-54. We were thinking of the Life which is still in the Son of God. John had had a revelation of Him and to him there was no doubt that Jesus was God. The people of Jerusalem had to accept Him as such or nothing at all. In Him was Life but it seems there had to be a contact, there had to be faith on the part of the individuals. There was a release of Life when contact was made. The Lord perceived that this man had the faith. That was the only requirement, to have faith in the ability of this Divine Person. Again the Life was released and entered into that child and the child was healed. That Life is not dependent on time or space. This is the power and it is just the same today. We may live in Him today – this relationship is essential. We must make contact with Him. We are not going to partake of this Life if we are not walking uprightly. Satan

would have us believe that this abiding is unnatural. Let's put it this way – it is the flesh that is the hindrance to us. We need to touch Him whatever is confronting us now.

"John 10:22-42. Jesus had performed works in Jerusalem that had never been done before; the works themselves were enough to substantiate His claims. He wants us to follow Him and to do those works that all those who believe in His Name were to do. Many men who are believing in a full Gospel today are being stigmatised by the Church – we want to identify ourselves with them. In these last days the Lord wants these works to be repeated and it is our conviction too, that even *greater works* are to be done today. Our prayers may not be spectacular but they may lead to something like that. We cannot jump into this life; it is a steady walk. A testimony is being raised here and we do not want there to be a single weakness. The devil would have us to think that this life of abiding is bondage. It is the old life that is a bondage."

Samuel continued, the hush of God's presence pervading the College prayer room,

"The Founder of the College had to spend days and days in prayer when he was 'climbing' in faith. Surely if he had to go back to God all the time, so must we. But it is worth living to raise a testimony. Shall we believe Him? Have we seen Him in all His majesty tonight, in His power and His authority? In the light of that can we believe Him? Let us tell Him tonight that we believe Him for all our needs, spiritual, natural and physical. We believe Him."

For some, Samuel's ministry did not 'tickle their ears' as they would have liked, usually those who were not used to trusting God even for their day-to-day needs, let alone in greater issues. Sadly, a life of prayer and faith holds little or no attraction for those who are *at ease in Zion.* Amos 6:1 (AV). It was not uncommon for him to read the Scriptures consecutively throughout a whole two-hour session, commenting here and there and pausing occasionally for a hymn. He would emphasise time and time again that a revelation is independent of every earthly circumstance and, in reading through the first four chapters of John's Gospel on one occasion, illustrated the point through the life and ministry of John the Baptist. Here was a man filled with the Holy Spirit from birth, whose revelation of Jesus as the Lamb of God launched the Saviour's public ministry. John was reluctant to baptise the Master for the remission of sins, when he knew that this peerless individual in the water was not guilty of one single sin. The cost of our redemption was beyond human comprehension or, in Samuel's words,

"It is beyond our ken."

Then, with a characteristic impassioned observation, he continued,

"You hear these commentators sometimes – they are so smart, aren't they – they think they have theological knowledge but as far as God is concerned their knowledge is practically nil – it all depends on Divine illumination."

At the end of a long day Samuel was now refreshed.

"We have been blessed again through reading these chapters. Oh, for the Lord to meet us all again."[2]

Engulfed in challenges of faith from day one as the Honorary Director in 1950, Samuel knew firsthand what stress and burdens were all about, but the Holy Spirit would not tolerate those 'tendencies' – as Samuel called them.

"No," he would say, "we must live in victory; according to the light the Spirit sheds on the Divine Person of the Son of God."

An ounce of experience is worth more than a ton of theory, was Samuel's axiom to live by.[3]

Samuel would have been so thrilled, in his own quiet way, to see the fruits of his ministry during those evening prayer sessions. In any ministry there will always be the 'wheat and weeds' growing together, as taught by Jesus through a parable.

> *The Kingdom of Heaven is like a man who sowed good seed in his field. But while everyone was sleeping, his enemy came and sowed weeds among the wheat and went away. When the wheat sprouted and formed ears, then the weeds also appeared.* Matthew 13:24-26.

In the parable, servants wanted to pull up the weeds but the Master advised that the crop should be left alone for fear of disturbing the wheat with them. Harvest time brought separation, when weeds were destroyed and a wheat crop gathered into the barn. Matthew 13:27-30.

In reflecting upon his years at the College, one former Korean student wrote:

> God sent me to the College for missionary training. I had a language barrier problem and found difficulties adapting to the strict regulations of the College. It was at that time that Rev. Howells taught me about a life of prayer. I learnt that he slept few hours and spent day and night praying for the whole world. I was surprised when he told me that he had been praying for North Korea for many years. Even though I was a Korean, I had never prayed for North Korea. His life of prayer inspired me.
>
> I woke up every morning at four o' clock and left the dormitories to pray for all parts of the globe as well as North Korea. Since that time I have always prayed early in the mornings for the work of God.

At that stage, God spoke to him one day in the College grounds and called him to serve Him in Africa. Because his wife could not speak English no missionary society would accept him, so the student bought a one-way ticket and began trusting God to guide him for the next step! He continued in his letter:

> When I came to Malawi, Africa in 1985 I was one of the poorest missionaries. God sent me to an area where poor people lived. My life became very difficult to live but I couldn't run away from the calling of God. I had to practise

what I learnt from Samuel Howells so I started to pray and fast. God touched Samuel Howells' heart and he often sent me letters of encouragement and money. Even though I never spoke to him about my lack of support, God communicated with him showing him my need when I was praying to God. Howells' prayers are bearing much fruit in Africa and I'm sure in other parts of the world as well. The Lord has established over five hundred churches through us in seven countries in Africa and used us to establish several kindergartens, primary schools, middle and high schools, a Bible College, a mission farm, a prayer mountain, one medical centre, two clinics – and we are still building an orphanage in Swaziland. We are also establishing a university, Swaziland Christian University, in cooperation with the government. Samuel Howells lived a simple and humble life but inspired and motivated many throughout the world. He taught me to think big and therefore pray big. Because of him, I do not pray only for local ministries but for ministries all around the globe.

That testimony alone indicates the impact Samuel's tireless ministry was to have upon the whole world and the emphasis placed upon young people learning, not only men's theories about the Scriptures, but to experience the challenges of a life of prayer and faith.

For those who had the privilege of knowing Samuel at closer quarters than most, here was a genuine, transparent individual, fully committed to God and willing to pay any price to see millions blessed.

Chapter Twenty-One

The Landing

As visitors entered the heavy studded door of Derwen Fawr House, the nerve centre of the College life and residence of the Director, they were met with an impressive hallway flanked with a large portrait of W. W. Lewis, an old revivalist preacher and early College lecturer. A wide staircase led up past an old grandfather clock to a balustraded landing. The now silent timepiece had once graced invalid Uncle Dick's home in Pentwyn, Rees Howells' grandparents' home in Glanamman. On Whit-Sunday morning, 15th May 1910, it had struck five resounding notes announcing Uncle Dick's complete healing, at the precise hour (5am) the Lord had spoken to Uncle Dick beforehand – quite a testimony when he walked down the hill and through the village to church that Whit-Sunday morning!

From this commanding position on the landing, overlooking the hall below in Derwen Fawr, every sound and conversation could be heard in detail and nothing was missed. When his father died, Samuel moved into one of the spacious bedrooms on that landing, although his daily business and interviews were conducted in the Blue Room on the ground floor. With its marble fireplace, long polished central table, enormous mirrored dresser and window seats, it carried its own aura. Here the Vision for the 'Gospel to be preached throughout the world in our generation' was given on Boxing Day 1934, and the nightly wartime prayer sessions took place. Entering was like stepping into another world. Samuel would spend his evenings there, reading and meditating into the late hours, huddled in front of a solitary one bar electric fire, under the glow from a standard lamp. There was no central heating in this large room with its decorative ceiling and heavy blue velvet curtains, and the cold winter temperatures produced chest and nasal problems which affected him for life. When his mother, Lizzie Hannah Howells, died in August 1972, Samuel eventually moved into the large bedroom immediately above the Blue Room, with its commanding view overlooking Swansea Bay. Samuel rarely shared his grief with anyone but withdrew quietly into himself, and drew comfort from the Scriptures. It was not until his later years that he was ever able to talk about his mother, who had proved such a rock of support during his initial years as Honorary Director of the Bible College.

Samuel Howells with his mother, Lizzie, 1965

The 'landing' served rather like the bridge of a battleship, with easy and direct access to the College office next door, where his personal secretary was always on call. Samuel had chosen Eva Stuart for this responsible position and when she eventually died of cancer on 4th August 1974, Ruth Williams, niece of Margaret Williams, head of the domestic side of College life, proved an able successor. Ruth was Welsh-speaking, from Treherbert in the Rhondda Valley, and had worked in the Civil Service during the war years. She taught Mathematics in the

Grammar School so was used to dealing with figures.

It was quite common on the 'landing' to hear the beckoning call for first Eva, then Ruth, to put everything to one side to attend to more important issues.[1] They were both very dependable confidants, with an appreciation of the spiritual aspects of College life. The telephone switchboard, controlled by a succession of secretaries, provided a link with all departments of the College and School, and the arrival of all visitors to the office was monitored by Samuel.

On Samuel's landing everything was convenient. There was a large reception hall for interviews, a nearby bathroom and an imaginative way of heating the landing from an airing cupboard with the doors left open! During the warm summer days, Samuel paraded the veranda outside. There was just one problem in the form of another landing on the floor above. Four large rooms and cloakroom facilities offered ideal accommodation for a bevy of enthusiastic lady students and some staff. The regulation 'Quiet Times' were kept upstairs, but the volume of sound did rise at times. As the years passed and the number of lady students in the College decreased, the landing became more tranquil, the only significant sound being the tape recordings of Samuel's own ministry meetings, as he rehearsed again those deep truths which were gripping him. All significant College services were by then transmitted to the different College buildings on the relay system.[2] Often he would listen to the Bible on cassette tape, given to him by his great friend and one-time trustee of the Charity, Raymond Stanbury, former student and Founder and Director of Valley Books. Raymond had pioneered this work in the Rhondda and through much prayer and vision had built up a large Christian book centre in Monmouth. He also owned other properties on the site, worth several millions of pounds, and also rescued a book publishing company in the USA. Sadly, Charity Commission laws did not allow for him to develop the work along the lines he had envisioned.

For visitors given the special privilege of being invited up to the landing and into Samuel's own room for private conversation, here was an experience never to be forgotten. This usually took place after the Saturday morning service or, briefly, after weekday services before lectures. A warm cup of tea was served with a biscuit or two, followed by relaxed conversation or review of the sermon content. Very little was actually shared about the College, but a deep interest was shown in the visitor and his or her particular ministry, usually with the promise of prayer.

Visiting speakers rarely, if ever, had an opportunity to sit under Samuel's pulpit ministry as he would give them maximum time both to share about their particular work and from the Scriptures during the Friday evening, Saturday morning, Sunday (two services) and Monday morning sessions.[3] However, he loved to talk with them in his room. One regular visitor vividly remembers those times:

> I would go upstairs to Samuel's room to say goodbye on Monday morning. In response to my knock on the door, that soft voice with a distinct Welsh lilt would say, "Come in, dear brother." Perched on the end of the table was the tray with tea and biscuits and an ample supply of sugar if required. Then a slender frail hand of welcome was extended and a finger beckoned to where I was to sit. Folders of letters filled the polished oak table near a neatly made up bed with shiny eiderdown. Piles of books were stacked precariously around the room on the cupboards and floor, but the predominant factor was the warm sense of peace and a Divine presence which emanated from this humble servant of God. He would listen intently to all I had to share and had followed the weekend ministry closely. He understood the problems we faced and the power of the Gospel to triumph in the darkest hour. He promised to pray and to write (his letters always contained substantial gifts for our ministry). Mr Samuel did not have a ministry of prayer – his life was prayer.

It was also known for individuals who sought to approach Samuel with complaints and grumbles to be asked to leave the room and to return only when they were in the right spirit.

Samuel was always dressed smartly, very rarely casually, if ever. His selection of good suits were sent to the cleaners regularly, and his watch and chain shone from his waistcoat pocket beneath his jacket. It was always the custom to wear ties and in the 1950s and 1960s separate white collars; several of the old wartime disposable cardboard variety were still in their packets ready for use in 2004!

Samuel Howells in the Blue Room of Derwen Fawr 1995

As the years passed, Samuel preferred to wear a dressing gown around the cold house, particularly in his own room, and it became an essential part of his uniform on top of his normal clothes. Expensive trilby hats were his distinguishing headgear outside, or a panama in the summer. Feeling the cold keenly as he did, he was always well padded. Once a week, a row of black leather lace-up shoes stood outside his door waiting to be cleaned, and loving hands dutifully obliged.

It was customary for the staff to contribute towards a birthday present each year. A pile of towels in their wrappings, or a new radio or cassette tape recorder or Bible, placed in prominent positions, for everyone to see, was Samuel's way of saying 'Thank you,' and as many cards as possible remained for many weeks crammed on the marble fireplace next to an easy chair. He would sink into this and rest his slippered feet up on a cushioned stool, which held nostalgic memories for him.

Samuel at Philippi, Greece in the footsteps of Paul 1962

As with everything else he did, Samuel was meticulous in financial affairs and, right to the end of his life, kept a very close eye on every penny that passed through his bank account. Every bank statement from 1950 onwards was filed in its envelope, so gradually the cupboards and cabinet drawers were filled up and new cabinets introduced to the room. Once bookshelves were full, new books were piled neatly around the room. It certainly gave the impression to the regular visitor that the room was shrinking! Central in the room was the table with its files and fountain pen and just enough tray space for a 'working meal,' and when the day was over, the matressed bed was calling. World history was being changed by the Holy Spirit and in this inauspicious room a humble man of God was deeply involved in prayer.

Chapter Twenty-Two

Saturdays

Saturday mornings were usually practical work sessions at the College, when students, as part of their training, helped staff members with cleaning, gardening, painting and a hundred and one tasks required to run a community.[1] For Samuel, it meant straightening his work desk and vacating his room while a team of selected ladies descended with dusters and clean bed linen, to make everything as shipshape as possible for the weekend.

After lunch, if there was a visiting speaker for the weekend, he was cordially invited in for a College cup of tea – always served in bone china cups and saucers in those days, never beakers (mugs) – and a long talk about the particular ministry that he represented. In his more youthful days, Samuel would take them for one of his famous constitutional 'marathons' and then, having assured them of his prayers for the ministry on Sunday, he would settle to his books. Throughout his life, Samuel was an avid reader and would invariably ask for a copy of a book if one was mentioned. His personal collection grew as friends sent him first editions, although he was reluctant to release them any further.

One former student vividly remembers a Saturday afternoon in the early 1960s, with the warm sunshine beckoning him to the beach for a free afternoon, following a busy morning of practical 'work out' around the College. Standing by the kitchen door near the covered archway, beneath which hung a large bell whose resonant strikes relayed meal times around the College throughout the week, stood Mr Samuel. He too, had noticed a large pile of sand straddled across the main driveway to Derwen Fawr House, and was looking for a willing volunteer to move it before an important visitor arrived. "My heart sank and bang went my free afternoon," quotes the student, "but really it was my privilege to serve such a humble man of God." In later years, it was Samuel's privilege to serve this same student and his wife as they ministered in Thailand. It was through receiving Samuel's regular gifts that they were able to purchase large numbers of Gospels, to blanket their whole area, where so many had never heard of the Lord Jesus before. This was so typical of the Holy Spirit's leading in Samuel's world ministry.

Early Saturday evening was usually an appropriate time to approach Samuel for a personal discussion or for counselling. He was a very patient, sympathetic listener, taking careful note of the spirit of his enquirer, and provided wise suggestions. Always aware that some thought he was old fashioned he would argue, with a twinkle in his eye, that sunshine, flowers and trees were old fashioned too!

It was that twinkle that revealed his deep inherent sense of humour, which he sometimes needed to disguise, when asked to speak a word of authority in situations referred to him. Some involved differences in opinions between staff members or the occasional student who was deemed to have 'misbehaved.' In confidence he would reveal how unnecessary these 'on the carpet' appointments were but, in each case, he always exercised much grace and gentleness, assuring the miscreant that if the Lord had forgiven him, then he surely had. Satan, with long experience of manipulating fallen human nature, was a master at seeking to create diversions from the main spiritual issues in the College, but Samuel, exercising much wisdom, sought to defuse them as soon as possible, covering each one with believing prayer. Often these problems concerned relationships between students who were unwilling to accept the College Rule 8. This forbade prolonged fraternisation with members of the opposite sex during term times.[2]

Contrary to many opinions, Samuel was not against marriage, which he recognised as a very solemn, life binding union between a man and a woman before God. The break-up of marriages, particularly among Christians, deeply disturbed him, since the union represents the relationship between Christ and the Church as taught in Ephesians 5:25-27, 32 (AV).

> *Husbands, love your wives, even as Christ also loved the church, and gave Himself for it; that He might sanctify and cleanse it with the washing of water by the Word, that He might present it to Himself a glorious church, not having spot, or wrinkle, or any such thing; but that it should be holy and without blemish. This is a great mystery: but I speak concerning Christ and the Church.*

Samuel's personal stand as a single man lay in the truths of Matthew 19:12 (AV).

> *...There be eunuchs, which have made themselves eunuchs for the Kingdom of Heaven's sake. He that is able to receive it, let him receive it.*

He also felt that a young man would be wiser to seek his own ministry first, and the Lord would then guide him to find a suitable, supportive partner for that ministry. Having sat under his father's ministry as a young man in his early impressionable twenties, during those important years in the College when the Vision was given, Samuel often reflected on the transactions made with God in his own life. On Boxing Day 1934, the Holy Spirit had placed the responsibility upon Rees Howells of laying the foundation and believing for the fulfilment of the Great Commission, spoken of in Matthew 28:18-20.

> *Jesus came to them and said, "All authority in Heaven and on earth has been given to Me, therefore go and make disciples of all nations, baptising them in the name of the Father and of the Son and of the Holy Spirit, and teaching them to obey everything I have commanded you. And surely I am with you always, to the very end of the age."*

Although a great spiritual challenge, Rees readily accepted the privilege, believing that God was God and well able to believe through him. After all, Abram had believed for the blessing of the world in his day.

Samuel was also aware of another aspect of the Vision, which the Lord had later revealed. The Holy Spirit had offered the little company of believers at the College the opportunity to be vitally involved in the Divine programme for these last days. Would they, in view of God's mercy to them in salvation, offer their bodies as living sacrifices, holy and pleasing to God, which would be their reasonable service (Romans 12:1). It had been clearly pointed out to those who were responding that intercession was required to bring to birth every stage of the Vision, right through to the end times. This is sometimes a neglected and overlooked spiritual principle today. Rees Howells had gained positions of authority in healing and finance already, and was always seeking to press forward in his walk with God.

Samuel faced with others the position of celibacy, and made an unqualified response. The 144,000 spoken of in Revelation 14:1-5 describes a company of individuals totally surrendered to God. Without dispute, even the highest qualities of our human natures have been corrupted through the fall of Adam and Eve in the Garden, so that a total cleansing would be required to produce a Bride fit for the Bridegroom. The totality of the atoning work of Christ makes complete provision for this, but it must be worked out in the reality of day-to-day life, stage by stage, not in our imaginations. Grace is available to satisfy every need of the human heart.

> *My grace is sufficient for you, for My power is made perfect in weakness.* 2 Corinthians 12:9.

In Revelation 19:7-9 the Marriage of the Lamb is outlined.

> *Let us rejoice and be glad and give Him the glory! For the wedding of the Lamb has come, and His Bride has made herself ready. Fine linen, bright and clean was given her to wear.* (Fine linen stands for the righteous acts of the saints). *Then the angel said to me, "Write: 'Blessed are those who are invited to the wedding supper of the Lamb!'"*

Jesus once told a parable of some virgins who missed the wedding feast because they were unprepared.

> *Therefore keep watch, because you do not know the day or the hour.* Matthew 25:13.

To Samuel, these were very sacred truths about which

he rarely spoke in public. They had been revealed when the Holy Spirit rested upon the Founder's ministry in a powerful way and were not for debate. However, there were times when Samuel shared them privately with those whom he realised would appreciate and understand them in the right way. To him, as always, to walk biblical truth was far more important than to talk about it – but only possible through the grace and power which God has provided for us in Christ through the atonement.

Occasionally, in Samuel's ministry, these deep truths were spoken about very sensitively, usually by way of a reminder to the staff who had been present in the College when the revelation was given. One such occasion was in the Thursday evening meeting of 2nd June 1955, when Samuel was considering the passages in John 6 where Jesus proclaimed Himself to be the Bread of Life.

> "A young man standing before them and saying, 'I am the Bread of Life.' They could not take that without a revelation. The whole world was to be satisfied with His Body. He was Life. Have we come to the position where we never hunger or thirst? Do we day by day feed on Him? Has He satisfied us? Ever since last Saturday afternoon, that company on Mount Zion who have followed Him all the way have been in my mind. Those who do not want any relationship but Himself. It is not anything ordinary. It fills our minds, our affections, which have been absorbed in His Person. He becomes all in all. There will be 144,000 who lived as He lived. Whether that is the exact number at the time of His return, or represents a complete number from all generations, is immaterial. There is a fellowship, a relationship that only the 144,000 will know anything about. Don't lose these revelations that we had on the Bride."

Then Samuel expressed an opinion that many of the early Church fathers had found their all in all in Christ. He recounted the life of Ignatius, at the turn of the first century AD, the Bishop of Antioch who lived a singular life to the

Lord.

"His one passion was to be conformed to the image of the Lord (Romans 8:29). He was a martyr and more than a martyr. Some of those will be among that company. Has the Lord set a higher standard for them and a lower standard for us? We want this to become real – that He is the centre of attraction in our lives. I do long that all of you will enter this now. Christ is the Bread of Life – feed on Him daily."

It was always very clear to Samuel, that for people to become part of the Bride to the Saviour, He must become all in all to them. It is a position gained only through the process of death to the self life. Unless that process is worked out in practical living, they can only claim that position falsely. A deep and solemn silence would pervade meetings whenever Samuel touched on the life of Esau, who sold his birthright so cheaply (Genesis 25:29-34). The Holy Spirit will never fully take His rightful place in a person's life unless that individual has 'died.'

Another often divisive yet biblical issue which emerged in the 1970s, and which passed through various phases, was the charismatic renewal throughout Britain. Staff and students had varying church backgrounds and all visiting speakers were welcome in the pulpit. Occasionally in services a message would be given in tongues with interpretation, and there were healings. Samuel himself at times pronounced a prophetic word, often concerning national issues. When very unwell he would call the 'elders' up to his room for prayer for healing, and the Lord would touch him afresh. Several of the former students such as Bryn and Keri Jones and Alan Scotland were associated with emerging leadership in these circles in the UK, so Samuel prayed earnestly for each one, recognising the pitfalls that they faced. In some instances, the movement was bringing great disservice to the Christian testimony. Samuel pondered over these developments in the Christian Church and sought to know how to pray for those involved.

The charismatic experience in 1 Corinthians 12, widely referred to as the Baptism of the Holy Spirit, accompanied by speaking in unknown tongues with interpretation, was manifested in the twentieth century at the Azusa Street Revival in Los Angeles, in 1906. Similar manifestations later attended meetings in the British Isles at Sunderland in 1907, from which the first Pentecostal movement in Britain grew under the leadership of an Anglican vicar, Alexander Boddy. In subsequent annual meetings at the Sunderland Convention, Thomas Myerscough and Smith Wigglesworth entered into a deeper relationship with God. Cecil Polhill, an original member of the Cambridge Seven, a group of seven Cambridge University graduates who served with Hudson Taylor as missionaries beginning their service in China in 1885, was greatly influenced and was himself baptised in the Holy Spirit in 1906.

With renewed spiritual energy and vision Cecil Polhill and his friend Alexander Boddy, vicar of All Saints Parish Church, Monkwearmouth, Sunderland, England, similarly blessed, founded the Pentecostal Missionary Union and soon a Bible School was opened in Preston, with Thomas Myerscough as its leader.

It was there that George Jeffreys, born at Maesteg in South Wales in 1889, and converted in the Welsh Revival (1904-1905) was prepared for ministry, alongside such great Pentecostal preachers and missionaries as W. P. Burton (who called himself the Tramp for God), James Salter, Percy Corry, Robert Darrah and E. J. Phillips.

George Jeffreys exercised a very powerful ministry in Ireland. His brother, Stephen, began working in the local coal mine at the tender age of twelve, as did so many young men in South Wales at the turn of the nineteenth century. Those long hard years put 'steel into his bones' which he later carried into his ministry. Stephen was converted at the age of twenty-eight, in the Welsh Revival in 1904, and soon wanted to preach. Although openly opposed to the new Pentecostal trends at first, he eventually sought seriously for the Baptism of the Holy Spirit. The Lord answered his prayers in a fuller way than he had ever anticipated, according to the promise of Luke 11:13:

> *If you then, though you are evil, know how to give good gifts to your children, how much more will your Father in Heaven give the Holy Spirit to*

those who ask Him.

Stephen's life was dramatically changed. Holding meetings at Cwmtwch, at the head of the Swansea Valley in South Wales in 1913, 145 people were saved. He called for assistance from his brother George in Ireland and from then on the pair conducted campaigns throughout Wales and eventually the whole of Britain.

Stephen's ministry particularly was renowned for its outstanding miracles of physical healing that demonstrated clearly the power of the atonement. He had never sought such a ministry, but when a young lady, due to have her leg amputated, asked for prayer, he anointed her and prayed. The healing was dramatic, the first of many that focused people's attention on Christ the Healer, and Stephen's life principle became: 'Pray – Preach – Persevere.' He poured his life into the work, earning the reputation of a fearless, tireless preacher. Following years of fruitful ministry when the spirit of healing flowed through him to thousands of people throughout the world, Stephen's health eventually failed and he moved to Mumbles, Swansea (after the death of his wife in January 1941, to be cared for by his daughter, May), for the fresh air, as it seemed to many.

Samuel recalled some Saturdays when he accompanied his father to the bungalow where Stephen Jeffreys was staying. Until then Stephen had never found liberty to pray for his own healing, but now he had called for Rees Howells to visit him, accompanied by Samuel, and told him on 11th October 1943, "I would like to be healed, and I came to Swansea to believe, and I believe you can help me." (These and other similar words of Stephen are recorded in notes of Rees Howells' meetings taken on 15th October 1943). He had swayed congregations of thousands for thirty years and here he was in Swansea seeking healing. For many years, Samuel had admired Stephen's fruitful ministry and would often refer to it when he preached himself. Samuel was firmly convinced that one day there would be a wave of healings across the world similar to that when the power flowed through Jesus during His Galilean ministry. To meet Stephen personally in Mumbles was such a great honour, but it was sad to see him so disabled and helpless.

Rees Howells appreciated that Stephen Jeffreys was a born evangelist and if the Holy Spirit came into Stephen's life in the profound way that had changed Rees' own life, Stephen would not only be healed, but would be transported into a completely different spiritual dimension, and into moment-by-moment communion with the living God. As Rees Howells said in his unpublished autobiography (which was used by Norman Grubb to help write the first twenty chapters of *Rees Howells Intercessor*):

> It was nothing less than a new creation. The feeling I had was, *He brought me to the banqueting house, and His banner over me was love.* Song of Solomon 2:4 (AV). It is impossible to describe the floods of joy that followed. Another Person came into my body and transported me into the realm where God is.

It is difficult to convey in words to the reader the depth of fellowship that Rees Howells enjoyed with God, but those who were his contemporaries spoke of someone who had obviously known an experience similar to Isaiah's in the Temple, as in Isaiah 6, yet was so natural and human. This level of fellowship transcended by far the charismatic experiences and giftings that the Holy Spirit was already exercising through men like the Jeffreys' brothers, Stephen and George, and others. Rees Howells realised that the whole of Swansea would be moved if Stephen were similarly blessed, and that blessing would send ripples all round the world. Stephen had once said that the world needs a new revelation of Christ who is the same today as ever He has been, and Rees Howells' personal desire was that Stephen would become one of the Holy Spirit's instruments to convey that revelation.

To see God work in answer to his prayers had been a personal challenge to Rees Howells, who was constantly convicted by the life of Moses, the first Old Testament character to perform miracles in the Lord's Name. However, he had learnt to pray only prayers given by the Holy Spirit. In this case he talked and prayed with Stephen so that he could be led to experience the transforming infilling that would be necessary to deal with the powerful demonic forces which had stifled his ministry through infirmity. Only the Holy Spirit could do that. Rees Howells had waited for the Lord to speak, but the Word did not come and Stephen died in Swansea on the 17th November 1943.[3] Samuel was learning all the time, as a young man in his early 30s, being prepared for similar tests as the future Director of the College.

The essential feature of Rees Howells' ministry was that the Holy Spirit is a Person, the Third Person of the Godhead, who had been operating on earth since its foundation. Using these resources gained through the atonement, which also acted retrospectively, He had taken full control of individuals for certain Divine interventions in the history of the Jewish nation, as recorded in the Scriptures. (e.g. Othniel, Judges 3:10; Gideon, Judges 6:34; Jephthah, Judges 11:29 and Saul, 1 Samuel 10:6). He witnessed and regulated every facet of Jesus' life and final walk to Jerusalem, culminating in the crucifixion. He empowered Jesus to rise triumphantly from death on the third day and indwelt believers after the ascension (Romans 8:11). The Holy Spirit then became responsible for completing God's work on earth and the fulfilment of all the prophecies concerning the end times. In a short autobiographical booklet, Rees Howells reminded his readers that when the disciples met the risen Saviour:

> They worshipped Him and returned to Jerusalem with great joy. Luke 24:52 (AV).

These men had joy before they had power, so joy in that case was not proof of power. They had this joy when they were waiting for the *power from on high* – the Holy Spirit, Luke 24:49.

That had been the state of the Church after the Welsh Revival (1904-1905). They had much joy in the risen Lord, but at the same time they felt the lack of power for service. This was the 'silver thread' of revelation that Samuel had received. Unless the Holy Spirit was permitted to deal with an individual's nature and replace it with Divine Nature, then there would be problems. In Jeremiah 17:9 it is clearly stated:

> The heart is deceitful above all things and beyond cure. Who can understand it?

In referring to the lengths that Judas went in his betrayal of Jesus, Samuel said,
> "It only shows the extent of the corruption of human nature."

Without doubt, there were many casualties in the developing House Church Movement of the 1970s, as giftings were sometimes being expressed through unchanged natures. So, without placing any restriction on the private exercising of the gifts of the Holy Spirit, which he had no authority to do, Samuel did express his wish, publicly and privately to some staff members who had been blessed through charismatic experiences, that the main College services should be focused around the intercessory ministry which was continuing all the time. Repeating truths he had heard from Rees Howells, Samuel stated that to step into the realm of intercession was as different as an unbeliever stepping from darkness into the Kingdom via the gateway of the new birth. As with everything spiritual, it comes by way of revelation.

In sharing his heart privately, he referred to his views in this way. Paul mentions in 1 Corinthians 12:31:
> *Eagerly desire the greater gifts. And now I will show you the most excellent way.*

"Sermons are very good," he would say, "but they do not touch the nature."

Then, quoting 1 Corinthians 4:15-16,
> *"Even though you have ten thousand guardians in Christ, you do not have many fathers, for in Christ Jesus I became your father through the Gospel. Therefore I urge you to imitate me."*

Samuel would add,
> "It is fathers the Church needs."

His aim, as his handwriting so eloquently indicated, was to reach upward and to believe for the *greater works* of John 14:12 (AV). That is exactly what was happening through his ministry around the world, although very few recognised the depth of ministry that was operating through him. A graphologist would perhaps also detect the vertical writing in Samuel's script and suggest someone who is reserved, calm and somewhat aloof. Emotions may be intense, but they are held in check by the mind which sits in judgement over the impulses. Here was somebody with a certain charm, the result of poise and good manners, whose friendliness would not permit intimacy on the part of others. That would be a fair assessment!

Samuel R. Howells.
Bible College of Wales

Samuel Howells' elegant signature

Saturdays were certainly days of relaxation and reflection, and Samuel would occasionally slip into a nearby sitting room to watch the news on television, especially if Wales was involved in an International Rugby Match!

For the students, Saturday afternoon and evening were the only official 'time off' periods in the week apart from Sundays – that is for those who were not allocated to specific duties in the kitchen or attending to central heating coal and wood burning boilers. Others would be on their knees preparing for local Sunday preaching appointments.

Mount Pleasant Baptist Church in the centre of Swansea was often the venue for regular Saturday Youth For Christ evangelistic rallies, or the annual Worldwide Evangelisation Crusade meetings, when the Bible College students assisted with musical contributions. Samuel gave his full prayerful support to these functions but preferred to slip in quietly and unobtrusively and to make a similar exit. It was the same for Emmanuel School Christmas concerts, always presented with precision and great talent, or the visits to Swansea by the Operation Mobilisation vessels *MV Logos II*.[4] Samuel was never one for projecting himself in public, even when the ex-USA President, Jimmy Carter was sitting in the front row.[5] In some ways, opportunities to greet Christian friends or to give a word of encouragement were missed, but that was always done privately afterwards, or via a staff member. The reason for Samuel's desire to retire from the chatter of the crowds lay in the fact that success in the intercessory prayers that he was carrying depended entirely upon an undisturbed relationship with the Lord, making possible the moment-by-moment access into the Inner Sanctuary where prayers are heard and answered.

Once a month, a staff member was asked to call in after supper on Saturday evening to 'give a little trim' – to act as professional hairdresser or barber, and smarten up a usually well groomed, 'Brylcreemed' head of hair. At the end he would ask just how much it would cost!

– And so to bed –

Samuel Howells recuperating c.1970s

Chapter Twenty-Three

The Young Generation

The majority of senior staff of the College, including Samuel himself, had reached their 70s. To modern youth they would be senior citizens and such words as 'cool' and 'stuff' certainly did not punctuate their daily conversations. However, they were by no means considering retirement, and were as enthusiastic and committed to the task they had dedicated their lives to as in the 1930s. There were logistical problems, however, which needed to be faced, one being the oversight of the students. On the ladies' side, in the late 1970s, Pearl Temple, a skilled shorthand typist and secretary, felt called at the completion of her student course to assist in the College office.

Some of the BCW ladies staff, July 1981. 1. Ruth Williams (Samuel's secretary and P. A.), 2. Valerie Sherwood, 3. Pearl Temple, 4. Joan Rush and 5. Primrose Thomas.

However, there was another need. When Dr. Joan Davies left the College in 1962 due to a serious illness, her sister Eira, a former Emmanuel Grammar School sports mistress, had assumed responsibility for the lady students until Janny van der Klis became dean for the next four years. Then Kathy Cowan, who had returned to the College from her missionary service in Korea, and several former younger lady students, on a temporary basis, took over the role. Now it was time for someone else to take over. Samuel felt led to ask Pearl to take charge of the lady students and promised to pray for her in this most challenging role. He was always ready and willing to carry the burdens of others. If someone was asked to take a College service or prayer meeting, he would enquire about the subject and provide helpful suggestions from his vast knowledge of the Scriptures and then say, "Now I will carry the burden for you; you just speak." Anyone taking the pulpit would certainly feel the effect of those prayers.

Pearl, with recent experience from her student days, made helpful practical changes and received support from her mother, Mrs Margaret Temple, who had 'sold all' to follow the Lord to the College, where she was a welcome addition to the kitchen staff. During ensuing years Pearl, despite a back problem which necessitated her wearing a plaster cast at one point, proved the Lord's help in healing and in many practical and teaching tasks that she undertook – all done as to the Lord.

The men students were being overseen first by Arthur Neil and then David Davies, following a recuperation period after experiences in the Congo Simba Uprising. Both, however, were not resident and, since Norman Madoc's departure from the College to be married, the men students were virtually unsupervised.

Samuel approached Richard Maton, then teaching in Emmanuel Preparatory School, in the summer of 1978 and asked him to consider taking on the job, plus continuing his teaching in the School. It was a formidable challenge but God spoke through reading the book of Ruth 3:3 (NASB).

Wash yourself therefore, and anoint yourself and put on your best clothes and go down to the threshing floor...

Ruth was to meet Boaz at the threshing floor. We meet Christ at the cross, our threshing floor. During Richard's waiting-upon-God period, Isaac Watts' hymn *When I survey the wondrous Cross,* On which the Prince of Glory died, My richest gain I count but loss, And pour contempt on all my pride – through which his original revelation of the Cross had come – was repeatedly sung or played throughout the summer. When Richard shared these confirmations with the Director, Samuel fully understood the truth from his own deep experiences that the only place where we meet with God and can go any further in our ministry, is at the foot of the cross. This was a call from the Spirit to enter a new ministry.

After the death of Dr. Symonds in 1970, it took several difficult years for Richard and Pearl (until the early 1980s) to re-establish a structured framework within the College, in which the principles of prayer and faith became priorities in the training. Samuel gave his full support to these two new young leaders.

Another new, very hard-working staff member was Michael Williams, a former College student (who had studied alongside Pearl Temple), with a degree in Civil Engineering. He had the capacity and strength to cover the work of three men. Mr Williams, as he preferred to be called, earned the respect of everyone. During the cold winter months of vacations it was he who ensured that the boiler fires kept burning and the central heating systems continued to function properly.

A rapid escalation of coal prices in the 1970s caused concern. Gas and oil-fired systems were introduced but the large system, a real museum piece which heated Derwen Fawr House, remained untouched. Samuel called for energy saving measures, including supplementary glazing and the use of wood in boilers, as opposed to coal. A new era had certainly begun!

Friday evening prayer meetings had so often been given to praying for specific College needs, including finance for College fuel bills, but now it was for new supplies of wood. Student teams scoured the district for trees blown down or branches needing to be lopped, and the introduction of chain saws onto the market soon saw the College proud owners of two Husqvarna chain saws! Out in all weathers, students became expert loggers and amassed literally tons of logs for Mr Williams' woodpile each year, ready to be split with axes and metal wedges into suitably sized slices for the boiler fires. This process continued, usually from October one year till April the next, seven months hard labour! The younger generation certainly proved their commitment to serve, and many have since become anointed ministers of the Gospel around the world.

As Samuel prayed about several pressing practical jobs which required attention around the College, particularly with new Health and Safety regulations coming into force in the United Kingdom, assistance came from unexpected directions. Over a period of several years, the Government Community Service Scheme, when offenders were required to give hours of practical help in the locality, provided valuable professional skills from stonemasons to carpet layers and carpenters. Then during the long summer vacations, teams from Helps International Ministries, an American based group of highly skilled men and their wives, covering a wide range of trades, stayed at the College and improved much of the ageing property. Through the kindness of John Mallett from Cardiff and his family, larger projects were accomplished including replacing roofs of Sketty Isaf and Derwen Fawr dining room. There was certainly a buzz about the place.

Throughout his ministry, Samuel never lost the sense of responsibility he felt for introducing the students to the deeper aspects of the Christian walk. He knew how essential was this section of the students' spiritual education, this window into prayer and faith. He himself was involved in bitter spiritual conflicts and he expected their full cooperation and attention in the meetings, in some of which he spoke for almost ninety minutes without a break. Normally such a quiet, gentle individual, in the pulpit he would speak straight,

> "Be careful how you conduct yourselves in these meetings. Be very serious. We are dealing with very serious matters tonight which require your full-time and attention. Behave yourselves, and (beckoning in one direction) I am speaking to you. There are great needs and it would be better if one spent time alone, but we have an enemy and we have to watch him. We cannot afford to have the spirit of levity when we are dealing with these weighty matters. He can come as a roaring lion, or he

may come as an angel of light, so we need the spirit of discernment."

A silence would descend on the meeting almost enough to hear a falling feather touch the ground. On the other hand he would give himself to prayer for anyone in the fellowship in need or trouble,0 and as many will testify, dealt with them in great tenderness.

Samuel would read excerpts from letters received from friends all over the world whom he was supporting. He was touched by their suffering.

> "Their concerns are our concerns," he would declare, "and we must stand with them. We think we are going to live normal lives, don't we? I don't think so. That is a false idea. Take heed to what the prophets said."

Satan constantly buffeted Samuel by asking him how he was going to cope, trying to do what large recognised missions were doing, by supporting so many individuals. His emphatic answer remained the same,

> "The Holy Spirit will help."

Samuel reminded his listeners that Satan would try to keep them busy all day thinking about themselves, when so many other people in need should have their prayers and support. However, to say words is one thing but to produce the finances was another. To take hold of the promises of God for finance when you do not have the resources requires faith.[1] In one meeting, Samuel thundered out,

> "Theories will not help you, I tell you that – you try it – you won't go very far, you have to live it out day by day, hour by hour. What I am telling you tonight is very elementary, very rudimentary compared with the intercessions for the nations."

Here was teaching in the Holy Spirit that the young generation of today would appreciate. There was a grip in it. Immersed in these intense spiritual conflicts and striving to believe God for complete victory in them was a realm some, even prominent believers, could not appreciate. He was often heavily criticised for being cold, aloof and distant, but he would recall comments once made by his father in similar tests,

> "When God is speaking to you and man speaks contrary, you don't want to be near them. I always keep those people at arm's length!"

Bursting into the Bible College scene during the years that were to follow came a young American, Dr. Sam Matthews and his wife Cathy, from Shawnee, Oklahoma. These were to become two very dear friends of Samuel and the College family and were always welcomed whenever their schedule enabled them to visit. Sam had read the book *Rees Howells Intercessor* many times. It had been a source of great strength to them when challenged with a prayer for Cathy's healing from a terminal illness. Their testimonies of God's dealings with them thrilled Samuel as he heard of the Christian School and Family of Faith they were responsible for back home, a catalogue of miracles. It was their emphasis on prayer, faith and intercession which impressed everyone.

Samuel Howells and Sam Matthews on the 'bridge' c.1989

Samuel would take his new 'young' friends up to the Black Mountain and the 'bridge' whenever possible, where they would enjoy deep fellowship together. Sam Matthews is currently a leader in a company of international apostles for over three thousand churches in more than fifty nations, and travels extensively.

One summer, a 'serving experience' team of young Christians and their leaders from Family of Faith spent a week at the College helping with the practical work, enjoying the beautiful walks around Swansea Bay and the Gower, and visiting Welsh villages where Rees Howells had learnt the principles of intercession, as well as taking a longer train journey to Llandrindod Wells.

During the next decade of the 1990s, Sam's fellowship and ministry in the College would prove a great blessing and strength to Samuel. Sam would love to spend his mornings alone in the Blue Room, the large downstairs room in Derwen Fawr House where the Vision was given to Rees Howells. Then the two men of faith, the younger and the older, would spend time together discussing matters concerning the Vision and the certainty of its fulfilment in these last days.

> *For the vision is yet for the appointed time. It hastens toward the goal and it will not fail. Though it tarries, wait for it, for it will certainly come, it will not delay.* Habakkuk 2:3 (NASB).

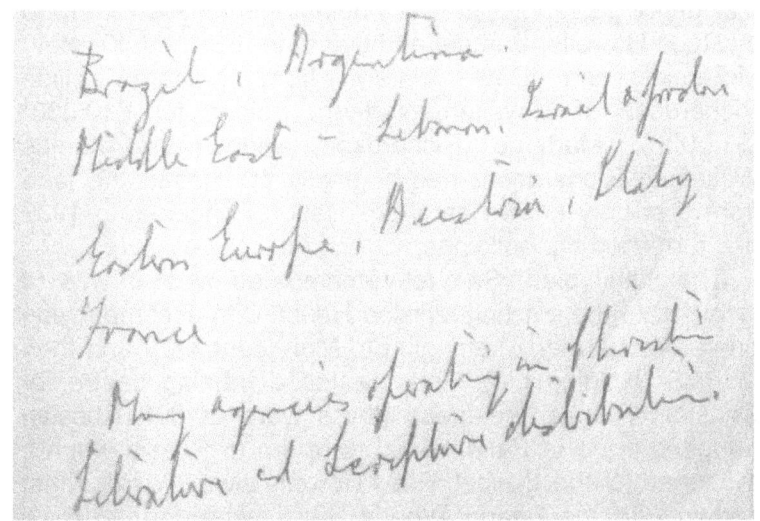

A section of one of Samuel Howells' 'country' prayer lists; found in his Bible. The last two lines reads: Many agencies operating in Christian literature and Scripture distribution.

Chapter Twenty-Four

The French Connection

It was often suggested by casual observers that Samuel and his staff were not living in the real world, yet that was far from accurate. Had these people committed themselves on the same terms and conditions as Samuel had accepted from the Lord, they would soon have discovered just how real and down-to-earth life was. Samuel's French connections will illustrate this point. There had been a real surge of adrenalin in the young Oxford graduate as in the 1930s he received the news from his father of a planned trip abroad, his first of many to follow. Passport photographs and a leather bound passport were purchased before they finally boarded the Paddington train from Swansea station, heading for Paris, France.

The College centre in Paris would eventually be in 1 Rue Georges Sorel, Boulogne-Billancourt and named Maison de l'Evangile. It was originally purchased in 1938 by Rees Howells, Samuel and two other trustees, Kenneth McDouall and Dewi Lintern from Madame Hilda Richardson of Moyallan, Northern Ireland for £10,000[1] ($16,000). Madame Richardson, widow of Thomas Wakefield Richardson, had originally purchased the land from a society known as d'Exploitation Foncières in 1930 and furnished the buildings.

The initial plan, Samuel remembered well. It was to incorporate the existing Mission House with accompanying properties, formerly belonging to Mrs Yasnowsky and then to RMS (Holding Ltd). This created a training centre for Christian Russian refugees (there were 30,000 Russian refugees living in Paris) ready to return to Russia when it reopened for the Gospel. Rees Howells always carried that certainty in his heart. Already there were former Bible College students running the Mission Hall and more were to follow. It is interesting to note that during their 1937 Paris trip, Rees Howells and Samuel met a student from Mount Lebanon who mentioned a vacant property in Beirut, Lebanon, which would be very suitable for a College. Since Lizzie Howells had been very impressed with Beirut as a possible site for a centre, correspondence was soon opened and offers made for the buildings. Samuel was taking careful note of the way the Holy Spirit guided so perfectly, and often smiled when his father was affectionately referred to as 'God's Real Estate Agent!'

Initially the Nazi occupation of Paris rudely interrupted any progress in the Mission House, whose latest occupants Leslie Ditchfield and Fred Ridgers, students from the College, had escaped for their lives. Their eventual return to England is a story in itself as they travelled south cross-country and, with the assistance of the brave French Partisans and the Tartan Pimpernel crossed the Pyrenees Mountains into Spain.

Maison de l'Evangile (The Gospel House) Paris, France

The Tartan Pimpernel was the name given to Donald Caskie, minister of the Scots Kirk (church) in Paris at the time of the German invasion of France in 1940. Although he had several opportunities to flee, Caskie stayed behind to help establish a network of safe houses and escape routes for Allied soldiers and airmen trapped in occupied territory. This was dangerous work and despite the constant threat of capture and execution, Caskie showed enormous resourcefulness and courage as he helped thousands of servicemen to freedom. Finally arrested and interrogated he was sentenced to death at a Nazi show trial, and it was only through the intervention of a German pastor that his life was saved. After the war, Caskie returned to the Scots Kirk where he served as a minister until 1960. This is an inspiring story of selfless commitment to others in the face of extreme adversity. Leslie and Fred were arrested in Spain as British spies. Samuel prayed much for his dear friends during their imprisonment and enforced starvation before their final release and return to England, and he assisted their recuperation at the College.

Freedom for Europe finally came in 1945, which enabled the work in Paris to find its feet again. Fred was very practical and transformed the buildings, bringing them up to standard and Samuel was more than impressed during his first visit en route to the Middle East, in 1951, even venturing to sample some of the French-style cuisine, beautifully cooked by Mair Davies. During the next years, Samuel was to build close relationships with several French Christian families because of Toby Bergin's love for France. Summer holidays often saw young people from France helping with the work in the College, and improving their English as they did.

Samuel Howells in Paris, France, (from left to right) Samuel, Mair Davies, Vreni Rossler and Fred Ridgers c.1962

Thirty years later in the 1980s, a wholly French congregation was established at the centre in Paris with their own pastor, and a fellowship of Russian believers, who had migrated into the district since the Russian Revolution in 1917, were able to use the buildings for their services. Mair Davies, through her persistent door-to-door Bible distribution ministry and her Christian bookstall at the entrance to the Paris market selling Christian books, in a not always too friendly environment, had established a good witness. Her strong Welsh accent merged well with her French, giving folk the impression that she was genuine Breton from the north of France.

These were Samuel's friends and he loved to see them again when they occasionally returned for a holiday break in Swansea, Mair in her 'Deux-Chevaux' the traditional French "two-horsepower" family car![2] Samuel took time to listen to their concerns for the future of the work, particularly as the years were telling on their health. Was it time to hand over to the French Christians themselves? Standing where it was in the suburbs of Paris, 1 Rue Georges Sorel was a very valuable property and, if sold, would provide a fortune that could be channelled into Samuel's worldwide ministry. Of the original four trustees of the French property, Samuel alone remained in office. It was a weighty decision to make and he was in no hurry to make it. Selling the property on the open market to developers would terminate the evangelical witness in the district and no one wanted that. Gifting it, without any financial returns for all the investment into it over the years, was another option, but differences between English and French laws were considerable for this approach. Once more, as he had been on previous occasions, Samuel was pressurised to make a hasty decision but he stood firm. Never one to be pushed into decision making without examining the situation carefully, and seeking professional advice whenever possible, he would weigh up all the pros and cons and legal issues and then wait for an inner assurance from the Lord before he acted. There are several warnings in the Scriptures about acting precipitously and the consequences for doing so. One is the impatience shown by King Saul in 1 Samuel 13:8-14, when he failed to wait for the prophet Samuel to arrive. Waiting for God's time is an essential lesson for every Christian to learn, and failure to do so probably accounts for many disasters that occur and dishonour the name of the Lord.

At the same time, however, legal bills in connection with sorting out the Paris problem were escalating, as one letter dated 14th June 1970 indicates:

> I should add that Reverend Samuel Howells is very anxious that the matter is now brought to a speedy conclusion one way or the other. He / the Bible College of Wales, has already incurred a liability of not less than £3,000 ($4,800) and I mean no discourtesy when I cannot allow this situation to continue further.

A significant development was that the fellowship of Maison de l'Evangile wished to become affiliated to the Christian and Missionary Alliance, France, a close-knit network of churches working under the oversight of the Christian and Missionary Alliance, an American Missionary Society. Samuel was pleased to correspond with a bona fide Christian society and invited their Director for France, Monsieur Fred Polding, to the College for talks in February 1989, when various proposals were considered closely. Time passed before Samuel was finally free in his spirit to step forward. In a typically gracious but clear letter to Monsieur Polding, he wrote personally:

> Thank you for your letters which I have read very carefully. In view of the fact that this valuable property, which would be worth thousands of pounds sterling today if it were sold in the open market, is being transferred as a gift to the Association of Alliance Churches (this letter accompanied an official legally phrased document gifting the property to the prospective new French owners) we are firmly convinced after much prayer, that it is the Lord's will for the sum of 50,000 dollars to be donated to the Bible College of Wales for its worldwide ministry, as a token of appreciation. I am sure you will be in agreement with this. We shall be much in prayer that the Lord will

overrule all these negotiations and that it will be brought to a satisfactory conclusion as soon as it will be possible to do so.

Wishing you every blessing in the Lord. S.R.H.

It took several years more to unravel all the legal complexities involved in making this very generous gift but eventually, early in 1994, a donation of £33,242 ($50,000) was gratefully received from the Christian and Missionary Alliance, France, in appreciation for the gift of the property known as Maison de l'Evangile.

Another chapter in Samuel's ministry was concluded.

Throughout this period, the intercession for the emancipation from spiritual slavery of the Eastern European peoples had continued, and it is worth spending a short while opening a window into his pulpit ministry at this time. From where was he drawing his strength? How did he cope? Speaking from John 5, he drew the College's attention to the man, crippled for thirty-eight years, who was healed by Jesus, after waiting unsuccessfully to plunge first into the healing waters of the Pool of Bethesda. Great as his physical healing was, it was the exact words spoken by Jesus that are most significant in verse 6 (NASB).

"Do you wish to get well? The Authorised translation: *Wilt thou be made whole?* is a little closer to the true meaning with its use of the Greek word 'hugies' meaning 'whole' because, in verse 14, Jesus continues the conversation with the man. *Behold, you have become well (whole); do not sin any more so that nothing worse happens to you.* In a moment, Jesus was able to deal not only with the physical condition, but with a whole lifetime of inbred sin. This is the power of God at work and Jesus was operating solely as God. No one can make Jesus any smaller than that. John's Gospel begins in eternity, not in Bethlehem, as do Matthew and Luke, and introduces Jesus as God from the very beginning. Then, through a series of powerful miraculous signs Jesus presents Himself as such to mankind. Those who believed were totally

transformed and there was no situation beyond His reach. It was not a theory or a doctrine, but Jesus was presenting Himself to people from all walks of life and had the power to say to them, 'Stop sinning now,' and they discovered that they could. He made new men and women of them."

At this point in his ministry, Samuel interjected,
"We are now on the threshold of another College year. There will be many difficulties, many trials, many testings and many needs. But is Jesus real to us? He is greater than them all."

Samuel developed the theme by examining other similar cases in Mark's Gospel. In Mark 2:1-5 four young men break through the flat roof of an Eastern house to lower their paralysed friend, expecting Jesus to heal him. Jesus' response in verse 5 was, "*Son, your sins are forgiven.*" Mark 5:1-20 records the remarkable deliverance of the poor man called Legion, possessed by many demons. He was given a completely new life and became an evangelist to his own people, speaking only of the power of Jesus to transform lives.

"The Holy Spirit is working all over the world today," Samuel added, referring to several recent letters sent to thank him for timely financial gifts sent to agencies distributing Scriptures to China, Russia and various countries of Africa and Indonesia. "Being one with Him is the secret," concluded Samuel.

To refer back to the first sentence of this chapter, who was really living in the real world is a question we can all ask ourselves.

Chapter Twenty-Five

The Wall Comes Tumbling Down

As God wove His tapestry through the lives of Samuel and the College fellowship the silver thread of intercession became more evident. Reports from Russia told of underground printing presses where young Christians were committing themselves to work for life in the secret hideouts, never again to see the light of day, if necessary. The Scriptures meant everything to the Russian believers.

Additional lunchtime prayer sessions were introduced at the College, and Fridays became voluntary fast days when staff and students could meet for prayer for Eastern Europe and the Communist World. For Samuel, carrying the full weight of the intercession, there was a bitter price to pay as one by one fifteen key workers in the College died either through illness or old age. News came that the young underground printers had been discovered and arrested, and Samuel was deeply touched for them and their families.

Good Friday of 1979 had proved particularly difficult, following the tragic death of a highly respected and much loved staff member who took his own life following a period of illness. In ministry, Samuel referred to Luke 22:31-32,

> "Simon, Simon, behold, Satan has demanded permission to sift you like wheat; but I have prayed for you, that your faith may not fail; and when once you have turned again, strengthen your brethren."

The mystery of God's ways was difficult to interpret, as He worked to enable Samuel and the College family to appreciate a little of what families of the Russian printers were experiencing. Here, with his own College family feeling the loss along with each individual's family and friends, Samuel drew those left together with consistent ministry from the Scriptures, bringing them back to the cross and the glorious resurrection. In each case it was an opportunity to remind his 'flock' of a wonderful, full salvation. The pangs of death were removed and an eternity with God was our goal.

Samuel had considered the growing trend for cremations in Wales, but held a personal aversion to anything other than the traditional committal ceremony at a graveside. Cremation seemed to him an attempt in people's minds to blot out any thought about the resurrection of the body when Christ will call forth all who have died through the ages to appear before His Judgement seat (John 5:28-29). Perhaps he was influenced by its associations with the nineteenth century Welsh eccentric, Dr. William Price. In 1884, at the age of eighty-three, dressed in a white tunic over green trousers, and claiming to be a true Druid priest, Dr. Price had on the hills of Wales cremated his young son whom he had named Jesus Christ, and his daughter, Mary Magdalene. In a final act of blasphemous defiance, Dr. Price threw the ashes towards the heavens declaring with a loud mocking voice, "Now You resurrect these." It was with that mocking affirmation that Samuel was familiar. Mr Justice Stephens, who presided over the resulting trial, finally declared cremation as legal for the first time in Britain, and then fined Dr. Price – one farthing (one tenth of today's penny, a fraction of a cent).

After each farewell service at the College and committal at a local cemetery, relatives and friends would join the staff in the large chandeliered drawing room of Derwen Fawr House. Carefully cut sandwiches were always served and a large assortment of delicious cakes, delivered that morning from Reid's, the Swansea confectioner. Then there were endless supplies of tea served in bone china cups with saucers, normally kept safely in the drawing room glass-fronted china cupboards. Death was never a defeat in the College but, through the grief and sense of loss, each one brought a wave of new life into the prayer.

Acts of kindness at such times always touched Samuel's heart profoundly, and he was always deeply sensitive to the way believers acted towards each other. Although he could not reciprocate every kindness shown to himself in a practical way, he would carry the giver on his heart in prayer, along with the many other prayers he prayed every day. To illustrate this, an interesting story from 1987 begins when a kind Gentlemen's Outfitters heard that Samuel was finding difficulty in acquiring the more traditional style of clothing, especially trousers, that gentlemen wore in their 75th year. Throughout his life, Samuel was always turned out well, despite the austerity of the war years. The outfitter arranged to visit Samuel at the College for 'measuring.' Just as he was about to leave, Samuel, after enquiring about the welfare of the outfitter's family, had one request,

"Please will you let me have a photo of your family, especially with your three daughters?"

The clothing, including the trousers, fitted well and the photograph was given a prominent place on the mantelpiece, among others of missionaries, all prayed for regularly. Those prayers have since had a profound influence upon the whole family. All three daughters have committed their lives to the Lord to serve Him in one way or another, and the Gentlemen's Outfitter has found greater fulfilment in his service for God.

Samuel as he really was, relaxed and happy mid 1980s

On the night of 7th January 1982, a freak blizzard swept across South Wales covering the landscape in over twelve inches (thirty centimetres) of snow, much deeper where there was drifting. Swansea, not used to such heavy snowfalls, was brought to a standstill for a whole week, providing the children with an extended dream holiday and the adults with considerable logistical challenges. At the College all the wood supplies were buried under snow and, once located and cut up, needed to be carried to the boilers, and even then the wet wood took a while to produce heat! Samuel was deeply concerned and prayed much for the small team of students who had remained in residence over the Christmas vacation as they helped staff members work tirelessly throughout the daylight hours to 'keep the home fires burning.'

Derwen Fawr Road after a blizzard, January 1982, taken from outside the main College entrance. Derwen Fawr Estate (left) with Men's Hostel in foreground (left), and Staff Hostel / library in background (left). Sketty Isaf Estate (right).

In his ministry sessions, Samuel continually stressed the importance of the Word of God and pointed out how one of Satan's strategies is to deprive people of the privilege of access to the Scriptures, as was the case in Eastern Europe. When the storms are raging around us God's Word becomes a rock, leading us to the Saviour. The importance of committing Scriptures to memory, especially in our childhood and youth, cannot be overestimated. Then, of course, it is the ministry of the Holy Spirit to bring revelation and understanding. Amidst his trials Samuel declared in one Friday meeting in April 1979,

> "It is all right in fair weather to say that Jesus is King and that He is on the Throne, but things were very rough when the Apostles wrote their letters."

Snowy view from the veranda of Derwen Fawr onto the BCW grounds (front right section of the Italian Gardens), roofs of bungalows (middle, the land was formerly part of the Derwen Fawr Estate) and Swansea Bay with Mumbles Lighthouse (far right, though not visible on this day), January 1982.

Friday was always set aside then in the College to pray for Eastern Europe, so Samuel read out many reports from friends who had risked border crossings to encourage the believers there. The news emerging was of such a phenomenal growth of Christianity in areas where it was hardly known a century before. The emptiness of life without God was a stark reality and proved the failure of Communism. Samuel solicited urgent prayer still, especially for the dissemination of the Scriptures. As a further stimulation for believing prayer Samuel, as was his usual custom, read out some reports from China where remarkable conversions and outstanding miracles of healing were taking place through the courageous preaching of God's Word.

Do not throw away your confidence, which has a great reward. Hebrews 10:35 (NASB).

It is interesting to note that Rees Howells in the late 1940s had prayed for China too, for weeks and months. America witnessed Mt. St. Helens' cataclysmic volcanic eruption on the 18th May 1980, which drove many to fear the approach of even worse natural disasters, and as Britain was gripped with a Royal Wedding (of Charles and Diana on the 29th July 1981), Samuel listened carefully for the Holy Spirit's whispers concerning world events.

An unexpected spiritual conflict arose on 31st March 1982 during Margaret Thatcher's term of office as Britain's Prime Minister. Having already earned the title of the Iron Lady for her Union reforms, she led the country into war against Argentina (2nd April), who had invaded the Falkland Islands, the British owned territory in the South Atlantic Ocean (known as the Malvinas Islands in Argentina). On 5th April a Task Force of over a hundred British ships, including two aircraft carriers, HMS *Hercules* and HMS *Hermes*, carrying twenty-eight thousand men and women, set sail from Portsmouth, the largest force since the Suez Crisis. A War Cabinet was set up as the country went to war.

This was just the tip of the iceberg and Samuel could see, in the Spirit, where the real conflict lay. For some years the Holy Spirit had been preparing for a wave of blessing to sweep through Argentina and now evil spiritual authorities in the heavenly realms were threatening to hinder the work (Ephesians 6:10-12). Once more, everything was laid to one side to seek the Lord's leading. Three specific petitions were given to pray. First, that there would be a minimum of bloodshed in the conflict. Second, that General Leopoldo Galtieri, the Argentinian military commander, would be removed from office. Thirdly, that there would be, as a result, a spiritual awakening in Argentina. Once more passages from the Scriptures, read carefully under the Holy Spirit's anointing with occasional comments, brought inspiration to the prayer. It was always a question of whether the Holy Spirit was able to deal effectively with the situation. Obviously, a group of Christians would unanimously declare that they believed without a shadow of a doubt that He could, but if challenged as to whether they were willing to be responsible to see that it happened through them, that would be another story. Most would baulk at believing even for something much less – £100 ($160) by the end of the week if they had empty bank balances and purses!

Samuel never treated these prayers lightly. Often he found great strength in considering the story of Gideon in Judges 6-7 as he ministered. This seemingly insignificant young man from the tribe of Manasseh was given the opportunity to deliver his whole nation from the scourge of the Midianite raiders, who would flood the land like locusts on their innumerable camels. He obeyed as far as he could, but it was not until the Holy Spirit came upon him that he entered a different dimension altogether. Judges 6:34, literally translated reads:

The Holy Spirit clothed Himself with Gideon.

The command of Jesus for His disciples to remain in Jerusalem until they were endued with power from above carries the same meaning:

But you will receive power when the Holy Spirit comes on you; and you will be My witnesses in Jerusalem, and in all Judea and Samaria, and to the ends of the earth. Acts 1:8.

From then on Gideon remained invincible and there was a resounding victory for Israel. Samuel was utterly convinced that if Gideon had gone alone against the foe, the victory would have been equally assured.

Events in the Falklands soon escalated when the Argentinian cruiser, *General Belgrano*, was torpedoed, and sank killing three hundred and twenty men on 2nd May. In retaliation, the British destroyer HMS *Sheffield* was badly damaged in surprise attacks by the courageous Argentinian pilots flying in French built Super Etendard aircraft. Launching their deadly AM39 Exocet air-to-surface missiles, twenty crew members were killed. These deadly attacks were launched six feet above sea level, below radar contact. HMS *Galahad* was crippled with one hundred and twenty killed. Ferocious hand-to-hand fighting, following the landing of five thousand troops on 21st May, enabled the British troops to gain a bridgehead at Port San Carlos in the south. Supply ships *Atlantic Conveyor* and *Sir Tristram* were crippled by missile 'chaff' and lives were lost. Their cargo of vital aircraft was destroyed too. HMS

Glamorgan strayed too close to shore and received a heavy mauling from the Argentine fighter planes. More men were killed and HMS *Coventry* was sunk. It was a very serious situation for the expeditionary force. At the Bible College where every BBC report was followed closely, Samuel led evening intercessory prayer sessions well into the night.

Then the mainly untrained ten thousand Argentinian soldiers, many of them young[1] men, conscripts (drafts), proved inadequate to contain the fully equipped British contingent, whose miraculous eight-mile march (nicknamed 'The Yomp') from San Carlos Bay through the marshes, to take the capital in a surprise attack, forced a quick surrender. Casualties were considerably reduced. Superior equipment played a significant part in the victory, especially the Harrier Jump Jets operating from aircraft carrier HMS *Hermes*. On 14th June the white flag was hoisted by the Argentinian garrison in Port Stanley and this brought the conflict to a speedy conclusion.

All three petitions regarding the Falklands crisis were answered. Every death in war is tragic. Numbers killed and horrific casualties were very high on both sides, and graphic scenes of carnage were viewed on TV screens as the fortunes of war were enacted before the world. Had the conflict continued, thousands more would have suffered and the bitterness and grief for those left behind intensified beyond measure. General Galtieri was removed from office and a real wave of spiritual blessing swept across areas of Argentina.[2]

During these years, Doris Ruscoe, previously introduced as the first head teacher of the Bible College School, was now bubbling over to share her reminiscences of Rees Howells, with whom she had spent many hours of discussion during her early days in the College. Her book, *The Intercession of Rees Howells* published by Lutterworth Press was released in 1983. Samuel had received many reports of its progress and was pleased to have the first signed copy, having previously been asked to write a suitable preface.

It was true to say that there was a 'real grip' in the prayer for the demise of Communism, and each victory on the way served to strengthen the main prayer. Evident changes came in 1986 when Mikhail Gorbachev, whose mother was an Orthodox believer, called for Glasnost (meaning Openness, a Soviet policy to allow freer discussion of social problems) and Perestroika (meaning Restructuring of the economy), a dramatic change from the old days. Then in 1986, an explosion at the nuclear reactor at Chernobyl in northeast Ukraine brought shudders to world leaders, as a radioactive cloud drifted across Europe as far as Britain. Immediate assistance was sought from countries outside the Soviet Bloc, as the scale of the disaster emerged. For some the word 'Chernobyl' was related to 'Wormwood' in Revelation 8:11. This up-till-then unknown region was certainly on the map.

Samuel's ministry through the book of the Prophet Isaiah became very relevant again as it had been during Rees Howells' ministry. God had met with Isaiah at the death of Uzziah, King of Judah, and introduced him to the realm where few are privileged to reach, even today. Before that becomes possible a deep inner purging and cleansing is necessary. With the threat of invasion from the Northern Kingdom and Syria hanging over the nation, God gave Ahaz, the new King of Judah, opportunity of help which he refused. This refusal, of course, drew out the renowned prophecy of the virgin birth, in Isaiah 7:14.

Therefore the Lord Himself will give you a sign:
The virgin will be with child and will give birth to
a Son, and will call Him Immanuel.

In chapter 8, the consequences of Ahaz's stubbornness are spelt out as the Assyrians would sweep across Judah like a razor. Like floodwaters, they would overflow the land and reach right up to the neck (v8) and then God would intervene. Samuel would relate Assyria to the Communist domination of Russia throttling the life of Eastern Europe as a whole. God had given Samuel three distinct prayers to pray.

- That God would grant religious liberty in these lands.
- That God would make it possible for the Christians in Communist countries to teach their children about God.

- That God would make it possible for Scriptures to be printed and distributed in these countries so that everyone could have a copy of the Bible of his / her own.

In Isaiah's case another forty years elapsed as the Assyrian threat increased, but his intercession continued. Hezekiah brought sweeping religious reforms into the land. Almost a revival in modern terms as detailed in 2 Chronicles 29-32 but when the full force of the Assyrian flood reached the gates of Jerusalem, he found the situation more than he could cope with. He appealed to God in prayer and solicited Isaiah's help. Isaiah remained unmoved throughout these years of intercession till the very end, because of his initial revelation of the nature and character of God, which is unfolded throughout his prophecy. He knew without any shadow of doubt that 'the flood would only reach the neck.' The word from God pronounced a conclusive end to Sennacherib King of Assyria's plans.

Because you rage against Me and because your insolence has reached My ears, I will put My hook in your nose and My bit in your mouth and I will make you return by the way you came.

He will not enter this city or shoot an arrow here. He will not come before it with shield or build a siege ramp against it. By the way that he came he will return; he will not enter this city, declares the Lord. Isaiah 37:29, 33-34.

Samuel could see clearly before him, in the Spirit realm, the picture of God putting a hook in their nose and a bridle in their lips to turn them back by the way which they had come. Communism was doomed and he knew it – it was a matter of waiting to see the Communist Empire crumbling. Samuel was able to declare with confidence that the impregnable 'wall' would crumble too. After seventy years of oppression, God's time had come.

The demise of Nicolae Ceausescu from office as Secretary General of the Communist Party ruling in Romania, witnessed publicly on national television in 1989, demonstrated the miraculous nature of his fall. Since 1947, when Russia had removed King Michael as Head of State, the once 'Bread Basket of Europe' was systematically stripped of all its wealth. When the Russians left in 1968 and Ceausescu came to power, he further impoverished the country and exhausted its economy. With a brutal enforcement of power, the Securitate (Secret Police) slaughtered two million of the population, with the Church as its main target.

The College had been blessed through visits from Romanian pastors who suffered under that regime, including Pastor Wurmbrand, whose paper *The Theology of Martyrdom* was an eye-opener. Now they were free and the College was later to welcome its first Romanian student, daughter of a pastor. The emerging Church would receive far greater accolades than Nadia Comaneci, the gymnast, had received in her outstanding Moscow and Los Angeles Olympic displays of 1980 and 1984.

Samuel's twenty-five years of intercession for Eastern Europe from 1962 to 1987 were complete, but there were others to come.

Dr. Sam Matthews was staying at the College when the Berlin Wall finally and officially fell in November 1989. The evening before, as he was ministering, there was such a release of the Holy Spirit in the meeting that everyone knew for certain that a significant event had happened in the Spirit realm. One staff member reported seeing Samuel later in ecstasy on the landing waving his handkerchief and declaring,

"The Wall is down, the Wall is down!"

The Wall certainly had come tumbling down – physically and spiritually. Samuel believed without doubt that many more walls would fall around the world as intercession is made through the prepared, consecrated lives of believers, and the Vision for the complete fulfilment of Joel's prophecy for the outpouring of God's Spirit on all flesh takes place.

Chapter Twenty-Six

Victory in South Africa

In South Africa the apartheid abuses sanctioned by Mr Verwoerd, following his withdrawal from the Commonwealth in 1961, continued at a lesser degree under the leadership of John Vorster (Balthazar Johannes Vorster). Elsewhere, Ian Smith claimed Independence for Rhodesia, to be renamed Zimbabwe, in 1979. During that troubled period when there were many brutal killings (including a massacre at New Adams Farm[1] in November 1987 by a highly drug-crazed gang), Samuel Howells responded to an invitation from Hans Von Staden, Founder of the Dorothea Mission, to speak at their annual conference in Pretoria, South Africa during the summer of 1986. The details of the trip had been discussed in Bristol the previous summer with Glyndwr Davies, UK representative of the Mission. Dorothea (the name of Von Staden's wife, and meaning Gift of God) was a multiracial evangelistic fellowship looking to God alone to supply all their needs, and placed great emphasis on weeks of prayer before embarking on any of their campaigns. Their teams worked in the dangerous, troubled areas of the townships like Soweto.

Samuel was deeply moved when he was introduced to Spirit-filled black African Christian women who had suffered much for their faith in that cauldron of unrest. Oblivious of all inner pain, their faces shone as they magnified the Lord Jesus Christ through their triumphant broad smiles, so much so that the visitor from Wales declared that it was worth travelling all the way to Africa just to meet them. He genuinely felt the great privilege that was his. They bore the true hallmarks of Spirit-filled servants of the Living God.

Commenting on the proceedings later, Samuel affirmed that he had never before experienced the Presence of God in such a manifest way in ministry as he had that night. A tape recording confirms his remarks, for here was a normally reserved and quiet servant of God, reading and expounding from the first five chapters of Daniel with such fluency and passion that his friends at home would have found it hard to credit that it was the same Samuel. The Holy Spirit had truly taken hold of him as he portrayed the vital part that Daniel's intercessory ministry played in laying the foundation for the Jews' return to their land, following seventy years of captivity in Babylon. Samuel had the witness that the leaders present in the congregation, and many others, had received the word and would be giving themselves wholeheartedly to see a turnaround in the destiny of South Africa. They would not be disappointed; the sinister system of apartheid was broken (elections were held in 1994) and a bloodbath averted. True intercession prevails every time, but remains a costly process.

Old Church at Rusitu, Gazaland (now Zimbabwe) where revival broke out in October 1915 under Rees Howells

During his trip, Samuel was driven to Rusitu, Zimbabwe, to the old mission station where revival first broke out in 1915, under Rees Howells' ministry. There he met Moses, an old blind African Christian with a glowing countenance, who was able to lead Samuel to a certain spot and say,

"Here the Spirit fell." He was referring to the moment when, like thunder and lightning, the power of God had fallen on the congregation. Heaven had opened and there was no room to contain the blessing. Samuel often referred to blind Moses when he recounted the story, and mentioned the outstanding manifestations of the Spirit that were evidenced during that spiritual outpouring. Always wary of the counterfeit, Samuel would recognise this as the genuine article for which he was praying.

Samuel returned to the College from his trip to Southern Africa renewed in every way, inspired by the deep response to the challenges of intercession by so many who were prepared to pay any price to see the evils of apartheid destroyed. He reflected on some of the salutary lessons on the ministry received through the life and example of Rees Howells who had made it abundantly clear that in the spiritual conflict between God and Satan, both must have channels. The warfare is fought through those channels. The Holy Spirit must find individuals who are totally committed to God's will, and they are bound to the will of God in every detail of their lives until the battle is won – or the intercession is through. The ministry cannot be undertaken without the Holy Spirit, who is the only living witness to Christ's atoning work on the cross, His resurrection and ascension. Only the Holy Spirit knows when the total victory is gained in each given situation. Unless the channel allows the Holy Spirit to deal with every facet of his or her life, the enemy will take hold and prevent victory. It is a very close walk with God leading to a complete destruction of Satan's power – a wonderful victory releasing much joy as the deliverance is witnessed on earth. The intercessor never comes out the same person; each intercession brings about a further radical change as the Divine Nature takes over.

> ...He has given us His very great and precious promises, so that through them you may participate in the Divine Nature. 2 Peter 1:4.

Samuel had seen this taking place in the lives of the Africans, and remembered his early days at the Bible College when the challenge went out for individuals to make a full commitment to serve the Lord. He had been in his early twenties then, when the transactions were made between the Lord God Almighty and the frail members of the College staff and student body. There was such a release of power and joy throughout the campus that everyone joined in unison for an hour at least, singing a familiar chorus of the time, welcoming the Holy Spirit. This was true worship from surrendered lives.

The reality of the walk with God was constantly being put to the test, and Samuel could never expect the African believers to face their challenges without his proving the Lord's power at work in the College. Amidst the turmoil of that period, one of Samuel's closest friends and a loyal staff member and Trustee, Idwal Thomas, was suddenly rushed into nearby Singleton Hospital with acute appendicitis and peritonitis. With this infection present, things took a turn for the worse and Idwal's life was in the balance. Samuel had first known Idwal in the early days when he visited his sister, Gwladys Thomas, a teacher who was one of the group who went to commence the School and Home in Jordan in the mid 1950s. Idwal came from Dowlais, near Merthyr Tydfil in South Wales, so was able to converse with Samuel in fluent Welsh, a rare luxury at the College in those days, sadly. With Idwal hovering on the brink of death, Samuel put everything to one side, including sleep, and waited on God alone, while other staff members joined in corporate prayer. Then the word of the Lord came to Samuel, as was so often the case, "Idwal shall live." That was the turning point, and Idwal remembered the Lord ministering to him when he was at his lowest, through the Welsh hymns which he had learnt as a young man in chapel. Full recovery took many weeks but, eventually, Idwal was back in the bakehouse, baking bread and pounding dough, a sideline he had learned at home. Death had been challenged and the victory gained. It was a seal on what God was doing in Southern Africa.

Through Rees Howells' ministry, they had been deeply taught that these God / Satan conflicts will only ever be won through the ministry of intercession. The offer is open to every believer, and the Holy Spirit will take us as far as we are prepared to go. Samuel was certainly resolved to go as far as possible.

Chapter Twenty-Seven

Retired!

'Retired' was never a word that either Samuel or the College staff had considered in their early days of enthusiasm and expectation. Carried along by the river of faith that the Founder's ministry had created, they could see all the time, with their spiritual eyes, the whole world being reached with the Gospel in their lifetime, to herald back the King. That was the essence of the Vision which took them through the darkest of days, similar to the hope which the Apostle Paul presented to the Thessalonians in their day (1 Thessalonians 4:13-18). But Jesus had declared quite clearly that,
> "This Gospel of the Kingdom shall be preached in the whole world as a testimony to all the nations, and then the end will come." Matthew 24:14 (NASB).

The nations must all be reached first and then the end would come – no retirement! However, in practical terms, the ageing resident teaching staff in a very vibrant Emmanuel School were being replaced by younger employed teachers, more able to cope with the changes in the developing educational system. Costs for running a modern school in a very competitive local environment were escalating. A newly formed combination of teachers and very supportive parents, keen to retain a Christian based school in the district, formed a Parent Teacher Association called the Emmanuel Association. A variety of activities drew great interest, and generous sponsors helped launch a Jubilee Fund to raise funds for building modern sports facilities and a stage for the school. A Jubilee Concert in 1984 attracted favourable publicity, showing the high standard of achievements in a wide range of creative skills of the pupils, and suitably depicted the progress of the school over fifty years.

The retirement of Dr. Kingsley Priddy as head teacher in 1980, at the age of seventy-two, affected Samuel personally, as he would have loved to relinquish some of the heavy responsibilities on his shoulders, but it was a very necessary step for Kingsley to make. Graham Lippett, a former student of the Bible College and teacher in Emmanuel, who succeeded as head teacher, was very capable, with work experience as a missionary in France and also as Head of the Mathematics Department in a school in Walsall, UK. He had a real heart of concern for the spiritual welfare of all the pupils in the day school, and in the home for missionary children.

Emmanuel Grammar School 1980s on the Glynderwen site. Glynderwen House (top middle), El-Shaddai (top right), grass tennis court (foreground left) which was later concreted and a high wire fence was erected.

For Dr. Priddy, of course, it was not a case of retirement but relocation and redirection. Never one to remain static, he embarked on two different journeys. One was to Australia and Tasmania, visiting relations and a former pupil of Emmanuel School, and the other to Pakistan in response to an invitation from Pastor Nathaniel Barkat to preach in his country district. Even at the age of seventy-two, here was an opportunity for Kingsley to put into practice his missionary principle skills in a dust-filled area where the only toilets were across the fields. His passion for souls in every nation drove him forward. Samuel was concerned for his friend and was relieved to see him arrive back at College in one piece.

Derwen Fawr Estate (edge of hospital on left), with old nursery and printing room (back middle), with edge of Conference Hall (back middle right), with (from left to right) Primrose Thomas, Mair Davies and Dr. K. Priddy c.1990.

Another of Kingsley's projects, which Samuel followed with great interest, arose when an African, Kofi, came to his notice through Leslie Brierley, a prominent WEC figure. Leslie's wife was Bessie Fricker, a real 'cockney sparrow' from London who had distinguished herself as a student at the College through her application to study, and had then gone on to pioneer the work in Upper Volta. Kofi, a Christian head teacher in an up-country school was in great need, so Kingsley set about doing all he could to encourage and support this man and his family, who were living in much poverty. An arrangement enabled Kofi to make his first visit to the UK, to Keswick and to the College on 31st October 1986, where Samuel was pleased to make him feel welcome. It was a sad day years later when Kofi died from tuberculosis. Support for the family, Kofi's wife and two children, continued for several years. Two of the sons were named Kingsley and Gustav, as Gustav Scheller had contributed generously in their support.

Gustav, another of Kingsley's newly formed friends, often visited the College during the foundation period of Operation Exodus, a ministry of assisting Jews to make Aliyah (to return to their Homeland from countries around the world) by ship. Gustav became the Founder Director and was much encouraged through Samuel and Kingsley, who had both received the revelation of the Jews' destiny under Rees Howells' ministry during World War II.

It was of further great interest to Samuel when Kingsley began sharing with the College fellowship in prayer meetings about a Nigerian pastor from the Moomye tribe who was studying in the UK. This was the particular tribe to which Kingsley was originally planning to go as a medical missionary doctor to establish a hospital there in 1936, when the College 'altar call' led him to lay his 'call' down, and to be involved instead in the intercession for the nations. Full circle – and he was thrilled.

The two issues of retirement of resident staff, and in many cases the death of key resident workers (another twenty were called Home during the 1990s), and also the escalating costs – were added burdens for Samuel. One obvious consideration was the sale of land. He pursued the idea of selling part of the Sketty Isaf Estate for housing development but those plans fell through. In the early 1980s he was approached by the then Land Authority of Wales who had spotted suitable land on the Emmanuel School playing field which they felt could be developed.

Another possibility was to loan some of the money held in the banks at comparatively low interest and receive better returns. However, Samuel needed to be absolutely sure of the trustworthiness of the person with whom he was dealing, and that the arrangement was completely secure, since he was totally against investing in the Stock Market with its element of risk. It would also need to have full approval from both the Charity Commission and the Inland Revenue.

He did find someone who, over the years, became a very trusted friend, a financial advisor, very thorough and diligent in his work ethic, and who sought no personal gain from the Charity other than legitimate expenses that were kept to an absolute minimum.

A proposal was made, and as none of the High Street banks would match the arrangement, Samuel proceeded with a pilot scheme, which proved very successful and financially rewarding. With the full written approval of the Inland Revenue in Bootle and the Charity Commission's Legal Branch, a loan of £75,000 ($120,000) was advanced as follows. It was:
- Made to the financial advisor's business.
- Fully secured by unencumbered freehold property.
- Producing interest up to twelve percent at peak.
- Short term.
- Being repaid into the Charity account on a weekly basis with interest.
- Fully repaid.

The loan was regulated by a legal document signed on 30th December 1994 and Samuel was pleased with its favourable return.

Throughout this period, Samuel was anxiously monitoring the rapidly rising costs. Even the increased School fees of 1993 would not be sufficient to cover all the expenses of Emmanuel School, especially as the necessity of paying fees was a deterrent in an area where local state schools were offering such an excellent free alternative of high quality education. As overseas educational facilities had improved so rapidly the number of missionaries wishing their children to be in the UK decreased. Emmanuel School boarding facilities closed when the last boarder finished her education, and the House parents, Philip and Ann Thomas, after years of faithful service completed their responsibilities. The closure of the School was announced causing great concern among many who recognised the School's value in the district. The Emmanuel Association stepped in, formed a new Charity known as the Emmanuel Trust, and volunteered to continue running the School from its own resources. A trial year with reduced teachers' salaries was attempted, but the full realisation of what it had meant for the Charity to underpin the School became evident. It was a very sad day in 1994 when the final closure of the School, with its excellent reputation built up over many years through the dedicated services of teachers and ancillary workers, was announced.[1]

It is hard to enter into the personal feelings of Samuel during this dark and difficult period since he shared his thoughts with very few. However, he conferred regularly on business matters with his trustees of the Bible College.

Aerial view of Emmanuel Grammar School (on the Glynderwen Estate) c.1955. Derwen Fawr Road runs along the bottom of photo between the hedgerows. El-Shaddai building where boarder boys slept (bottom left), Glynderwen House where boarder girls slept with roundabout (bottom middle). Other buildings are classrooms.

One particular incident is worth noting. Although financially the right decisions were being made, the spiritual ministry of the School was an important consideration also. One Trustee involved in the process was deeply troubled through the night in an unusual way concerning the situation. He eventually found strength through Isaiah 30:21 (AV).

Thine ears shall hear a word behind thee saying, "This is the way, walk ye in it, when ye turn to the right hand and when ye turn to the left."

Early next morning he received a message asking him to visit Samuel before the College programme commenced.

"I hardly slept all night," Samuel told him, "and I believe the Lord was speaking."

Before he could continue, the staff member shared his experience, and they found an agreement in the Spirit concerning the decision they were to make.

If two of you shall agree on earth as touching anything that they shall ask, it shall be done for them of My Father which is in Heaven. Matthew 18:19 (AV).

It was the strength given through that occasion that later provided stability and confidence in an Industrial Tribunal in Cardiff, following appeals by teachers against unfair dismissal, and the inevitable strong feeling among Christians locally that a vital ministry to young people was ending.

Emmanuel School Badge (from a banner)

Several years previously, Samuel and the trustees had been led to engage the services of a national legal organisation which provided round the clock professional advice and legal services. Every step in the School closure had been monitored by this group, who finally represented the Charity successfully in the legal wrangles, which ensued. It was even suggested by some that Samuel had a million pounds secretly hidden away somewhere, and that this could have been used to perpetuate the Emmanuel School ministry in the district. The Charity assets were clearly represented in the Annual Accounts available for all to see. They consisted of a large proportion of gifts committed for overseas missionary work. At some point, they may well have reached the million mark, but no hidden hoard ever existed.

Bible College School Inter-House Work Shield

Throughout this period, the College services were recorded by Ruth Williams on cassette tape, as they had been since the mid 1970s. This practice was continued until Samuel's public ministry ended in December 2002, so an accurate record remains of his words and the prayers that followed.

In these conflicts it is imperative that the Lord is allowed to speak Himself beforehand concerning the final outcome, because the 'going through' can become very dark and depressing at times.

Samuel's close walk with God throughout this decade shines through his pulpit ministry in evening prayer meetings and Sunday services which were all tape recorded. Familiar phrases still echo in the minds of those who heard him,

- These men of the Bible were dwelling on the Person of Christ, not on their misfortunes.
- The emphasis all the time was 'Walk in Christ.'
- I am sure you are all familiar with the content of these chapters.
- I know there are these testings but there is no need to dwell on the testings but rather on Christ; that's a miracle in itself, isn't it?
- As I said before, if God has revealed these things to us we will spend every moment of our lives in worship and thanksgiving undoubtedly.
- What privileges the Lord has conferred upon us.
- Have you thanked Him and worshipped Him today?
- We firmly believe.
- These are very familiar words to you, I am sure, *Let us draw near.* Hebrews 10:22 (AV). We do so through the rent Body of our Lord.
- When He begins something He always makes an end, undoubtedly. We haven't got time to read the whole chapter now.
- Let us ask the Holy Spirit to help us understand these deep things so that we do not read them superficially.
- Only one glimpse of the cross is sufficient to change us completely; undoubtedly.

"Undoubtedly" was always said with great emphasis.

In one series of the services, Samuel focused attention on the dramatic and fundamental changes that took place in the Apostle Paul's life over a ten to twelve year period. Here was a prominent Jewish Pharisee, steeped in Judaism and every facet of the law, who met with the risen Christ and, through the power of the atoning work of the cross applied to every area in his life, was dramatically changed, so much so that he became prepared to risk his life to go to all the Gentiles. He was equally convinced that the same power which had transformed his life, was able to lift the Gentiles out of their sin and give them the power to live entirely transformed lives. Paul was pioneering a new pathway and even Peter and Barnabas wavered (Galatians 2:11-13).

When confronted by a situation where converted Jews and converted Gentiles were together, Peter's Jewish background still lingered in his mind as he lost sight of the 'new man in Christ' that the work of the atonement had created. It had been about five years from the Day of Pentecost before Peter had approached the Gentiles with the Gospel in the House of Cornelius (Acts 10). Even then, it had only been possible following visions from God on the rooftop of Simon the Tanner's house outside Joppa where he was staying. The great Apostle had chosen to stay with Simon at the tannery, a place usually built at a safe distance from any town because of the pungent smells which pervaded the countryside around – certainly not a five star hotel!

In Peter's visions he clearly heard a voice telling him,
Do not call anything impure that God has made clean. Acts 10:15.

So when messengers, sent by Cornelius, a Gentile Roman centurion, arrived at the tannery, Peter readily responded to the invitation to visit his home and to share the Gospel with the household there. The Holy Spirit came upon the Gentile gathering, and through Peter the keys of the Kingdom conferred on the Apostle by Jesus (Matthew 16:19) – the revelation of the truth of the Gospel – enabled the door of faith to be opened to the Gentile world, as it had been opened to the Jewish Nation in Jerusalem on the Day of Pentecost (Acts 2).

But Peter's ministry to the Gentiles was confined to that one household. The revelation Paul received enabled him, now that the door was open, to penetrate the whole of the Gentile world of his day. Although he never forgot his own Jewish nation, and was prepared to pay a great price to see them saved, Paul strove for the salvation of the Gentiles more than any other. In Romans 8:11 he declared that the same power of the Holy Spirit that raised Jesus from the dead was at work in the lives of the Gentile believers to lift them from their sinful lives.

And if the Spirit of Him who raised Jesus from the dead is living in you, He who raised Christ from the dead will also give life to your mortal bodies through His Spirit who lives in you.

In praying for the believers in Ephesus, he requested that the God of our Lord Jesus Christ, the Father of glory, would give them the spirit of wisdom and revelation in the knowledge of Christ, that the eyes of their understanding would be enlightened. He prayed that they would know what was the hope of their calling and what were the riches of the glory of His inheritance in them. Then he prayed that they would experience the exceeding greatness of His power according to the working of His mighty power – the same power that raised Christ from the dead and set Him at His own right hand in Heaven. He referred to the *incomparably great power for us who believe* (Ephesians 1:19). This was radical teaching for those days, but do we really believe and experience it today, as we should? Exceeding great and precious promises have been given for believers to be lifted up out of themselves by the ascended Christ within them.

As Samuel read passages from Ephesians and Colossians, familiar truths took on a new meaning, particularly as he pointed out that, although a prisoner for some five years, Paul was not mentioning the conditions of his imprisonment. He was not confined to the measurements of his cell but was living above his circumstances – a man in Christ. Samuel continued,

"The emphasis is on revelation all the time. The great mystery is that the Gentiles will be fellow heirs with the Jewish people.

"The mystery that has been kept hidden for ages and generations, but is now disclosed to

the saints. To them God has chosen to make known among the Gentiles the glorious riches of this mystery, which is Christ in you, the hope of glory. Colossians 1:26-27.

"The burden now," Samuel continued, "is that the dear believers around the world should be able to share these blessings with us. It is forty-four years now since His servant (Samuel sometimes referred to Rees Howells, his father, as 'His servant') was taken. It was very dark then but God spoke to us, 'The gap is there. Will you fill it?' The voice of God that day was very clear. Since then grace has been commensurate with every test. One outcome has been the publishing of the book *Rees Howells Intercessor*. Christian leaders all over the world are being transformed through reading it, as they testify in their letters that I am continually reading.

"God again spoke to one as clearly as He spoke at the beginning, *'Give ye them to eat.'* Mark's Gospel says *their heart was hardened.* Mark 6:52 (AV). Make sure your minds are not closed to these things. You take this week – there are very heavy expenses to be dealt with. The electricity bill for three months is £2,400 ($3,840) for these buildings alone. I do trust we use electricity with care. We would be failures every day apart from the Holy Spirit. There is greater truth than you realise in the words that Jesus spoke – *'Without Me ye can do NOTHING.'* John 15:5 (AV). Nothing is done without Him. There are other bills to be paid tomorrow also.

"Whatever the domestic needs, however, are we still remembering the ministry which God has given us to the world? I have letters ready this week for the Gulf States where believers have prayed through to see Saddam Hussein giving permission for Bibles to be distributed in schools in Iraq; for India (Every Home

Crusade), for Moxam – a man in the Holy Spirit who has assumed responsibility to take the Scriptures to every home in India, and he is getting on with it; and for Israel; and for Croatia (Dr. Branko Loveric from Zagreb). To read letters from Branko would break your heart. Ministering to refugees who have literally lost everything of this world, he is at it by day and by night, and also providing food for the public food kitchens. He appealed to us to continue interceding for them so that they, by their lives, could witness to these dear people.

"Further letters are going to Mozambique, Zimbabwe, China, Israel, Cambodia, Poland, Mongolia and Russia. And so it goes on, week by week. Do not be too active and then miss out on prayer. It is better to drop activities and to make time for more prayer. Spend time, not to pray for our own blessing, but to pray for others of the household of faith."

Samuel was always very sensitive on this point, recognising that in some Christian groups the focus is upon what the Lord has done for 'us' alone. He pointed out that there is an element of selfishness and self-centredness generated. In his experience, and that of his father, Rees Howells, the Holy Spirit had always sought to reach out through them to others for whom Christ died. As they did so, their personal joy and worship increased all the time.

"We do not want to forget these objectives," Samuel continued in his ministry. "If we seek first the Kingdom and His righteousness all these things shall be added. It is not what a person says that counts. No, you watch their conduct."

Throughout the 1980s Samuel had become a regular supporter of Christian workers, some of whom were former students, in about forty countries in the world, as well as sending substantial gifts to agencies distributing Scriptures particularly in India, Africa, Eastern Europe and China.[2]

Samuel regularly kept a small pocket diary in which he recorded the names of speakers in all the services, including bookings for later in the year. Where he was the speaker the initials SRH only were included, plus the passage of Scripture from which he ministered. For some unexplained reason he also recorded any gifts larger than £100 ($160) received during the 1980s, given specifically for the ministry. With the value of the pound having fallen so much since those days, the reader can not easily appreciate just how much Samuel was praying in each year to manage the ever increasing College expenses, and to pursue his ministry of support across the world. In one year, he recorded the following gifts.

- Twenty large gifts received, totalling £10,310 ($16,500). (If these twenty gifts were received in 1989 it would be worth £21,050 / $33,680 in 2012).
- Twenty-one large gifts received, totalling £21,180 ($33,890).
- Twenty-four large gifts received, totalling £24,937 ($39,900).
- Eleven large gifts received, totalling £13,300 ($21,280).
- Fourteen large gifts received, totalling £17,180 ($27,490).
- Thirteen large gifts received, totalling £21,770 ($34,830).

It was a mammoth task, repeated throughout the 1990s. There was further work to do – for everyone! Therefore, with Emmanuel School closed, the world ministry was intensified and there was to be NO retirement.

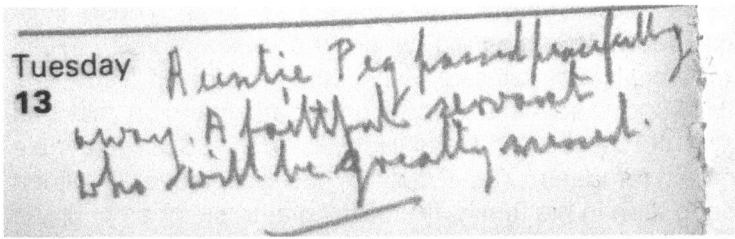

Entry in Samuel's very small pocket diary (2.5 inches in width, 6.3 centimetres) 13 January 1987. Entry reads: 'Auntie Peg passed peacefully away. A faithful servant who will be greatly missed.' Aunt Peg (Margaret Williams) was one of the first students who studied under Rees Howells in 1924.

Chapter Twenty-Eight

Ethiopia

Nestling among the College archives lies a letter from Addis Ababa, the capital of Ethiopia, addressed to Samuel Howells and dated 23rd June 1990. Signed by the widow of Brigadier General Abye Abebe, the Ethiopian Minister of War, it recalls days when he and several other notable sons of Ethiopia, were educated at the Bible College School.

> My late husband, who until his untimely death, had maintained great affection and respect for the Bible College of Wales, used to tell us all about the College's helpful staff and his wonderful schooldays. We recall times when tears used to come to his eyes.... This letter is, therefore, duly inspired by the truly special remembrance of the almost time immemorial friendship which the family of your dear friend still cherishes....

The letter was signed by Tsige Ayenalem.

The deep links forged in the Spirit with Ethiopia since 1936, when the Holy Spirit had led Rees Howells to pray for the preservation of this ancient people so often mentioned in the Scriptures, were threatened by invading Fascist forces under Mussolini's command. These links had been strengthened when the beleaguered, exiled Emperor, Haile Selassie visited the College in 1939 and 1940, and marvelled at the Penllergaer mansion that had been purchased by Rees Howells in his desire to help Jewish refugees. The Emperor had sent several refined young men in his family, from Ethiopia, to study as pupils in the School. Samuel was a member of the College staff by then and, always keen to welcome visitors, had taken a personal interest in their welfare. There was Lidj Asrate Kassa (a relative of the Emperor and later to become a

Governor General of Aroussi, an Ethiopian province), H. H. Ras Asrate Kassa (the Emperor's Private Chaplain), Abye Abebe (the Brigadier General, husband of the writer of the letter) and Dejazmach Hailou Desta Kassa. Hailou, as he was generally known, began the first Christian Union in the School. It was very much through his influence that a fresh touch from God was experienced by many pupils.

The Howells Family (plus a staff member of BCW, far right) with Emperor Haile Selassie (sitting) at Penllergaer Estate October 1939 with his two nephews, students at the School.

Although not participating in the venture, apart from visiting with Rees Howells for photographs, Samuel always smiled when asked about the two weeks of camp at Penllergaer for the senior school pupils in October 1939. The star attraction on that occasion was the Emperor himself who travelled from Bath, England, to share the experience with his nephews, pitching his own canvas tent along with the others.

> "In Ethiopia," he said, "we were in the war zone with war planes flying overhead and in immediate peril from bombardment. At Penllergaer it is beautiful and quiet and I hope to rest."

Life under canvas, however, did not appeal to Samuel! Samuel was deeply touched by the tribute in a national newspaper, following the death of his father, Rees Howells, in 1950 and written by his young friend, Hailou.

> I had the privilege of seeing our most beloved Director when he called on me on the Tuesday before he was taken ill, and as we spoke about Ethiopia it seemed that he himself grieved for all the wrongs that were done to her, and with a sorrowful groaning that was beyond explanation he added, "Prayer is what we need." Yes, it was prayer he recommended to us Ethiopians. The last word he left us – "Victory!" Ethiopia, take the medicine this friendly physician prescribed and the victory is ours!

Throughout his lifetime, Samuel never lapsed in his prayers for Ethiopia, which Satan is constantly seeking to wrest from the hands of God.

God had assured Rees Howells of future blessing in Ethiopia through the promise of Psalm 68:31 (NASB):

Ethiopia will quickly stretch out her hands to God.

So that victory was assured and the Emperor returned to his people in 1941. It was to remain a troubled land fiercely contested in the heavenly realms and many would pay a heavy price, even to this day, to ensure that the flame of God is not extinguished.

In 1950, Hailou's daughter, Sophie, was sent to the School and was much loved. On 24th November 1974, some of these young men were among sixty leading figures in Ethiopia executed in a political upheaval. As Samuel led further prayer at the College for the Ethiopian people, so many still living the simple lifestyle of their forefathers in the beautiful rolling hills of the north, or scattered across the arid lowlands in the south, the oldest of the three FitzHerbert sisters teaching in the School, felt an urge to work in Ethiopia. So in February 1950, Dr. Margaret FitzHerbert, a highly qualified physician and gynaecologist, joined a medical team in Addis Ababa at the express invitation of the Emperor, and helped to establish The Haile Selassie Hospital, giving special attention to the care of lepers. When she died in 1971 leaving only five hundred Ethiopian dollars[1] of this world's goods, fellow workers wrote of her:

> She lived entirely and untiringly as a channel for Christ's love and compassion. Living in such close fellowship with God she was given special sensitivity to the needs of people.

Capable of experiencing intense feelings of compassion toward those who suffered for the name of Jesus, Samuel knew he had met a man with a true spirit of intercession for Ethiopia when he welcomed Gerald Gotzen as a visiting speaker to the College during the 1970s. Here was a dear brother who also recognised the important role that Israel was to play in these last days, and was also involved in highly sensitive missions across the borders into Communist controlled Eastern European countries. When Haile Selassie died in 1974 after being deposed, and the Russians helped Mengistu Haile Mariam to quell neighbouring Somalian and tribal faction opposition, to set up the local People's Courts known as the Kebeles, Gerald's involvement in Ethiopia deepened. He did his utmost to encourage a persecuted Christian majority in the land and earned the reputation of 'Mr Ethiopia.'

A terrible famine swept across areas of Ethiopia in the early 1980s, and the Christians in the West were alerted to pray for the thousands who were fleeing persecution and an acute shortage of food and water, to refugee camps in neighbouring Sudan. Among these were residents of the Beta Israel Community, known as Falasha Jews by their enemies, Falasha meaning aliens or invaders. Living in thatched huts around Lake Tana in Gonda, this unusual group of people with distinct Jewish origin had been discovered in 1769 by the Scottish explorer, James Bruce, when he stumbled across them while looking for the source of the River Nile. Now Mengitsu was destroying their villages and herding them into communes. Samuel, alerted to their plight most probably through Gerald, who kept his ear to the ground as far as Ethiopia was concerned, prayed much for them.

Meanwhile, behind the scenes, the Israeli Defence Forces, working alongside the Central Intelligence Agency and the Sudanese State Security Forces, began operating a plan to escort members of the fleeing Beta Israel community across the mountains to the Sudanese capital Khartoum and to transport them, by covert means, into Israel. It was a slow process and only eighteen hundred reached their destination safely in 1983. It was then that a carefully devised initiative named Operation Moses (Mivtza Moses), using Hercules Transport aircraft fitted to carry two hundred refugees at a time, snatched eight thousand emaciated, destitute Beta Israel citizens from Khartoum airport and flew them safely home to Israel. Flights continued from 21st November 1984 until 5th January 1985, when the operation was brought to a sudden end as a result of leaked news published in an American newspaper. Arab nations objected to this mass exodus, and over one thousand refugees were left behind. For many who had never seen an aircraft before, Exodus 19:4 took on a new meaning.

> *You yourselves have seen what I did to the Egyptians and how I bore you on eagles' wings and brought you to Myself.*

The small remaining remnant was later retrieved in operations Joshua and Solomon. For Samuel, this was yet another wonderful answer to prayer, for this ambitious deliverance could never have proved such a success without the assistance of the God of Heaven, and it had been a further opportunity to believe God for the impossible.

In a service prior to the beginning of the new Spring Term in College on 3rd January 1985 Samuel read from Jeremiah 32 and 33 and stressed again how, through their close walk with God, these great prophets were able to discern and speak out God's purposes and believe Him for the impossible. Even at that juncture Samuel spoke knowledgeably about Operation Moses, stressing that although the refugees were returning to Israel in unbelief, it was the Holy Spirit's desire to reveal the atoning work of their Messiah to the whole nation. Then Samuel rose to his full stature in Christ, as so often happened when he was involved in these intercessions, and declared,

"The two greatest intercessions of the Director

during the war years and afterwards were for the preservation of the Jews during the Holocaust and the establishment of the nation."

He always made it abundantly clear that the two main issues for these last days, and they run concurrently, are for the Gospel to be preached with disciples made in every nation, and for the blessing of the whole Jewish nation. Samuel held tenaciously to these two spiritual targets, without wavering once, throughout his whole ministry.

These were not just wild declarations plucked out of the air, for Samuel himself had sat in the back corner seat of the Conference Hall, as was his custom in those war days, when his father was fighting through in those historic intercessions, both during the war years and afterwards.

Despite the sentiments expressed in the Balfour Declaration in 1917, for self-determination to be granted to Jews and Arabs in two agreed states for the people, Jews, Christians, Turks and Arabs living in the Middle East, a lasting settlement had never been achieved.

President Truman had initiated the Anglo-American Committee of Inquiry in 1946, but by February 1947, the fragile situation had collapsed once more, so it was referred to the United Nations for their decision.

Samuel remembered how his father watched every move in the Holy Spirit, discerning that God was on the verge of making a significant mark in history. To begin with even the motion needed acceptance by the UN Assembly, so a vote in its favour was crucial.

As the weeks had proceeded, every meeting in the College was charged with the presence of God, and Samuel, with senior staff members, recalled the quality of faith that was being generated by the Holy Spirit through Rees Howells. Here was one individual just reading passages from Daniel 3, Ezra 1, Joshua 5 and 6, Acts 10 and Exodus 10, interspersed with additional comments, and each passage seeming as though it was written solely for this international situation,

"Faith inspired by the Holy Spirit will bring the same blessing as people received from being with the Lord Jesus.

"The enemy that attacked Moses when God

sent him to be the deliverer, is attacking today, when God's will is that the Holy Land should be given back to the Jews."

Such phrases made an indelible impression upon Samuel at that time.

Then, on Monday 24th November 1947 in the 9am meeting after reading Isaiah 59, Jeremiah 33 and sections from Romans 8-11, Rees Howells had declared with typical measured words,

> "Only the Holy Spirit can really carry a burden and intercede. Paul made a wonderful intercession for the nation and if we make the same intercession today we will be bound to go through."

There were further meetings that day as the motion was being considered. Would it be thrown out even at the start? One young person, Kristine, the author's wife, in the late meeting at the College that night, recalls vividly the electric atmosphere as the Holy Spirit lit up the Scriptures afresh to everyone,

> "In the first prayer meeting that evening we had prayed earnestly and believed that God's will would be done, as the motion was being discussed. In the short break after that meeting we fully expected to hear that the motion had been granted, but the radio news was not good. In the second meeting we read 2 Kings 6:8-17. The Syrian king, Benhadad had sent a host of horses and chariots to surround and kill Elisha and his servant, who became distraught with fear. Elisha prayed that the Lord would open his servant's eyes to see God's protection. The Lord did, and he saw that the mountain was full of chariots and horses of fire, which completely protected them. As Rees Howells read this passage under the anointing of the Holy Spirit, we 'saw' the hosts of God's angels surrounding the United Nations building, and knew without a shadow of doubt that God's will would be done when the votes were counted. It was no surprise, though a source of great rejoicing,

> when we listened to the radio after the meeting
> and heard that the motion had been passed."

Once more the Holy Spirit had triumphed, but there was a further step to come, with a United Nations vote to secure a two-thirds majority in favour of Israel. The voting was postponed for three days, but Rees Howells had always emphasised – and this was another truth that Samuel never forgot – that delays are never denials in the life of prayer.

There were further excursions into the Word of God, with great inspiration drawn from Deuteronomy 30, extracts from Jeremiah and Psalm 118:19-23,

> "We want to tell the Holy Spirit – You are God, move that committee tomorrow – give us that faith. It isn't in man, but it is in God. We want to put this through. We have a chance to believe today."

Here was a further lesson which Samuel learnt and later applied to his own ministry. When the Holy Spirit gives a Kingdom prayer it is always essential to be found believing God 'today,' no matter how difficult or impossible the situation may seem.

Midnight on 29th November 1947 brought the news that the United Nations Assembly had voted by thirty-three to thirteen for the partition of the land, a clear two-thirds majority. A wonderful answer to prayer. After nearly two thousand years, the nation was back in its own land and it was one of the greatest days in history, a victory for the Holy Spirit. Samuel had witnessed for himself the power of God at work in the world at the highest level, and was strengthened to the core of his being in the parallel prayer for the completion of the Vision, the Gospel to be preached throughout the world, often termed the Every Creature Commission. As with this prayer, which was not answered without a battle, some stiff contests would follow.

In some College meeting notes, later discovered in Samuel's room and obviously read by him during times of testing, were the following words of exhortation.

> Abiding. John 15:1-8. When the abiding is perfect and the connection between the Vine and the branch unhindered, we can prevail

according to God's will and get answers to our prayers. Abiding means that you allow the Holy Spirit to live in you exactly as the Saviour would live if He was on earth. While we are praying now it would be worth for every one of you to get a place of abiding every day. I used to be before Him every morning and every evening and He would tell me what He wanted me to do and it was perfect fellowship. You lose sight of everything else in His presence. Unless the Holy Spirit is in you all your prayers are guesswork and not half are answered. The simplest person can understand that unless the life runs through the Vine without a hitch, there will not be fruit. Not a single person has any excuse for prayers given by the Holy Spirit, not to be answered.

No wonder Samuel's ministry became so powerful as it was built on such a solid foundation and grew from strength to strength.

At midnight on 14th May 1948, the Provincial Government of Israel proclaimed the New State of Israel which was recognised by the United Nations. Sadly, on the 15th May there was a violent reaction from countries whose end is clearly revealed in the Scriptures.

To return to the story of Ethiopia, the country was devastated by long hard years of famine and poverty in the 1980s, but God was still at work, and when the Communist backed dictator finally fled to Zimbabwe, his successor Meles Zenawi, set up a multi-party democracy allowing steady growth in the churches. Samuel would again give himself to pray for Gerald Gotzen, who took full advantage of the country's new found freedom to arrange for consignments of Bibles, New Testaments, Christian booklets, translations of well known Christian books and children's books to be printed and distributed in the land. A wave of blessing would pass through the Orthodox Coptic fraternities, and the evangelical churches would experience remarkable growth. It would not be uncommon to find passengers reading Bibles on Ethiopian Air flights, groups reading in the streets and children, taught to read, slowly rehearsing the Gospel stories to grandparents who had never known schooling themselves.

Ethiopian Coptic Christians reading the Word of God

When Gerald was to show his video, 'Window Over Ethiopia' on the prayer room screen showing all that he had witnessed, Samuel was animated. Calling Gerald straight into his room after the service, Samuel could hardly wait to declare with such excitement,

> "What my father prophesied I have seen and witnessed today."

This was the beginning of the fulfilment of Psalm 68:31. Ethiopia was stretching out her hands to God. Gerald's life from those days has shone, as though Heaven has come down and touched him. In a letter written to a friend and supporter in October 2010 Gerald writes:

> 'The first occasion when I visited the Bible College was in the autumn of 1973. I praise the Lord for this wonderful association over many years with Mr Samuel, Dr. Kingsley Priddy, yourself and so many other beloved Christians. It was also the connection with Ethiopia and the regular support for the ministry, especially the Bibles that I received from the Bible College. I am firmly of the conviction that the Bible

College under Rees Howells and then continued by Mr Samuel and the staff in the ministry of intercession for Ethiopia, is definitely one of the main factors of the tremendous movement of revival and renewal. The seed of intercessory prayer was sown in tears of time over seventy years ago, and now we are witnessing this wonderful harvest and the Kingdom being established in Ethiopia today.'

የኢትዮጵያ መጽሐፍ ቅዱስ ማኅበር
BIBLE SOCIETY OF ETHIOPIA

Bible Society of Ethiopia in the capital, Addis Ababa

In 2007 an unexpected imprisonment in an Eritrean gaol (jail), where he met many of the persecuted Christian prisoners rejoicing in their risen Lord, would spur Gerald on to see even greater blessing. Intercession would again be in operation, and the outcome assured.

To witness heavy rains in an Ethiopian village after months of drought was another miracle. Challenged by the pagan elders as to God's existence and ability, Gerald was led to declare the authority of God over the elements. That night the heavens opened. The whole village turned to Christ. That God is at work in Ethiopia there is no doubt.

Gerald's poignant words describing Samuel, when friends gathered in the Conference Hall following Samuel's death in 2004, were that he was a gracious man who never sought the spotlight or limelight; he lived in the shadow of the cross; he had a world vision, and when you were with him you caught the vision. Here was a true, close friend of Samuel.

Chapter Twenty-Nine

Operation Desert Storm

The final decade of the century had hardly adjusted to the many changes that were taking place across the world, when ominous events clouded the Middle East once more.

On 17th July 1990, President Saddam Hussein of Iraq, accused Kuwait of oil overproduction and theft of oil from the Rumaila Oil Field and, despite United Nations' pleas to withdraw, invaded the region, seizing the oil fields there.

Samuel followed the progress of this rapidly escalating situation prayerfully, as the UN Security Council issued an ultimatum for Saddam Hussein to withdraw by 15th January 1991 or face military action. On the surface, it seemed to suggest a face-to-face conflict only, but the Lord's hand came powerfully upon Samuel and steered his attention in a different direction. Having enlarged his borders into Kuwait, Saddam was turning towards his western neighbour, Israel. Lethal Scud missile launchers, hidden in skilfully disguised bunkers, were poised to release their deadly weapons on Jerusalem.

At the College, about to enter its new term in 1991, special prayer sessions were convened to consider this crisis as the United Nations deadline approached. In a late night session on 15th January, Samuel commenced his reading from Ezra 1,

> "In the first year of Cyrus King of Persia, in order to fulfil the word of the Lord spoken by Jeremiah, the Lord moved the heart of Cyrus King of Persia to make a proclamation throughout his realm and to put it in writing."

In his typically thorough manner Samuel reminded his listeners how Isaiah had declared the Lord's word that Cyrus would be raised up in righteousness, as an instrument to perform God's purposes (Isaiah 44:28 to 45:1). Now, eighty years later, this hitherto unknown monarch, showing such a magnanimous spirit, had emerged from Media and conquered the invincible Babylonians. God's revealed will became reality through the intercessions of Ezekiel and Daniel who, like Isaiah and Jeremiah, knew the mind of God for their generation.

"They were pure instruments, there was no hindrance in the flow," continued Samuel.

As Samuel developed his ministry, those present in this late meeting sensed again that God was speaking through him, and guiding him in focussed prayer as General H. Norman Schwarzkopf, the Commander in Chief of U.S. Central Command for Operation Desert Storm, signalled the launch of a military offensive to liberate Kuwait from the Iraqi aggressor.

When the Holy Spirit came on Samuel in this distinct way, each phrase rang out from the depths of his being and gave no quarter for unbelief. He had seen the hand of God stretched out in the Communist world, following twenty-five years of intense intercession, when satanic forces had resisted stubbornly. Now there were other spiritual forces to be broken in the Middle East countries, to enable tens of millions of people to receive salvation through Christ. It was to be a work of God.

"I believe we have the mind of the Lord in these matters, as Paul mentions in 1 Corinthians 2:16 *But we have the mind of Christ*. We cannot place our weight on anything else, only on the Divine Word. How could we deal with these world matters – it is hard enough to deal with ordinary domestic matters?" he continued.

To the casual reader, some of Samuel's statements may seem presumptuous, but to those present at the time there was no doubt at all who was actually speaking; just using the voice and emotional expressions of a humble servant.

He stressed throughout 'this great crisis,' as he called it, the need for strength to believe God beforehand and, in a late prayer meeting again, on 17th January, he developed the theme he had touched on previously. As soon as the returned Jewish exiles from Babylon commenced the rebuilding of the Temple in Jerusalem, Satan came in with all his force to prevent the progress. He does that vigorously, for every phase in the development of God's plan, even today.

Quoting from Samuel's emphatic words,

"In face of what is happening, we feel that Israel is in mortal danger. What does the enemy desire to do? To destroy Israel, and in the event of destroying Israel, the Word of God will not be fulfilled. We have seen in recent meetings again that it is God's will not only to restore Israel to the land, and that constituted a great miracle, didn't it, dear friends? We remember the prayers that we offered to that effect during the war years and in those succeeding years. The faith that God gave at that time to see them, for the most part, back in the land. But Zechariah has told us what will happen in the land when God visits them, when the people are to see their Redeemer. It will be a wonderful day when the arm of the Lord will be revealed. The iniquity of that land will be removed in a single day. A Divine act – and they will repent and will be born anew as a nation. These are the ultimate purposes of the Almighty. The enemy at this time is challenging. Don't take it for granted because I tell you that prayers, even ordinary domestic prayers, sometimes baffle us. I wouldn't be honest if I told you otherwise. How many times during these past weeks we've been baffled – we've been at the end of ourselves – that is our experience. We only speak experimentally, not theoretically; we've proved it. We've gone back to God in our extremity and we have seen, not the hand of man but the hand of God, as it was manifested in the days of Haggai and Zechariah. Now there is an enemy," Samuel continued, and he was speaking very clearly, "and he is satanic and once he will see that the day is turning against him, what is the danger? He will unleash everything that he has in his armoury."

Samuel was obviously covering new ground in his intercession now, and he was totally dependent upon the Holy Spirit to inspire and lead him through,

> "We are treading a path that we've never trodden before, and we do not know exactly how much faith we require to believe these things."

Apart from the men in the Scriptures there were very few to whom Samuel could go back for inspiration in similar circumstances. He did, however recall those critical days during the war years when his father, Rees Howells, had led the College in prayer in the battle for an Allied victory on the beaches of Salerno in Italy. Historians record this as an amazing turn around in what threatened to be 'a near disaster' according to General Mark Wayne Clark, Commander of the American 5th Army, in his memoirs. The Germans were anticipating a second Dunkirk. However, at the College, prayer meeting notes (taken from when Rees Howells preached) tell a different story:

13th September 1943

> Judges 7. You leave all now and come back to this battle. Don't allow yourselves to be slack. Every second of the day this is on me. There is not one thing we are doing here tonight that will count much in Italy, only what we are doing by way of the Throne. When a man fights you know how he fights. Every Nazi tonight fights for his life. It is the most fierce battle that has ever been. You feel tonight that you are afraid of the next news. Don't you put importance now on anything, only on this one. In a fight there are laws where God doesn't feel it right to intervene until a man gets to his extremity v35. England and America are only fighting for one thing – the end of the Nazis. If you are of value to God in this He will keep you here as an intercessor, otherwise He will put you where you will carry more of a burden. We must pray now as we did when we were nearly invaded.

14th September 1943
Daniel 5. We are running into a greater test now than ever before – the Spirit witnesses this in me – and there will be no refuge only in the Holy Spirit. I am not fighting with small or great, only with the enemy over there. I have died to everything the world can offer; I have seen men as men and God as God. The prophets were not shallow men.

7pm meeting
1 Kings 20. Hitler and his troops have gained more ground and our troops have been told to prepare to re-embark. Benhadad sent that challenge and God heard it. Are we going to reclaim? Does God hear the challenge tonight? Remember you all have a chance to take part in this battle. The last time we fought like this was for Stalingrad and what a victory that was. We don't want to retreat and we don't want thousands of our young men to be killed. After Alexandria and Stalingrad we can stop the enemy tonight. The next thing is to be the Divine intervention. You must always fight where the Holy Spirit is fighting.

10pm meeting
1 Samuel 14. The Allied soldiers are fighting for the doom of the Nazis. I would be sorry to find that they have put more time into it there, than I am doing here. The Germans are much stronger but we read in the Scriptures that one man, Jonathan and his armour bearer got through. Tell the Lord tonight, *There is no restraint to the Lord to save by many or by few.* 1 Samuel 14:6 (AV). Have we the faith tonight that this man had? His faith is most perfect.

Samuel spoke of those wartime battles in private talks with his closest staff friends and it was obvious that they had made an indelible mark upon his spirit. They helped him find strength to press the spiritual battle to its end in this 1991 challenge, although every step forward required Divine inspiration.

Speaking from the pulpit Samuel reminded those present in the prayer meetings,

> "A real burden descended upon us when we prayed during the war years, and God worked and preserved the Jewish Nation when it was facing annihilation in the gas chambers."

Rees Howells in the summer of 1949 (approximately six months before his promotion to glory) aged by his intense intercessions during World War II and beyond.

He recalled how he would slip quietly into Rees Howells' room at that time and find him slumped and exhausted in his armchair, as pale as death and bathed in perspiration, such was the agony he was experiencing as he carried the intercession. It eventually broke him physically, as up till then he was such a strong person with incredible stamina. Yet whenever Samuel had asked him if it was worth carrying such a burden, or whether he was all right, his answer was invariably that he was perfectly fine.

"Couldn't be better," he would say.

Now Samuel was locked in a similar spiritual conflict with the powers of darkness. It was not to be a general prayer, however. Those in the meetings were asked to consider placing their lives in the prayer, to allow the Holy Spirit to deal with any part of their lives. Samuel was deeply concerned too for the ordinary people who would be caught up on the ground, and for the many young men flying dangerous missions in the air in over 110,000 sorties, and who would be facing death. Then there were the innocent civilians invariably caught up in these carnages of war. He solicited earnest prayer for them all, with the same sincerity and passion as we would like people to plead for us if we were facing similar conditions. It was in these situations that the real Samuel emerged from his seemingly distant, even cold and hard image perceived by many who were still not allowed to draw close to him, such was his shyness.

He reminded everyone how, during the twenty-five year intercession for the demise of Communism in Eastern Europe and Russia, it had meant a day in, day out involvement. The evil spiritual forces behind the scenes had to be bound, and only the Holy Spirit could do that, but the blessing that ensued across Siberia and the northern regions was beyond imagination. Earl Poysti had sent him a letter describing a recent visit when he found revival blessing wherever he went in areas once known only for their oppression. Then, in a powerful prophetic utterance from within, Samuel spoke again,

> "We firmly believe that through the agency of the Holy Spirit that power is to be manifested again in the Middle East," rang out across the

room. "We are not praying in a fog; the Word of God will never fail."

It was certainly a Kingdom battle and many participated in it during the following weeks and months. When these opportunities are given by the Holy Spirit to enter into Kingdom intercessions, personal response is very important and it is relatively easy to discern those who are 'in' and those who are not, even in a Christian community. How essential it is for the believer to be walking daily in fellowship with the risen and glorified Lord Jesus Christ through the ministry of the Holy Spirit. There were those in the Founder's day, Samuel recalled, who had been asked to leave the College for not showing interest or response in these vital spiritual exercises.

The prayer deepened in the lives of those who were responding, and Samuel set some very pressing domestic prayers aside as he reached out to God for the faith required to see God's purposes fulfilled. Great strength was drawn through considering how God had worked in order to breakthrough the barriers necessary to introduce the Gospel to the Gentile world. God had prepared Saul of Tarsus from his mother's womb (Galatians 1:15). When Stephen, no doubt a fellow student from the synagogue of the Freedmen, was martyred, the arrows of conviction had struck home into Saul's heart. His passions roused, Saul wrought havoc on the church, but he was broken by the revelation of the risen Christ outside Damascus, and was transformed and commissioned. The door was finally opened through Peter's visit to Cornelius, but God broke through. It was all beyond human comprehension.

"God will work again in that way," declared Samuel, "and we can never tell who He is preparing at this time."

Into the New Year of 1991 and the return of students for another term of preparation for Christian service. Samuel exhorted them to follow the prayer diligently and God would bless them. As always, he urged them not to pray 'stray prayers' – that is, their own ideas, but what God was giving through the ministry. Stray prayers weaken a prayer meeting and should be discouraged, but you must be importunate, persistent, explicit and direct. During the

Christmas break he had spent protracted periods in God's presence and came out with 'all guns firing!' Powerful ministry from Exodus showed the faith that Moses exercised to see the children of Israel through the Red Sea when the waters were 'torn apart,' and then into the book of Numbers, sometimes referred to as the 'Book of Murmurings and Complaints.' Unbelief completely ruined the wonderful opportunity the people were given to enter the Promised Land at Kadesh Barnea. It was theirs, and God promised He would defeat every enemy who opposed them. Sadly only two, Joshua and Caleb, believed God but had to experience the pain of turning back and wandering for forty years in the wilderness. It was a failure to believe the covenant given to Abraham that resulted in such a tragedy. Now, at the College, everyone was being asked to believe the covenant given by the Lord Jesus for blessing the nations. In reality, it is not an easy thing to do, only with the help of the Holy Spirit, but if we show any tendency to believe God He will make up for every deficiency.

On the ground, Iraq responded by creating a massive oil slick in the Gulf of Arabia, and ignited seven hundred oil wells in Kuwait, as a combined military force began an assault on 24th February 1991 to liberate Kuwait.

In a further declaration of faith on 11th March 1991, clutching the pulpit firmly, Samuel spoke these prophetic words,

> "We are convinced that the time has come for the Lord Jesus Christ, who has died for mankind, to be uplifted not in some parts of the world, but in all parts. *He shall see the travail of His soul, and shall be satisfied.* Isaiah 53:11 (AV). There will be no rivals to the peerless Son of God. Abraham's covenant is still valid and also the covenant that God has made with His Son. In the validity of that covenant we are believing tonight and basing our full and entire confidence in it."

Further excursions were made into the life and ministry of Joshua, before the College reverted to its normal programme. God dealt so graciously with Joshua, when he succeeded Moses, and no doubt Samuel could empathise with his feelings, having faced a similar challenge himself when Rees Howells completed his earthly ministry in 1950. Joshua was led into the realm of the supernatural where the faith of God operates. The costly prayer for the Communist world had drawn a cry from the intercessor as he had been identified with hundreds and thousands of suffering saints, all of whose cries had not gone unnoticed by the covenant-keeping God. Now the Holy Spirit was broadening the challenge and Samuel was not to be deflected by lesser issues,

"We have all got a long way to go," he added.

"We haven't exercised the faith that Joshua exercised that day," (referring to the miraculous crossing of the River Jordan) "no, not one of us. It was the faith of God."

With the end of the financial year looming, the domestic pressures were mounting, and Satan was telling Samuel all the time to neglect praying these Kingdom prayers and attend to the financial needs.[1] This was pressure that few of us have experienced, but Samuel reiterated the truth that it is easy to be deflected, but he had persisted. Then, in one late evening meeting he paused,

"There have been some wonderful deliverances this week. We have never appealed to anybody, our minds have been engaged in prayers of the Kingdom. The week is not complete; there will be more deliverances on the way."

God was fulfilling the promise:

Seek ye first the Kingdom of God, and His righteousness and all these things shall be added unto you. Matthew 6:33 (AV).

As staff and students stood with Samuel, the believing of God would descend in the services, with the assurance that God had everything in hand. Hostilities were formally brought to an end on 28th February 1991 and cease-fire terms negotiated on 1st March, but these were not officially accepted until 6th April. Operation Desert Storm had liberated Kuwait, but a deeper spiritual conflict had resulted in a more significant victory for the Kingdom of God. How was this victory gained, we might ask? But this was not the end. There were other spiritual goals in Samuel's mind and he was prepared to do whatever was necessary to see them established in the world.

One of the significant revelations given to Rees Howells, was what came to be known in the College as 'The revelation of the blood-washed continent.' It was revealed as Europe was experiencing its darkest moment in history when Adolph Hitler had invaded most of Europe and held further evil intentions in his mind. Rees Howells had predicted that Hitler would not invade Britain, but the spiritual battle was intense and history records how slender was the cord that held things together. The war continued longer than anyone anticipated, but Rees Howells never once doubted its final outcome. Europe one day, he declared, would experience a spiritual awakening when its citizens would once again know the cleansing that the precious blood of Christ could give to all who call upon his name.[2] Hence the name, blood-washed continent. It would not necessarily take place in times of affluence or abundance, but possibly when persecution and oppression brought despair to the nations, but it would come.

Samuel often referred to it and prayed much for every development across Europe, particularly since 1957 when the Treaty of Rome was signed and the concept of the Common Market grew. Then, in 1992, the Maastricht Treaty was signed and Britain was really committed to a closer link with Europe. When Queen Elizabeth II and Francois Mitterand officially opened the Channel Tunnel on 6th May 1994, and the Eurostar (Le Shuttle) commenced its regular trips beneath the English Channel, a permanent bond with Europe was forged. By the turn of the century, even the Euro currency would link most of the mainland European countries.

As with his father, Samuel could read the spiritual significance of all that was taking place, and it all placed an urgency upon his spirit which drove him further and deeper into the costly realm of intercession.

Chapter Thirty

New Developments

Throughout this period of the 1990s, Samuel remained focused on his world ministry and endeavoured to send support gifts, backed by his prayers, when he was able. He greatly appreciated the new young staff members, mostly former students, who were seeking to work alongside him during difficult days. He prayed for them. He was reminded of the time when Ezra requested permission from Artaxerxes, King of Persia, to return to join the Jews who had already resettled in Jerusalem (Ezra 7 and 8). Permission was granted, and also for others of the young generation who were of their own freewill determined to go up, and ample gold and silver was loaded into their hands. Before starting the journey together they prayed and, as Ezra had assured Artaxerxes that the hand of their God was upon them for good, he was ashamed to ask for any military protection en route.

There is an interesting story told by one of the former students (let's call him David) from this decade, which illustrates just how the Lord had conditioned Samuel to cope with the mounting pressures of the day. David was on security duty one evening when the telephone rang. He had promised to transfer the call but became terribly confused with the system, especially as Samuel arrived on the scene to answer the call as well. David was desperate and explained his problem to Samuel who sought to assure him that it was not the end of the world.

> "Don't worry, David," he said, "I've given up worrying about anything. All I have is my Bible and the quietness of my room and that is enough."

In telling this story years later, David himself was severely tested and could appreciate the depth of that advice. David, recalling difficult years in his own childhood was then prompted to inquire, "Mr Samuel, did you miss your parents very much?"

Many have wanted to know the answer to this very poignant and personal question, realising that Samuel's childhood must have been very confusing, to say the least, no matter how much love and attention was showered on him by his foster parents, Moses and Elizabeth Rees from Glanaman.

Lizzie Howells 1965

"Well," Samuel thoughtfully replied after a moment's pause, and then continued to explain that, as a child, he had never felt close to his real father but missed his mother dearly. He was deeply attached to her, especially as she had maintained a regular postal contact with him and, in later life, when Rees Howells had died, Samuel appreciated his mother's sterling support in the College. He had finally spent many long hours with her when she was confined to her room right up to her death on 9th August 1972.

An unusual event occurred in late August 1994, which deserves mention. For several days, staff and students were suddenly alerted to the presence of police with sniffer dogs visiting every room and corridor in the College. A mixture of excitement and apprehension filled the air. Then came the announcement of a visit from Dr. Ian Paisley, who would be in the district to open two churches in the locality, one in Pisgah, the "home" chapel of Evan Roberts the revivalist, in Loughor, which he built before the revival of 1904.[1] Dr. Paisley, this colourful and often controversial figure from Northern Ireland, had been the Democratic Unionist Party representative in Parliament since 1970, but was also the founding member and elected moderator of the Free Presbyterian Church in Ulster. The son of an Independent Baptist minister and with three of his five children in the ministry, Dr. Paisley was a real family man with a deep understanding of the fractious situation in Ulster, so he had much to share with Samuel during the time available. Samuel welcomed his distinguished guest and his wife, Eileen, and they were ushered in to the front drawing room with its glass chandeliers and best china tea service, while the police chauffeur was provided for next door with a selection of similar iced cakes and shortbreads.

Samuel sat back and enjoyed the conversation as Dr. Paisley relished the congenial atmosphere and was as free as a bird, his sonorous tones filling the room. Dr. Paisley had been trained originally in Barry Bible College, with its slightly different practical and doctrinal emphasis, but those issues would never cast any shadows over the great fellowship that these two very different figures were enjoying in the Lord Jesus Christ. The visit ended all too quickly with handshakes and farewells, but not without Dr. Paisley commenting about his accompanying police officer who had found faith in Jesus. "Law and Grace met together!" laughed Dr. Paisley as the limousine glided off down the drive.

It was not always easy for new students arriving at the College to identify immediately everyone on the campus, particularly as the older members only seemed to appear in the evening and Sunday morning services in the prayer room. Many, by this time, preferred one particular seat, earmarked with a special cushion, so that newcomers were cautioned not to occupy those prime positions!

On one occasion, in 1999, Samuel was returning from his afternoon prayer walk and, in order not to draw attention to himself, took a route via a side gate and crossed the lawns through the flower gardens. In a respectful approach to an elderly gentleman, characteristic of the country from which he came, a new overseas student stopped to speak to this 'unknown visitor' to the College. Inquiring as to the age of this gentleman and what he was doing, he evoked a friendly response and, with a twinkle in his eye, the stranger answered the student's last question, "What is your name?" It took several days for the student to recover!

Looking back over his shoulder, as he was for a brief moment in the year 2000, Samuel could trace the good hand of the Lord upon his fifty years of ministry, and would have been ashamed, just as Ezra had been, to ask for any protection other than that provided by God Himself. Those years had certainly not proved plain sailing, but God had remained faithful to His promises in a big way. For many this would be an ideal opportunity for a biblical Jubilee away from the onerous responsibilities that he still carried at the age of eighty-seven years, but he settled for a modest celebration in the prayer room of Derwen Fawr House, where staff and students gathered informally to sing and pray, and enjoy cups of tea and a slice cut from a special iced, and suitably decorated, celebration cake. Anything more elaborate would have seemed incongruous and Samuel thoroughly enjoyed it. Photographs were taken, some with him holding one of the seven handwritten Bibles that Joan Rush specialised in producing during her morning Quiet Times with the Lord. It was artistically inscribed on the flyleaf, and is still a constant reminder of Samuel's love for the Word of God and his passion to see it distributed throughout the world.[2]

**Fifty years as Honorary Director celebrated, February 2000
Samuel receives a handwritten Bible from Joan Rush**

As Samuel grew older, it was interesting to note how Samuel's attitude changed towards having his photograph taken. During the earlier years of his life and ministry he seemed uncomfortable and even embarrassed, but later in life whenever visitors requested an opportunity to be 'snapped' alongside him he took it in his stride and rather enjoyed it. Across the world today there must be many memorable shots of him, hidden in personal albums.

During this period, Samuel's physical health was showing the impact of long years on the 'spiritual battleground.' Summer months intensified his hay fever and a fresh irritant, eczema, on his pale skin found him often without a tie and wearing an open necked shirt –

quite uncharacteristic! Even shoes for walking became unbearable sometimes.

Samuel Howells with Richard Maton. Richard is holding the handwritten Bible, which took nearly three years to complete

Always friendly, always encouraging always grateful for kindnesses shown to him, Samuel would quietly appear anywhere in the main Derwen Fawr building, curious to know what was happening and wrapped in one of his long warm dressing gowns over several further layers beneath. Students often puzzled why Mr Samuel was always wearing his slippers throughout the day, except on Sundays or when in the prayer meetings. Few people ever realised that his suffering was quite acute at times. Never a hint of complaint ever passed his lips, just adoration and praise for his wonderful Saviour and Lord. A cataract operation on his left eye restricted his ministry for a while. Samuel had several short stays in Swansea's Singleton Hospital, where he earned the reputation of being a model patient and was much loved by all the nurses. Whenever he visited a hospital, either for treatment or for admission, he was in prayer for the other patients whom he considered far worse than himself, and they soon became aware of the inner presence that he carried with him. He was always full of praise for the dedication and commitment of the consultants, doctors and nurses who treated him with such respect. Although of a quiet disposition, he was never one to refrain from speaking a word for the Lord when the opportunity arose.

Young men staff, affectionately called 'my boys' by Samuel helped him on several occasions when needed and he adapted his style of pulpit ministry, condensing what would have previous needed several sessions into one meeting only. The indelible lesson, permanently etched upon the spirits of staff and students who were in those meetings, has been that the pure reading of Scripture alone under the anointing of the Holy Spirit is far more effective than hours of hermeneutically correct sermons seeking to explain the meaning of the text depending on scholarship alone.

This point was exemplified on an occasion when a visitor arrived at the College one August weekend and was given the opportunity to share his testimony in the Sunday morning service. A complete tearaway and rebel as a child, he soon ended up as a habitual jailbird and reject from society, beyond redemption. Prison was his life. Remembering a Bible his mother had given him, he read it through, over and over again to no effect; it simply had no meaning for him. The visitor then reminded us that a baby takes milk from its mother's breast day in and day out, without understanding why, or what it is made of, but it is necessary for growth and the baby knows instinctively where to go. Similarly the Scriptures teach us that the Word of God is like milk and through drinking it we can grow.

> Like newborn babes, crave pure spiritual milk,
> so that by it you may grow up in your salvation.
> 1 Peter 2:2.

The College visitor shared how, one day, the Holy Spirit quickened the Word that he had been drinking for weeks and he was dramatically changed. His present ministry, having gained confidence from prison governors all over the world, was to stand in the exercise yards of gaols when high-risk prisoners took their daily exercise and simply read aloud the Scriptures, with no comments. Results were phenomenal as the Holy Spirit drew the prisoners together to listen and many were being saved as a result.

Samuel was equally confident that what people needed most in the world was the Word of God, not sermons, so he pressed forward, despite his frailty and the buffetings that he was experiencing on every hand, to send gifts to agencies and individuals around the world who were involved in taking the Scriptures, 'Bread of Life,' to the people.

A series of falls produced by sudden shifts in Samuel's blood pressure caused him to black out, often with dangerous consequences as he struck his head somewhere. It was obvious to everyone that realistic preparations were required for the future.[3]

New trustees were then appointed including Alan Scotland.[4] In Alan's own testimony, he recalls a time when, standing alone in the College library in the late 1980s, the Lord drew very near and planted a witness in his heart that the day would come when he would be entrusted with the responsibility of the College. This he kept hidden for many years until Samuel, while he was sitting one day with Alan quietly in the car near the 'bridge' on the Black Mountain, asked him if he felt God was speaking to him about anything. Alan was able to share those deep spiritual issues and Samuel responded warmly to them.[5]

Tentative plans were drawn up for the possible upgrading and use of existing College buildings. Student life too, was enhanced by younger staff leadership and a lively student evangelistic outreach in Swansea, developed.[6] It gave Samuel much joy to see the younger generation being actively engaged in this way.

Being responsible for a registered Charity, Samuel and his trustees had to always show due diligence in their management of College affairs. This included their financial resources. The concept of faith would not easily fit into rules and regulations governing charities being introduced. The Holy Spirit must guide them again. They were led initially, by making a small secure loan offering very favourable returns. The results earned the Charity Commissions approval.

In 1996-7, Samuel and his trustees had approached a

local surveyor for the sale of the School playing fields at Glynderwen for housing development. The principle of selling off superfluous land was not new to Samuel who had previously sold a large plot in front of Derwen Fawr property for development in order to contribute towards the £100,000 ($160,000) which he had promised his father he would raise. The idea was floated on the property market and six of the major housing developers were interested. Eventually it was felt that retail development would prove the best option. Samuel was faced with a difficult decision requiring more than a mere nod of approval; the sale of Glynderwen Estate, the first property bought by 'raw' faith in 1924 for the establishment of the Bible College. Was that great landmark of faith to be sold? It was clear however, that the old buildings required large sums of money to upgrade and maintain. As was his custom when faced with complicated issues such as this, his only response when presented with these suggestions, which had taken long hours to think through and prepare, was, "We'll see!" This was Samuel's way of saying, "I am not really keen on the idea at all, but I will consider it prayerfully."

Also on the agenda was the urgent need to update Derwen Fawr and Sketty Isaf properties. This would also prove very expensive. Would this be wise stewardship of the Lord's resources when the burden to supply millions of Bibles to the world pressed heavily upon Samuel's heart?

A new chapter was about to commence!

Entrance to Derwen Fawr Estate c.1940, bungalow and hospital (left); the two stone pillars were later removed

Chapter Thirty-One

The Achilles Heel

In ancient Greece, folk stories and legends were collected into two famous books, the *Iliad* and *Odyssey*, written by Homer. One great fictitious hero was Achilles, whose heel was the only unprotected part of his body. In the battle of Troy, a poisonous arrow entered his heel killing him instantly. Some story! To this day, any vulnerable part of a person's character is known as their 'Achilles heel.'

In any individual's walk with God, particularly someone vitally involved in affairs and interests of the Kingdom of God, Satan will always search out and seek to penetrate vulnerable areas in that person's life. It was certainly so in Samuel's life as we shall endeavour to illustrate.

Throughout his years, Samuel had always remained very reserved, and the added personal attacks upon his character and the work he represented, familiar to all Christian leaders, made him extremely cautious. He rarely contributed in a round the table business discussion or expressed his opinions, but preferred to speak to people on an individual basis in private. No doubt in Samuel's mind it was the application of the principle of Matthew 6:3 (AV).

Let not thy left hand know what thy right hand doeth.

Realising his age and considering the future role of the College carefully, Samuel made detailed preparations to ensure that it could continue and that the world ministry which he had built up over the years would be safe. Writing to a solicitor, skilled in charity law, he explained that he was convinced in his spirit that the ministry must be established for the very near future. There was a job to be done and much had been sacrificed to prepare for its undertaking. Nothing that could be avoided should be allowed to compromise the work. Samuel was now prepared to sell the Glynderwen Estate, this monument of faith. How could it happen, everyone thought. Unbelievable! It was a bitter decision for everyone concerned, especially the residents of Glynderwen, some of them who had lived there for over fifty years.

Schoolchildren of Emmanuel Grammar School on the Glynderwen Estate c.1955. Slope (back left) is the main entrance to the school with end section of El-Shaddai building (back right). Edge of photo (right) is Glynderwen House showing archway to the front door.

However, Samuel's vision encompassed a whole world and not just a College. He shared very little other than with his trustees and with their full support, he wrote to his solicitor that once the Glynderwen Estate had been transferred (to a newly set up Christian trust), the Sketty Isaf and Derwen Fawr Estates would follow and he reaffirmed his commitment to this. He was totally convinced that God would bless the world ministry and his present transactions with Him would one day release much money for the Kingdom. The door to Heaven's treasury was open for financing the Vision to complete the Matthew 28 Great Commission. After some intense bargaining, a substantial agreed price was reached for the development of

Glynderwen, and the College of the Derwen Fawr Estate would continue in perpetuity, as long as it was needed. The heavy burden resting upon Samuel would be removed.

Samuel measured this proposal very prayerfully and in the light of the cross. He was facing laying fifty years of costly ministry on the 'altar' just as his father had done when he was prepared to sell Glynderwen, Derwen Fawr and Sketty Isaf Estates in May 1939 to release £100,000 ($160,000) to take care of more than one thousand Jewish refugee children.[1] The 'altar' is an expression used throughout the Scriptures referring to the practice used by individuals wishing to show their allegiance to God through burning the pieces of slaughtered animals on an altar. It meant death to the animal, its blood being collected as evidence, and smoke rising from the pyre represented the true worship of the individual ascending to God. The animal was always in perfect condition so proved a costly sacrifice for the offerer.

Abraham was asked to sacrifice his son Isaac to demonstrate his devotion to God, believing that the Lord could raise him from the dead to perpetuate the covenant promises given earlier in his life, no matter how difficult that would prove to be. The New Testament parallel for this truth is demonstrated when God leads Christians to allow certain areas of their lives to be permanently forsaken. As a sacrificial offering they are set to one side, never to be owned again. They are symbolically laid on an 'altar' and the equivalent of death is experienced. In Romans 12:1 Paul refers to this process.

> Therefore, I urge you brothers, in view of God's mercy, to offer your bodies as living sacrifices, holy and pleasing to God – this is your spiritual act of worship.

In the lives of believers, it takes place in stages as they seek to worship God in obedience to His will. Samuel, at the high point of his ministry, was truly walking a deep path.

With the full approval of his trustees, Samuel proceeded, and a legal transfer document was carefully worded so that, in perpetuity, the Bible College only would derive the full benefit and use of the assets for as long as it needed it. Before taking this step Samuel wrote to his solicitor along these lines: 'I want to know that I am legally correct and beyond reproach, before taking this step.' The reply was in the affirmative.

Samuel Howells at the grave of his parents 1973

Now, in the College prayer meetings, Samuel was reading through the story of Abraham, through whom the covenant promises were given for the blessing of the world through a 'seed' – who would be Jesus Christ, the Son of God – and a land for a nation to dwell in, as recorded in Genesis 17-18. Following further visitations from God, when Abram and Sarai's natures were changed radically (as indicated by their change of names to Abraham and Sarah) Isaac was supernaturally born, when Abraham was one hundred years old and Sarah, ninety (Genesis 17:17). It was then that Abraham was asked to worship the Lord on Mount Moriah and to offer a sacrifice. That sacrifice was to be his only son, Isaac (Genesis 22:2). Abraham was challenged on a particular personal issue concerning his belief in the resurrection, Hebrews 11:8-18.

> *Stay here with the donkey while I and the boy go over there. We will worship and then we will come back to you.* Genesis 22:5.

This is a truth easily discussed among Christians, but often a problem when we are asked to lay aside important sections of our lives, our family and friends, our health, our homes, our possessions, our gifts, our ambitions. To us, it is the end!

Samuel had often ministered from this passage of Scripture with great solemnity, pointing out that true worship must always carry with it the element of costly sacrifice. He would point out that lip service does not impress God at all, but rather what is going on in our lives. He would remind the College that the Saviour laid down the conditions for service very clearly.

> *If any man will come after Me, let him deny himself, and take up his cross and follow Me.*
> Matthew 16:24 (AV).

A solemn hush rested over the prayer room one evening as Samuel finished reading the story of Abraham's steady climb up Mt. Moriah. With measured step and eyes fixed on the summit, the father of the faith sought strength from God. There was little said, as Isaac followed in obedience and helped to erect the stone altar and collect wood. The crucial moment of truth arrived for Abraham to explain the nature of the sacrifice. Isaac showed his true spirituality, bowed his head in total submission to his father's will and was bound to the altar. With perspiration pouring from his brow, Abraham raised the knife ready to plunge it into his only son's breast. To believe the resurrection in truth is a costly process.

> "Today," Samuel pronounced to the group in the College prayer room, "I have placed the whole of the properties and the work here, on the altar. It is all entirely in God's hands now."

That very sacred transaction marked a pinnacle in Samuel's walk with his God. It has also secured the future of the essential ministry to the world in line with the Vision, just as Abraham's obedience secured the blessing of the world through the Promised Seed.

Samuel's secrecy (in the process of working with the new Christian trust), provoked much speculation among his critics. False accusations were made against him and it took some damaging years before they could be conclusively disproved. A seemingly reclusive nature and the difficulties with which he shared with others proved to be his Achilles heel. But that was not to be the end. Although Satan is very skilled and ruthless in his activities he never, being only a created yet fallen and rebellious servant angel, can outwit the mastery of the Holy Spirit. Samuel was God's servant and the Holy Spirit was completely in control.

In his typically ruthless manner, Satan unleashed a series of schemes in a determined effort to destroy the Lord's work as it had developed over the years through Samuel's ministry.

It was not a case of frustrating the progress of a Bible College because there were other similar colleges throughout the world that provided excellent training for students wishing to be prepared for Christian service. These attacks were designed to block the ministry of prayer and practical support directed towards Christians working in many countries around the world. Some were former students, others were nationals in difficult areas hostile to the Gospel, and many were nationals involved with agencies distributing the Scriptures where they were desperately needed. Manipulating ordinary people and officials as pawns, Satan used every means possible to paint a convincing but completely false picture of what Samuel was actually doing, and Satan appeared to be having great success.

However, the strength of Samuel's position lay in the fact that he had already relinquished every hold he had on the ministry in his personal climb to the summit of his spiritual Moriah. Everything was now totally in God's hands and nothing could touch it. It is always a very important lesson for Christians to learn that, until everything is totally surrendered into God's hands, there is always room for Satan to work. He is no gentleman and will trample over everything to obtain his ends. However, he has no new tricks and is no match for the Holy Spirit who is the Master every time.

Samuel often recounted an illustration of this point told by his father, Rees Howells.

A desert nomad bought a tent but the old owner insisted that he retained one small peg on the pole in the centre of the tent in case he ever passed that way again. This condition seemed harmless enough and appeared so for a whole year as there was no sign of the old owner. Then one day while the desert nomad was with his family in their spacious tent, with carpets down and everything comfortable inside, the old owner called in and politely asked if he could hang his coat on the peg which was his on the tent pole, while he was in the district. That seemed harmless enough. The following week the old owner called again, requesting more baggage to be attached to the peg. Each week for the next month more was added and the tent was filling up with items hanging from the one peg. Finally, the old owner popped his head through the tent flap once more, and led in a camel which was then tethered to the peg. The new owner remonstrated angrily, "What are you doing? This is my tent." Back came the reply, "Ah, but it is my peg." By the end of the following week the tent was full of ill-tempered camels all tethered to the peg. They trampled over everything in the tent as the old owner tethered them to his peg on the centre pole, eventually forcing the desert nomad and his family to leave in disgust. This is exactly what Satan will endeavour to do in the life of any person who is not totally surrendered to God. He will trample over everything sacred to reach the unsurrendered property which still remains his.

Satan would find nothing in Samuel's ministry, now totally surrendered to God, for him to destroy and Samuel rested in that safe position. There was no room for camels!

Then there followed a protracted period when the

Charity Commission examined every aspect of the Bible College affairs (they have the right to monitor all its registered charities) and discussed everything in-depth with the trustees. It was then that Samuel found strength in some of Rees Howells' potent sayings,

> "The Holy Spirit does not know doubt, misery or worry, these are of self...Unless we believe in a test we have never believed...If I only take a thought that the Devil is stronger than the Holy Spirit I can close this Book (the Bible) once and for all."

The future of the ministry to the world was already secured as Samuel placed his total confidence, not in man's efforts but upon the Person of the Holy Spirit, whom Jesus had sent into the world to complete the work, and there was no doubting that.

Samuel Howells (left) with his good friend and trustee Norman Grubb c.1975. Norman Grubb had special fellowship with Rees Howells (whom he first met at the Keswick Conference, England in 1928) and Samuel Howells. Norman and Samuel (alongside other BCW staff members) worked on *Rees Howells Intercessor* (1952) together.

Chapter Thirty-Two

Handing Over the Baton

The Charity Commission was concerned that the new Christian trust was not suitable and the process had to be reversed. Negotiations for the sale of the Glynderwen Estate had to begin again. They also recommended an improved method of management of College finances, to solve accountancy problems. The College was already implementing these. With all in order, the Charity Commission was now satisfied with BCW's affairs. By this time, younger trustees were in place who would take everything forward into the twenty-first century. Among these was Alan Scotland[1] who, since his student days in the College had shown himself very responsive to the Lord's dealings in his life, and was prepared to shoulder different responsibilities involving unpopularity. He had related well with Samuel, who was pleased to welcome him as a staff member while Betty, Alan's wife, completed her Bible College course as a student. Samuel had prayed much for him as he developed the student evangelistic outreach in Swansea (beginning in 1971) and exercised a fruitful ministry in the local churches and chapels up and down the Welsh valleys. Now, with years of hard experience under his belt and a clear appreciation of the Lord's Great Commission for His followers to make disciples of all nations, he stood alongside Samuel to encourage and assist in any practical way that he could.

Samuel had conveyed to Alan, as he had to so many of the young men and women who sat under his ministry, the burden to see the Vision completed, given to Rees Howells on Boxing Day, 26th December 1934. The College was to remain a House of Prayer for all nations as it had been intended. Although Samuel was never convinced that the student training should necessarily continue in the form that had developed, prayer was the essential, together with providing practical support for those being prayed for. Samuel was assured in his spirit that Alan should be the appointed person to take the work forward into the twenty-first century, and this appointment was readily accepted by those who were to remain.

Remembering his own beginnings half a century before, Samuel knew that he had been far from the finished article then, and much 'honing' had been required. He would often refer to Jesus' teaching, known as the Sermon on the Mount, when the Kingdom laws were spelled out clearly for those who wished to follow the Lord. "Only the Holy Spirit can live these out through an individual," he would say and point out how ridiculous it would be, as in Matthew 7:1-5, if someone endeavoured to correct the sight of someone else while having a major impediment in his own sight. How spiritually blind people are when they criticise and pass judgement upon others, when they have never embraced for themselves similar responsibilities on the same terms as those they are judging.

As long as he had the strength to do so, Samuel would continue to appear at the pulpit, although his delivery was much slower and, with fewer additional comments, he would read the Scriptures under the Holy Spirit's anointing. Probably his last public service was on Boxing Day morning in 2002, when he followed the Christmas story, stressing again the greatness of the virgin birth and the essential need these days to emulate the believing of Mary in the face of impossibilities. Concluding his hour-long ministry, interspersed with suitable chosen carols, he read excerpts from chapter 30 of *Rees Howells Intercessor*, entitled 'The Every Creature Commission,' when the Vision for the Gospel to be taken to the ends of the earth was given to the Founder in 1934, sixty-eight years previously to the day. Then, with a final public declaration of faith he closed,

> "We believe in the fulfilment of this Great Commission more than we have ever done. The Holy Spirit will be poured out on all flesh. There may have been unexpected delays, but there is not a shadow of doubt in our minds; God will intervene."

Samuel never lost that passion which, by the strength of the Holy Spirit, had brought him through the severest of trials to a place of unassailable faith and confidence in God's revealed will for the future of this age.

At the College, there would obviously be outward changes as there had been since the foundation of the work. It was time to reassess the educational programme of the College to meet the ever changing demands even within the Church. The trustees voted unanimously for Alan to become the Chairman of the Charity and with Samuel's wholehearted blessing, the new Director.[2] He already had experience with Bible College ministry elsewhere and could immediately draw upon qualified lecturers from across the world to provide a similar teaching programme. Samuel was assured that there would be as smooth a development of the course as possible.

The new staff who joined the work came in, from various corners of the United Kingdom, with very deep commitments and a close walk with the Lord. There was also a depth of experience and gifting. The seeding of the nations was their goal, and a warm spirit of love and unity prevailed.

Samuel, in his enforced retirement at ninety years of age, was cared for most admirably by Les Johnson and other kind friends. He was given a large room in Sketty Isaf building – Room 8, a much sought after room by visiting speakers, and the once retirement quarters for Dr. Kingsley Priddy – now equipped with Samuel's favourite comfortable chair and a large television to provide him with the six o' clock evening news. Meals were served in his room as usual, at a table providing him with an excellent view of the trees and grass outside. Late at night, other residents in the building would hear him parading the large landing outside, on his nightly prayer vigil, sometimes with his lately acquired Zimmer frame. He enjoyed the early morning bird song, and the changing colours of the trees in each season, and he spoke often of the Lord to his many visitors.

Physically, life became gradually more and more wearisome for Samuel, but he remained very alert mentally and with complete understanding of all that he discussed.

Interestingly, Samuel very rarely spoke about his death, most probably because he knew that, for the true believer through the completed atoning work of Christ on the cross, there is no death. Obviously, there is the step forward out of an ageing body into eternity, but for one who had been living in eternity for many years that was a very small step. He was also totally convinced that the Holy Spirit, who had led Rees Howells in 1924 and then enabled Samuel himself to negotiate many fierce spiritual storms, would also guide perfectly in the future and complete the Vision, as it involved the covenant purposes of God. Any future arrangements for a funeral service were left entirely in the hands of the staff who were already managing the College.

Samuel's health gradually deteriorated in March 2004 so he was admitted to Singleton Hospital, Swansea where he stayed for several days, seeing close friends before finally falling into a deep coma from which he never recovered. He finally fell asleep in Christ early on Thursday, 18th March 2004, aged ninety-one years.

On Wednesday afternoon of the 31st March 2004, a simple Service of Thanksgiving was held in the Conference Hall. Gordon Williamson, Dean of Students, welcomed two hundred friends who joined Samuel's cousins, Allan Howells and Professor Howard Evans and their families to sing two of Samuel's favourite hymns, including *Jesus the Sinner's Friend*. They heard tributes from Dr. Sam Matthews (Founder and Director of Family of Faith, Shawnee, Oklahoma), Gerald Gotzen (representing the many visiting speakers to the College) and the author, representing the Bible College staff.

Rev. Geoffrey Fewkes, Minister of Pantygwydr Baptist Church and a former lecturer, read from a selection of Scriptures, and George Verwer prayed. Alan Scotland, Chairman of the board of trustees, spoke briefly from the Scriptures, although he was emotionally moved by the loss of such a special friend and role model. His thoughts are expressed in his tribute printed in the Order of Service booklet:

> Mr Howells stood out to me as one who cultivated a profound prayer ministry of intercession. His journey throughout ninety-one

years was not walked out on great platforms of this world. However, from a little room in the Bible College of Wales, he reached and touched the lives of many across the globe.

His responsibility in bringing leadership to the College and its family of intercessors was greatly challenging, yet he remained true to the Vision to reach every creature with the Gospel of the Kingdom. He went beyond the superficial; when he said, "I will be praying for you," he really did intercede. Intercession was not just another word for prayer – it was his life.

There are many memories I cherish of Mr Howells and his example is a continuing provocation to us all today. He was a very gracious and humble man and often reminded us that if we do err, let it be on the side of mercy, not judgement. His life was rich in spirit and in word, and though often preferring to withdraw from the crowd, he was a deeply affectionate man and knowledgeable of world affairs.

There were times that Mr Howells felt his own weaknesses, yet he continued to pursue the purpose to the very end. He was truly a man of God and it is our great privilege to have known him and to have worked with him.

The world did not deserve him. Hebrews 11:38 (The Message Bible).

His was a life of purpose under-girded by prayer; such a powerful combination has changed the lives of many. His life has deeply influenced, motivated and inspired many. We mourn his passing.

Also in the booklet were several photographs, one a final glimpse of Samuel waving from the bridge in the Black Mountain, under girded with caption, *'To be with Christ ...which is far better.'* Philippians 1:23.

The interment was with Samuel's parents in the family grave in Penllergaer Church graveyard, South Wales, UK, which is marked by a stone, engraved with the words:

Samuel Rees Howells
Born August 31st 1912
Glorified March 18th 2004
Honorary Director Of The
Bible College Of Wales
From 1950 to 2004
"With Christ which is far better" Phil. 1:23
"Well done, good and faithful servant" Matt. 25:21

The grave of the Howells family

Samuel's pathway to victory had been by the way of the cross all the way, and this had made his ministry so powerful. In his public prayers and devotional sessions, Samuel would always draw the congregation's thoughts towards the bitter price paid by the Saviour in order to redeem mankind. For the eternal Son of God to be ignominiously scourged by the Roman guards, His royal blood shed, and to be publicly hung on a wooden gibbet in all His shame, confirmed the truth of Deuteronomy 21:23.

Anyone who is hung on a tree is under God's curse.

How could One so pure and transparent be cursed? He willingly accepted the curse placed upon mankind in the Garden of Eden (Genesis 3:14-19) and offered complete freedom from sin to every person. Here was love in action at the deepest level and Samuel knew that it required a wholehearted response. He had given that unqualified response and appropriated the blessings that it brought.

Throughout his ministry, Samuel had frequently closed a Communion Service by reading the benediction from Hebrews 13:20-21 (AV).

Now the God of peace, that brought again from the dead our Lord Jesus, that great Shepherd of the sheep, through the blood of the everlasting covenant, make you perfect in every good work to do His will, working in you that which is well pleasing in His sight, through Jesus Christ; to whom be glory for ever and ever. Amen.

Somehow, he was able to communicate a sense of refinement and purity as each phrase found its place in everyone's life. The congregation sat in contemplative silence for several minutes before Samuel slowly gathered his notes, closed his Bible, placed a slender white hand upon the lectern, levered himself to his feet and quietly left the room. It was some time, even then, before there was movement or talk from those present. Never one to engage in mindless chatter after a service, Samuel preferred to savour the anointing and sense of God's presence for as long as possible. With measured steps, he would walk through the dining room once more into the main hall and place his hand on the bottom banister of the carpeted stairs leading up to the seclusion of his room. No longer able to scale the flight two or three steps at a time as in more agile days, each step was made in quiet contemplation. Once inside, with Bible temporarily placed carefully on his bed, and jacket replaced by a warm woollen cardigan, he sank back into his armchair, unlaced his shoes and soon had his slippered feet on his stool. A warm drink and a light 'repast' as he called his supper, and then the day or night lay before him for further reflection on the Word and prayer. Finally, with his earthly jacket and shoes removed, he rests with all the saints who have gone before, waiting to be part of God's final acts before the New Heaven and the New Earth replace the old, and God Himself will dwell among His people.

Verses from a hymn, which he included regularly in his choice of hymns on Sunday mornings, written by Mrs A. R. Cousins, express the immortal truths which influenced Samuel's ministry:

> O Christ what burdens bowed Thy head!
> Our load was laid on Thee;
> Thou stoodest in the sinner's stead,
> Did'st bear all ill for me.
> A victim led, Thy blood was shed!
> Now there's no load for me.
>
> Death and the curse were in our cup;
> O Christ, 'twas full for Thee!
> But Thou hast drained the last dark drop,
> 'Tis empty now for me:
> That bitter cup, love drank it up,
> Now blessing's draught for me.
>
> For me, Lord Jesus, Thou hast died,
> And I have died in Thee:
> Thou'rt risen – my bands are all untied;
> And now Thou liv'st in me,
> When purified, made white, and tried.
> Thy glory then for me.

Such memories of Samuel's ministry linger long in our

minds.

Throughout his years Samuel always felt, as did his father, that people are too easily satisfied with little time spent with God and much activity to influence a few, rather than much time spent alone in the Divine Presence to see the strongholds of evil broken, and millions released from spiritual darkness and bondage. As a wise sage once aptly said, "Before we speak to men about God we must learn to speak to God about men." So as was Samuel's custom, he had prayed for 'young Alan bach'[3] whom he loved with fond affection, appreciating to the full what it would cost his successor to ensure that the Vision of the Founder was perpetuated into the twenty-first century and inculcated into the daily life at the College.

Samuel Howells as a young man c.1929 – The Vision of giving the Gospel to EVERY CREATURE consumed his life

Chapter Thirty-Three

Epilogue

Rising from his feet one Friday morning, in the closing session of an annual Every Creature Conference in the College Conference Hall during the late 1950s, Samuel walked quietly to the pulpit and opened his Bible at Ezekiel 22. Each day during the Conference, he had sat prayerfully throughout the morning sessions in a corner seat of the front platform while the notable preachers of his day endeavoured to deliver their half-hour messages. Now in a hush of expectancy the congregation's thoughts were directed to verse 30.

Samuel began by setting the text into its background when Ezekiel and Daniel, both captives during the seventy year period when Israel was taken to Babylon because of their stubborn and sinful living, undertook their role as intercessors, and saw a dramatic turn around in circumstances, culminating in Israel's return to the land.

And I sought for a man among them, that should make up the hedge, and stand in the gap before me for the land, that I should not destroy it: but I found none. Ezekiel 22:30 (AV).

Then Samuel reminded his silent listeners, some hearing the sermon relayed to other buildings in the College, that the Holy Spirit was ever looking for a man to *stand in the gap*. The need was great, the labourers few, but God can do much through one surrendered individual. In a most uncharacteristic manner, certainly unknown to any of the College staff who had known him for many years, Samuel then made an appeal for all those who felt the Holy Spirit prompting them to make this deep commitment to stand. He reminded them to consider carefully all the implications and changes in their lives that this would mean, before they did so. Practically the whole congregation rose quietly to their feet, as one man, and the solemn meeting was closed in prayer.

The Holy Spirit searches to and fro across the earth to find His man or woman. He found the man in Ezekiel and Daniel's days. He found them in the twentieth century. He will find them again in the twenty-first century.
Perhaps you, dear reader, will be one too.

On reading through these life memories I do feel that they will, for some, provide a different perspective of life in the last century. As someone reminded me, there will be many who will like the book and some who will not. That encourages me, as it may stimulate thought and discussion.

One helpful suggestion was to remind the reader that the ministries of both Rees Howells, and his successor, Samuel, were not the end of the story. Those seeds sown into the lives of students throughout the century, through years of dedicated ministry of all the staff at the Bible College, are producing a bumper crop around the world. I can trace direct ministries through students into at least eighty-five different countries. Many are, or were, involved in literature, radio, TV, teaching, publishing and a host of other ministries involving new technology, covering almost the whole globe. Global Horizons is certainly totally committed to see resources set aside by Rees and Samuel Howells used for the fulfilment of the Great Commission of Matthew 28. Add to that the ministries from other colleges plus that of national Christians in most countries, and there is the potential, with the Holy Spirit's anointing, to see mankind reached for Jesus Christ.

No wonder there are stirrings throughout the world at this time. God is at work fulfilling His plan.

And He said unto them, "Go ye into all the world, and preach the Gospel to EVERY CREATURE" **Mark 16:15 (AV).**

Richard Maton has also written: *Samuel Rees Howells: A Life of Intercession* which documents in detail the powerful story of intercession in and through Samuel's life, and traces its effectual legacy into the twenty-first century. These books are also available as ebooks.

The Views of Two Visitors

The following are two cameo pictures written by close friends associated with the College. The first is from Michael Howard, who has exercised a powerful ministry in many African nations, and always proved such an encouragement and blessing to Samuel himself. His contribution was recorded without any consultation, or knowledge of what had already been written.

The measure of the stature of a great man of God is that characteristic of taking interest and pleasure in the little things and above all, in people. Spiritual giants are real men and Mr Samuel was a real man. I knew him intimately for over two decades as a great intercessor, passionate watchman, revivalist and great lover of God. Most of all, I knew him as a true friend. He was practical and down to earth as behoves a spiritual giant. In many ways he reminded me of what I read of the Indian Christian and intercessor, Sadhu Sundar Singh. It is recorded of him that on a trip to Wales he particularly enjoyed staying with a family where there were two little boys. He would enjoy playing games with them on the carpet. After one particular session with these boys he departed up to his room to pray. Not long after he left the lounge the boys ran to their mother and asked, "Mummy, Mummy where did Jesus go?"

Each time I arrived at the Bible College of Wales it was always with the greatest excitement and anticipation of seeing Mr Samuel and finding out what the Lord had been saying. There was one most memorable occasion that I shall never forget. I was taking tea in the drawing room. Tea for me at the Bible College was a most wonderful affair and always done properly with the fine bone china and biscuits, making each occasion a real event. I adored those dedicated ladies, Mr Howells' armour bearers, and would count how many cups of tea dear, precious Miss Williams had poured in her lifetime. I know it surpassed a hundred thousand but each cup was poured with the same love and dedication to service as the previous one. Again, as is the head, so is the body. In the natural, Mr Samuel was very much the head, but the real head is Christ and it was Christ for whom Mr Samuel lived. As I sat sipping my tea Mr Samuel walked in with his ever warm and most generous Welsh greeting, "Ah bach!" His face was really shining like that of an angel. I sat bolt upright and was riveted to my seat for a moment, for it truly felt as if Jesus had just entered the room. At that particular moment there were no formalities. Great political events were taking place in the world. President Reagan had begun his second term in office but the Lord had been hearing the cries of His intercessor.

"Mr Samuel," I asked, "what has the Lord been saying to you?"

With his hand raised in a familiar gesture of love, joy and victory he responded, "It is too wonderful. Too, too wonderful indeed!"

I was all attentive for I knew what an enormous burden Mr Samuel had been carrying for many decades for Eastern Europe and the Soviet Union. It was an agony that had consumed him, as does any burden that an intercessor carries from the heart of the Father.

"The Berlin Wall is coming down!" he declared most precisely and significantly. "The Lord has heard our intercession. Eastern Europe and the Soviet Union are free." What a real, genuine prophecy. It was done and accomplished so significantly that it was as if it had already happened. This prophecy of Mr Samuel was two years prior to President

Reagan travelling to Berlin and declaring, "Mr Gorbachev, tear down this wall." This is the victory of the intercessor. He knows that he can claim no glory for his travail, for all glory belongs to the Lord. But the intercessor has the deep satisfaction of the tremendous breakthrough and the task accomplished for the King. There was not a shred of doubt in Mr Samuel's mind, and neither in mine, that this spiritual giant had heard from God and gained the place of intercession after some twenty-five years of battle. It was not simply about Eastern Europe and the Soviet Union being free politically, socially and economically but of the glorious Gospel having free access into these lands which for so long had been bound by satanic Communism. This was the great victory of light, order and freedom over darkness, confusion and bondage. Yet again, true intercession had prevailed. Many may ask, "But what a price!" Yes, but the fruit of that price can never be measured in earthly terms. What a price Jesus paid for my redemption. Ah, but what fruit for such a price for the Lord. *He shall see of the travail of His soul, and shall be satisfied.* Isaiah 53:11 (AV).

Mr Samuel loved children and always had time for people. That says much about the quality of the man. Jesus loved children too. Nobody was treated differently. Every visitor I ever took to the Bible College was warmly and graciously welcomed. It somewhat troubled me that students often felt themselves distanced and alienated from this Bible College Director. How shall any intercessor who carries the great heartbeat of God ever be unapproachable? God is love and they that live in love live in God and God lives in them. Real prophets, intercessors and revivalists are men of genuine love, though often misunderstood and feared for their close proximity to the Lord. There is always something mystical about them and there was certainly a mystical air about Mr Samuel, but he was a lovely man. A particular student I recommended to the Bible College, who, after six months, screamed, "I hate this place. Why on earth did you send me here?" ended up staying for years. My simple answer to that student was, "DIE!" I then proceeded to give some solid advice. "Get to know the staff and love them and spend time with them because they are really lovely people. Listen to their accounts of the great sacrifices they have made for Christ and their amazing life stories." That student listened and by listening, changed his whole life by loving instead of being irritated.

Samuel loved to walk on the Welsh mountains and it was always at a brisk, healthy pace. I enjoyed walking with that giant of a man. Fellowship was not having to chitchat for endless hours but simply revelling in the presence of the blessed Holy Spirit. Mr Samuel certainly carried that 'air' of the Holy Spirit whom he knew as a real Person in a most intimate way. This is the lot of the true intercessor to whom the Holy Spirit becomes a distinct friend. Real fellowship is intimacy. It is to understand another's burdens and heartaches, joys and victories and to become wrapped up with that person's life. This is what intercession is all about. The intercessor, through deep intimate relationship with the Lord, carries the heartbeat of God and the burden of the Lord, and expresses it back to Him by the power of the Holy Spirit, who with Christ alone, knows the mind and will of the Father. Mr Samuel was down to earth, I guess, as much as Christ must have been. He loved the streams, the flowers and grass, appreciating them as the great panoply of the Father's handiwork. Outside of the walls of their deep travail, great intercessors are real men who appreciate the small things perhaps because they see the greater picture of world events as revealed by the hand of the Almighty. In the midst of international issues, there is always time to appreciate a flower, play with a child, laugh with a teenager, or care for an aged.

The Bible College of Wales was a 'School of Dying.' It was not that the rules were too many or too strictly enforced. The making of an intercessor or any man of God for that matter, is the degree to which he is willing to die and allow the blessed Holy Spirit to have His way. Whenever the Holy Spirit comes into the equation of any human life, He spells death to self so that Christ may live in all His fullness through the broken, yielded life. Stepping on to the grounds of the Bible College was stepping on to Holy Ghost territory and His powerful conviction was evident everywhere. The blessed Holy Spirit is comfortable with a certain environment and that environment had certainly been cultivated over many years at the Bible College. All of this points to the man who is leading, for as is the head, so is the body. What a commendation of the Director.

Another most significant and memorable occasion was being present at the College when Mr Samuel ministered one Tuesday evening. He had been in deep travail for a long time and it was evident from his stature that this was the case. I will always remember his ministry from the book of Isaiah. It was not that he really preached but simply read the Word, stopping every now and then to comment. It seemed as if I had never before read or heard the Word that Mr Samuel was declaring. It was so infused with pulsating life for it was read with the utmost love, reverence and conviction. It was breathed forth from a vessel so saturated with the blessed Holy Spirit that the Word sounded altogether different. I was both fascinated and captivated by this amazing rendition. I realised that the Spirit-breathed Word is life, and the more of the blessed Holy Spirit breathed upon the Word, the more is the explosion of that life. What truth and light are locked up in such principles.

Great servants of God are mostly misunderstood, except of course by those who speak the same language and live similar lives. Paul the apostle has been greatly misrepresented as a hard man, a woman hater, insensitive, as well as a number of other epithets. But, in Paul was a man of such deep love that he was prepared to become accursed for the sake of Israel. Mr Samuel was just such a man as well. His travail for the lost and dying of the nations, for the multitudes in the valley of decision, and his commitment to the Every Creature Commission, revealed the magnitude of the love of a man who walked and lived in close proximity to the Lord. His passion for natural Israel was manifested in the years of deep intercession for the nation and for Jerusalem. That passion continues in the hearts of many who sat under Mr Samuel's ministry, and who carry the same burden and passion.

Mr Samuel left this earth having accomplished the task assigned him by the Lord. His legacy continues in the hundreds of former students planted in the nations of the world, who continue to carry the baton of the blessed Holy Spirit as revealed through the Lord's servant, Mr Samuel Howells.

Such was the challenge that Samuel of Swansea left to the twenty-first century Church.

From Wales in nearby Llanelli, eight miles from Swansea, Rowland Evans, the Founder of the worldwide missionary movement known as World Horizons, and also of a more recent expression of faith called Nations, adds his own personal observations. Having sat under Samuel's

ministry for many years and finding in the College a spiritual home, his life was profoundly changed. He writes:
> It is clear from my personal knowledge of Mr Samuel that he was a man who held two views of the world at once. It was as if, for him, there was a translucent veil between the parallel courses of time and eternity. He had climbed his own mountain of transfiguration and, under the Lordship of One who was equally familiar with both realms, saw and overheard those things which provided the direction of his prayer.
>
> Like an Old Testament prophet, Mr Samuel was firmly at home in the presence of people and profoundly aware of the significance of world events. Yet, like his Lord, he developed a lifestyle where separation and silence could play its vital role.
>
> Even so, such a praying figure could not function in isolation. He needed the sympathetic environment of committed people who could confirm his words and will him to succeed. Together they shared a crucial understanding of their times and became an intercessory base which profoundly influenced the levels of spiritual life among many nations.
>
> The crowning genius of this base was that it was also a Bible College which could absorb into its family life students from Wales and the rest of the world. The essence of discipleship is always to show rather than to tell and on the basis of this principle, staff and students alike lived and prayed together in total dependence on God.
>
> The contribution to the world made by the faith-based, praying missionaries they trained is not easily evaluated except perhaps through the numbers of their disciples and the disciples of their disciples who returned to Wales to drink deeply from the same source. Perhaps since the days of the early Moravians, this faith-filled stream of young men and women had hardly

been exceeded.

Why did such a movement flourish in the soil of Wales? To answer this question I have to ask another. Why did Wales experience a spate of Holy Spirit visitations ending with the mighty 1904 Revival? I express a personal opinion but it is based on more than forty years of building world mission from a Welsh base. Revivals serve as windows into an even deeper revelation of Divine purpose that affects the destiny of a nation and the role of its young people in the evangelisation of the world. Could it have been Rees Howells' insight into this destiny that fired his passion for the Every Creature Vision?

My conscious personal journey with God began in the secret dreams of moments of childhood solitude. It was during my years of military service in Asia (1955-1958) that I was challenged to become accountable for what I believed. In time, this led to a missionary career. My introduction into the College environment came through the gift of a well-thumbed copy of *Rees Howells Intercessor*. My wife, Anne, read the book through five times in succession. I took longer, sometimes pondering my way through its chapters line by line. We were never officially students but felt that we had found our spiritual home among its community. Prayer, faith and inspiration from a wide range of missionary contact consolidated our formative years into a lifelong pursuit of God.

It was during a hidden five year period of intensive prayer that we moved to Llanelli, an unlikely setting to fulfil a missionary dream, but slowly and strongly a new world missionary movement began to grow around us. In time it encircled the globe and we named it World Horizons. Gradually hundreds of missionaries settled in many countries and the branch movement, Nations, with a family of new African and Asian indigenous missionary movements, also began.

In later years, I rediscovered that Rees Howells, after missionary experience in Africa, had founded the College to train young men and women who had been influenced by the 1904 Revival to follow through the revival's purpose – world evangelisation. Today I am convinced that it has been through the prayer of those who recognised the purpose that lay beyond revival that I, and those who have travelled with me, received the vision to build World Mission out of Wales and beat our own path to earth's furthest bounds.

They were sad days when we learned of the death of Mr Samuel; a warrior who, in spite of his advanced years, still held out his spear in the direction of progress. Yet, at the same time, we were deeply encouraged by the thought that many hundreds of second and third generation missionaries of many nationalities have echoed his faith and prayer as they have stood in the full light of their day as his worthy successors.

As I watch the demolishing of Wales' last great prayer base and weigh up its loss to our nation and the world, my grief drives me back to where the source of all wisdom waits for my visit. There I ask myself the question: Can what God had promised and was received by faith, ever really be lost?

The answer that biblical wisdom provides is a resounding 'No.' Abraham tramped the boundaries of Israel's land and sealed the promise of it for himself and his descendants, though through the tides of population's flow, his inheritance has been seeded with the values and religions of other peoples. Yet, four thousand years later, Israel once more stands where Abraham once stood. The boundary stones have not been moved. Similarly, the College imprint on the spiritual world will again emerge through all that is natural. It is a fundamental missionary principle that promised goals taken by faith are not reversed; they are never lost.

The consequences of the period of our history covered by this book can never be lost. As change takes place and the use of grounds made holy by the feet of naked faith become subject to different usage and values, we are aware that a world-shaping event that has absorbed so many lives may, for the moment, have reached a plateau or even its completion. Yet the currency of its faith will never lose its value, but will continue to be a hidden resource for those who will dare sail out of sight of land and continue in the Every Creature Vision on course bearings set by the same prayer and faith.

Good Friday, 10th April 2009.

Such stories could be multiplied a hundred times over as around the world God is raising up men and women and using them as His channels to bring blessing to a needy world.

BCW Vision – *Go ye into all the world and preach the Gospel to EVERY CREATURE* **(Mark 16:15), 1937 Annual Report**

The Every Creature Conferences
(From the Publisher)

In 1932, a Missionary Conference of the Evangelical Union of South America was held at Derwen Fawr from 24th to 28th June. One week later, Rees Howells held a Summer School for Ministers at Derwen Fawr from the 2nd to 8th July. These were a precursor to the Every Creature Conferences that were first called the Every Creature Missionary and Intercessory Conference. These were held in July / August when staff and students would vacate their rooms for guests. A big marquee (tent), additional toilets and catering facilities were all rented. The first Conference (1936) could accommodate three hundred guests. Rees Howells in a reply to a woman in Ireland in 1936 (who was writing on behalf of a man) stated that they could not allow additional people to attend for free as it resulted in overcrowding and was an additional burden upon the College, who were already charging less than cost. Rees also stated that if God wanted the man to come then He would have to provide the finances; that would be a seal (sign) that he was meant to be there.

In 1938, the name of the Conference was shortened to Every Creature Conference, then later, Missionary Conference. The WEC held a Conference at BCW in 1937, they had eleven types of booklets published by a printer and sent to BCW on the 2nd July 1937. There was also an Intercessory Conference held in 1941 at Derwen Fawr. The Every Creature Conferences were initially held for two weeks spanning July and August but were later reduced to one week in duration. The 1938 Every Creature Conference had seventy booklets printed in the German language, thus German-speaking guests were attending. The 1939 booklet had a print run of 1,250. After WWII, these booklets were reduced in size from an A4 booklet (often twelve pages) to A5 size (of eight pages), and were two A4-size papers folded together. These booklets often gave an overview of the previous years giving in thousands of pounds (1960s) often towards Bibles or missions in general. The last Conference was held in 1964.

Bible College Students and Publications
(From the Publisher)

Students of the Bible College of Wales (BCW) have come from or gone to at least eighty-five different countries of the world during BCW's seventy-eight years of active studies (1924-2009). BCW was closed for training in 1925 due to a cleavage and six years during WWII because of conscription. There have been at least 1,170 students trained at BCW from two to three years in duration. An average of fifteen per-year, some years had a high of sixty new students (pre WWII), others had a low of eight; many of whom have gone into full-time Christian ministry. In 1928, one student left for missionary work amongst the Berber Bedouins of Arabia and another in 1936.

The springtime College booklets of 1934, 35 and 36 reveal that in total there were 60, 80 and 120 students in those respective years. In 1936, thirty graduating students joined the WEC missionary society. In 1939, BCW had ninety-five staff members. It also had its own printing press and published a number of booklets and pamphlets: the Annual Report, sometimes known as the Whitsun Meetings or Anniversary / Session booklet, the Every Creature Conference (various editions), plus notices and Reports of the various College Sessions (six were published over a two year period, one every term). The 1937 Christmas booklet went through four editions. Print runs were sometimes 500, 600, 1,000 and up to 1,500 for the fourth edition! The 1941 Seventeenth Anniversary Whitsuntide booklet had a print run of 2,900. The 1936 Twelfth Anniversary Booklet (1st June) stated that 120 (students) were 'called out' (surrendered their mission calls to God) and the 'fire of God fell on the 29 March 1936' (revival!). It also stated that 170 (staff and students) were praying and interceding three hours a day for the Every Creature Commission to see its fulfilment. The first BCW student reunion took place in 1948, the second in 2007. BCW saw its last graduation in July 2009, before relocating in September to England, as Trinity School of Theology; renamed Trinity School of Ministry in March 2012.

Global Horizons

The Bible College of Wales was founded in 1924 by Rees Howells and became a registered Charity in 1955. In 2003, it became the Rees Howells Trust and is now, Global Horizons. Rees Howells' Vision was to 'seed the nations' with the Christian message as was his son and successor, Samuel Howells, in their obedience to the Great Commission of Matthew 28:18-20 and Mark 16:15. Global Horizons, under the leadership of Alan Scotland continues the work begun by Rees to 'seed the nations' so that *every creature* can hear the Gospel. Today, many of the world's seven billion people, which includes every tribe, nation and tongue, have not yet heard the Good News of Jesus Christ. Jesus told His disciples that the *harvest fields* were vast and ready, *white unto harvest* (John 4:34-38). He urged them to pray that the *Lord of the harvest would send labourers into the harvest fields* (Matthew 9:38). Global Horizons, an apostolic company of believers (Ephesians 4) is at the heart of Lifelink churches, and is committed to training such workers with the necessary skills for the twenty-first century. This is made possible by the provision of theological training and ministry delivered through a variety of partnerships with the worldwide Church. Global Horizons Lifelink represents a group of churches across the UK, the USA, and on mainland Europe, with further church relation-ships into South America, southern Africa, India and China, all of whom have chosen to work together in different ways for the advancement of God's Kingdom. Each church that affiliates with Lifelink is unique and has its own character and mission.

Trinity School of Ministry (TSM) formerly known as the Bible College of Wales is a non-denominational, non-residential Bible Training Centre based in Warwickshire, England. At the centre in Rugby, TSM seeks to train the whole person for ministry and outreach through a blend of sound Bible teaching and practical ministry training. TSM offers a variety of courses, with built in flexibility to cater for individual circumstances. TSM's name was changed to Global Horizons in autumn 2017.

Sources and Notes

The Sources and Notes have been compiled by the Publisher to give additional information, some cross-referencing and to clarify some points that may be unfamiliar to those not closely connected or familiar with the life and ministry of Rees and Samuel Howells and the Bible College of Wales.

Many Welsh place names from the 1900s have had a letter dropped from their name as can be seen in the spelling on old maps and old postcards. Places familiar to both Rees and Samuel Howells, such as Glanamman and Brynamman are now spelt Glanaman and Brynaman. With other Welsh place names, letters have been changed. Llanelli, a town, just eight miles from Swansea was formerly spelt Llanelly.

Foreword
1. For the past two decades, the American Dollar ($) has fluctuated from $1.3-2.0 against the British Pound Sterling (£). Within this book alongside the values in British Pound Sterling is the *approximate* value in American Dollars based on £1 to $1.6. Inflation has not been calculated into the values except where noted. Where inflation rates have been stated (e.g. the value of £10,000 / $16,000 in 1962 is worth £166,400 / $266,200 in 2012) these figures have been computed from the Bank of England's online inflation calculator which is based on accurate inflation rate data. Please note that inflation and the price of buildings and land can vary greatly, from one year to the next and between countries.

Introduction
1. Certain stories of Rees Howells' early years and intercessions frequently reoccur during the sermon notes that were documented largely from 1938-1950. Rees Howells frequently spoke about his life experiences to each successive batch of Bible College students as a means of encouragement, practical education and as a challenge for others to fully surrender themselves to the Holy Spirit. So that they too would walk in the Spirit, be obedient to Him at all times (even in the smallest of matters); to glorify the Father and exalt Jesus Christ through their daily living. Rees Howells often said, "An ounce of experience is worth a ton of theory."
2. This story, from the Bible College archives is also related in *Rees Howells Intercessor* by Norman Grubb, 1952, chapter five.
3. This Vision became known as the EVERY CREATURE Commission which was given to Rees Howells on Boxing Day (26th December) 1934 when it was believed that the Gospel should be given to all mankind (every tribe, nation and tongue) within thirty years (a generation). They were to take personal responsibility to intercede for the Gospel to go to Every Creature and to live sacrificial lives in order to train and prepare people for the mission field. By June 1936, there were one hundred and twenty students who had been called out by the Holy Spirit (to lay down their mission callings to intercede for others to go) because the fire of

God had fallen on the 29 March 1936 – this was revival! By June 1936, there were one hundred and seventy staff and students praying and interceding three hours a day for the EVERY CREATURE Commission to see its fulfilment. Once every tribe, nation and tongue had heard then Jesus could return – the Second Coming, see Matthew 24:14, Mark 13:10, 2 Peter 3:12, Revelation 5:9b and Revelation 14:16. Second, Rees believed that 10,000 people would be raised up like himself, *full* of the Holy Spirit to go into all the world and preach the Gospel in the power of the Spirit. Third, God would finance these men and women and as a *sign*, a gift of £10,000 ($16,000) would be given to the College. Up until this time, the largest gift the College had ever been given was £1,000 ($1,600). The £10,000 gift was received in July 1938 and made newspaper headlines in at least three different publications. £10,000 ($16,000) from 1938 is worth £525,000 ($840,000) in 2012. Rees Howells was not the first person to believe that the consummation of the age would be in "this generation" (thirty years), as others Christian workers had mentioned it from the 1860s onwards. Men such as Hudson Taylor (founder of the China Inland Mission), A. B. Simpson (founder of the Christian and Missionary Alliance) and John R. Mott (missionary statesman) all preached the possibility of evangelising the world in their generation. In 1910, the first International Missionary Conference was held in Edinburgh, Scotland, its motto was: 'The Evangelisation of the World in this Generation.' The Vision Rees Howells received added great emphasis on individuals, for their responsibility in world evangelisation which meant a full surrender and consecration (Romans 12:1), coupled with an enduement of power for service (Acts 1:8). *Go ye into all the world and preach the Gospel to Every Creature* (Mark 16:15) became the motto of the Bible College of Wales (BCW). The Vision was presented to the staff and students of BCW on the 1st January 1935. The story of the 'Vision' can be found in chapter thirty of *Rees Howells Intercessor* by Norman Grubb, 1952. Rees Howells shares the Vision in chapter two of his only published work, *God Challenges the Dictators – Doom of Nazis Predicted* by Rees Howells, 1939. In the 1960s, Samuel Howells gave the College a renewed sense of vision and leadership, as he prepared them to continue to be responsible for the Vision of world evangelisation, not in a limited time, but for the rest of their lives. The intercession was now a lifetime commitment to pray, give and go until all are reached. (Samuel always remained committed to the distribution of the Scriptures). A modern interpretation of the Vision can be summed up as: Go ye (Mark 16:15), give ye (Luke 9:13), pray ye (Matthew 9:38) and ideally do all three, in the power of the Spirit (Acts 1:8), for the glory of God and the exultation of Jesus Christ. Serve Him, obey Him and abide in Him (John 15:1-11). Go and make disciples of all nations.

Chapter One
1. The Bank of England's online inflation calculator suggests an overall inflation of 837 percent since 1950. £100,000 in 1950 is equivalent to approximately £2.7 million ($4.32 million) in 2012. Planning application for a retail superstore with 433 car parking spaces on the 6.67-acre

Glynderwen Estate site was rejected. In 2006, a housing developer bought approximately half the site (the upper level above the stream) and built twenty-nine properties that went on sale to the approximate value of £14 million ($22.4 million); these homes were completed in early 2012. Originally, a planning application for fifty-four homes was submitted but rejected by the council as the lower level was once flooded in the early 1980s. This twenty-nine home estate is called Bryn Newydd and consists of twenty-nine two to four bedroom homes with a list price *from* £294,995 ($471,990) to *from* £549,995 ($879,990) per home as stated in the 2011 brochure. The year 2008, saw a collapse in property and land prices across the U.K., which at the time of publication have not recovered.

Chapter Two
1. The author notes: 'The writing was being observed purely from a scientific perspective which can be very accurate if used by an expert. Beyond this is the discernment the Holy Spirit gives, delving deep into the spiritual realm where the real action takes place.'
2. Glanaman is a village next to Garnant. Garnant can be defined as being in the district of Glanaman, hence why Glanaman was Samuel's home even though his foster parent's home was in Garnant.
3. Oxford University fees for the 2012-2013 academic years were £8,600 ($13,760) for British students. For the previous academic year (2011-2012) the fee was £3,000 ($4,800) the maximum amount a university could charge until the British Government recently changed its rules.
4. La Maréchele, was born Catherine Booth, better known as Katie, the third child of General William Booth, founder of the Salvation Army. She pioneered the Salvation Army work in France (as well as Switzerland, Belgium and Holland) and married Arthur Sydney Clibborn, she took the name Booth-Clibborn.

Chapter Three
1. An archaeologist is an anthropologist (social scientist) who studies prehistoric people and their culture.
2. Rees Howells had the assurance of the Holy Spirit that no bombs would fall on the grounds of the Bible College and services continued as normal, even when Swansea Docks and city centre (just two miles away) were being bombed. Rees Howells by law was under obligation to the day school pupils (then numbering around 300) and provision was made for them. No provision was made for the College staff, students and around sixty missionary boarder children as the Lord has told Rees that 'neither shelters nor gas masks' were necessary, however anybody that wanted a gas mask could get one for free. This is also covered in *Rees Howells Intercessor*, chapter 35. Girl boarders at Glynderwen used to go down to the cellar during night raids, there were very few day raids. Boy boarders used the back corridor of El-Shaddai on the ground floor. Prep Schoolchildren went into Sketty Isaf corridor.
3. Any waste of water and electricity was anathema to Samuel Howells. The publisher remembers Mr Maton (author of this book) and then Principal of the Bible College of Wales informing the student body in

1999 that a quarterly water bill had been received for £10,000! ($16,000) and Mr Samuel was not happy. This was (and still is) a lot of money and would students try to conserve water. It did not help that many of the baths were old and large (cast iron and covered with enamel) so that a 6-foot man could have his feet flat against one end and his head still nearly under water! The bathroom of Samuel Howells located in Derwen Fawr House along with its antique bath and large showerhead was valued at £5,000 ($8,000) in 2001 as told to the Publisher by Miss Ruth Williams, Samuel Howells' personal secretary. The student body were frequently told to turn off unused / unnecessary lights to save money.

Chapter Six
1. On the 17th February 1950, one week after the death of Rees Howells, Dr. Priddy became School Head as Kenneth McDouall (of fourteen years service) had recently resigned because of 'great and unforeseen changes of December 1949 to February 1950.' He felt a call to the mission field and subsequently went to the Sudan under the auspices of the Church Missionary Society (*Emmanuel School 1933-1983*, Jubilee booklet).
2. In 1940, due to World War II, conscription of men (staff, students and prospective students) and with the redeployment of women (all essential to the war effort) led to the temporary closure of the Bible College of Wales for six years. All lectures ceased, however the meetings (services and prayer meetings) did not, they increased! Annual conferences were still held. Many of the male staff and students were conscientious objectors and had to stand trial before a tribunal. A number of the men students felled trees for the war effort at the Penllergaer Estate which Rees Howells bought in November 1938. Other College staff served in a number of non-combatant roles.
3. £20,000 at the end of 1938 (the liability for the Penllargaer Estate) is worth £1,049,900 ($1,678,800) in 2012. Nearly eleven years later, having been through WWII, the £20,000 liability that was cleared in 1949 would be worth £551,200 (£881,900). The phrase "I have looked forward for ten years to the day" spoken by Rees Howells on the 8th September 1949, was in relation to the first week of WWII when Britain entered the war on the 3rd September 1939.

Chapter Nine
1. Whilst the County Council agreed in 1950 to purchase the stately Penllergaer mansion (the Big House) on the Penllergaer Estate, this was just one plot sold from a total of 270 acres. Glamorgan Council Offices resided on this plot of land until October 2016, quite near to where the Big House once stood. On 30th June 1962, the trustees of the Bible College of Wales proposed a sale of 236 acres and on the 24th October 1962 received a cheque (check) for £10,600 ($17,000).

Chapter Ten
1. In October 1952, the British Empire declared a state of emergency in Kenya, as demonically inspired Mau Mau fighters intensified a brutal campaign of terror against political opponents, white settlers and farming

communities. The Mau Mau's sought to highjack this transition for their own political advantage. The brutality of their oaths and practices were shocking. They covenanted that they would be cut off "from all hope, outside Mau Mau, in this world and the next." The spiritual rituals of the Mau Mau involved digging up human corpses and eating the flesh, drinking human blood and many other unspeakable practices. Their vows became a renunciation of all Christian belief and morals.

Chapter Twelve
1. Norman Brend became a student at the Bible College of Wales in 1935, whilst Nollie became a student in 1937. Norman was at BCW during some of the war years though not all of them (WWII 1939-1945) whilst Nollie left in 1946. It was accepted practice at BCW, after graduation to stay on as a staff member until God called you into your next sphere of ministry; unless you had decided to get married or were asked to leave! It was not until the early 1970s that it was proposed that young married couples should be welcomed onto staff. During the war years, Norman helped decorate the Big House (stately mansion at Penllergaer) before felling trees on the Penllergaer Estate for his time of service during the war effort. Nollie worked in Derwen Fawr and would ask the "boys" (men students) for wood chippings from Penllergaer for use in helping start the fire in the Blue Room of Derwen Fawr House. They returned to the Bible College of Wales as Mr and Mrs Brend in 1957 and became members of staff. They moved out in October 2005 (staying with friends in the Sketty area) and in 2007, they moved into a Christian nursing home in Cardiff, Wales. Mr Brend was promoted to glory in Oct. 2012 aged 98, and Mrs Brend in Aug. 2015 age 100!
2. The students listed within this paragraph represent at least four decades of musically talented students ending in 2002/3.
3. Girolamo Savonarola was a Dominican friar in Florence (Italy) who preached against sin and corruption and was an anointed prophet and leader of the Florentine Revival (c.1493-1497). Savonarola's famous slogan was, "I warn you Italy, I warn you Rome, that nothing can save you but Christ." His sermons also warned of great judgement and then a golden age when Florence would unite Italy in a just commonwealth. In May 1498, Girolamo Savonarola and two monks were martyred in the Piazza della Signoria, the same square where a year previously, a 'bonfire of vanities' had taken place, as people threw their sinful objects into a huge fire.

Chapter Thirteen
1. Special prayer for India in her hour of crisis. India had been at war with China since the 20th October 1962 when Red Troops overran India's northeast border in a bid to extend its territory. India's 4th Division fell on the 20th November. It was India's darkest day since her independence from Britain in 1947, when ethnic violence came to the fore and the country was partitioned with Pakistan becoming a new nation. Peking, China announced by radio a ceasefire to begin at midnight on the 21st November 1962! The prayers of the saints of the Bible College of Wales (and around the world) prevailed again! Glory to God.

Chapter Fourteen

1. In the late 1990s, two different 'songs' of grace were sung before the midday and evening meal. One of these went, "Be present at our table Lord, Be here and everywhere adored, These mercies bless and grant that we, May feast in paradise with Thee." Previous to the late 1990s, the men and women students had breakfast together in Derwen Fawr dining hall. The men had to wash up (do the dishes) and dry the plates and cutlery. The women students had to clean and lay the tables for the next meal. Sink one, was for the plates, sink two, for the cutlery and the dreaded sink three was for the big pots and pans which often got burnt at the bottom and they were often very hard to clean! Samuel Howells whose first language was Welsh was never happy when any language other than English was spoken at the meal tables. In 1999, Samuel ceased having his midday meal at the staff table (staff sat at one table and students at another) and had them in his room. However his place at the staff table had been on and off for all his life as Director.
2. The footbridge spanned a gap of just three metres though was five metres in length. Since Rees Howells first made his declaration on the bridge in 1906, photos reveal that it had been replaced (or its handrails repaired) at least three times before being completely removed in 2008.

Chapter Fifteen

1. See *Revival Fire – 150 Years of Revivals* by Mathew Backholer, ByFaith Media, 2010, which covers the Congo Revival (1953-1957) in one chapter and details the story of David and Anne Davies. Mathew Backholer interviewed them in 2006.
2. In the mid 1960s, independence, followed by civil war tore the Belgian Congo apart under the Simba Rising. *This is No Accident* by Leonard C. J. Moules (1965) gives testimonies of the trials encountered by WEC missionaries whilst the *Congo Saga* by David W. Truby (1965) focuses on those connected with the Unevangelized Fields Mission.

Chapter Sixteen

1. The oak tree (if facing Derwen Fawr House from the front lawns) stood to the left of Derwen Fawr House. A poor quality photo in *God Challenges the Dictators* (1939), with only half the tree in view (on the edge of the photo) shows clearly that it has been lopped as had all its large branches. One of the elderly female staff, Ivy Impey told a visitor (the publisher's father) that the oak tree (which she saw everyday from her window) had been dead a long time. The tree blew down in a storm in the mid-90s. When the publisher first visited the Bible College of Wales in July 1998, the root ball of the great oak (about 8 feet in diameter) was on its side with the sawn-off stump remaining.
2. Rees Howells was a very well known man of God across Wales and Britain. He was often in all the local newspapers and occasionally in the national ones. For the local papers, nearly every prediction, word or prophecy was newsworthy and often made a front-page headline or the side banner. Newspaper reports with a word from the 'Welsh Prophet' or 'Welsh Pastor' as some headlines ran or a piece relating to the Bible College of Wales were bought and the articles cut out and presumably

sent to friends and supporters. The archives reveal that more than twenty-three copies of one newspaper were bought (and not given away) when Haile Selassie, Emperor of Ethiopia visited Penllargaer in August 1940 – this was his second visit to this Estate, the first was in 1939. When WWII began in September 1939 and continued past Whitsun 1940, when Rees initially believed the war would be over (See Doris Ruscoe's *Intercession of Rees Howells,* chapter two) there was a falling away of visitors and friends. In Ruscoe's words, 'for the next few years we were truly shut in with God.' This thinning out allowed those who were truly called, committed and consecrated, the fully surrendered staff and students of BCW to unite in corporate prayer and intercession as they were the ones who truly believed and *walked by faith, not by sight* and had the assurance of the victory in Christ Jesus by the power of the Holy Spirit living in them as surrendered vessels.

3. The exact number of deaths in the gulags is unknown. Under Stalin from 1923-1953 the statistics of those who died in gulags range from one to three million. However, others researchers say that out of the eight million that went in, only ten percent came out which means the deaths of 7.2 million people.

4. The importance of baptism and its accompanying teaching is an essential ingredient in the new birth process linked with repentance and can be seen in: Mark 16:16, Acts 2:38 and 1 Peter 3:21.

5. Whilst China has the largest printing press in the world – Amity Press in Nanjing, Bibles are still desperately needed in China, but especially amongst the unregistered House Churches whose leaders and evangelists are unable to give a Bible to each new convert for lack of availability. The vast majority of Bibles printed on Amity Press are for the Western world. A full Bible, printed and delivered within China costs just £1.20 ($1.80) as one Christian ministry states, who through their networks have the printing and delivery capacity of 300,000 Bibles per month, subject to finances. To date, they have printed and distributed 7.5 million Bibles (Dec. 2013) among the House Church brethren largely in rural areas; just less than 1.6 million in 2011 alone! One Chinese leader wrote: 'New believers need the precious Word of God to keep them from being deceived by cults. For each new believer in our network to have their own copy we need 683,923 Bibles.' (Feb. 2012). The ministry keeps precise records, knowing exactly how many Bibles have been delivered to each province. If a Christian was to go into a shop or a church and try to buy more than a handful of Bibles it will arouse suspicion and can lead to reprisals. The Christians in China are still persecuted for righteousness sake, some are tortured and many are imprisoned. Please remember these brethren in your prayers, our fellow brothers and sisters in China and beyond. See Hebrews 13:3, James 1:27, Matthew 25:36 and Proverbs 31:8.

Chapter Seventeen
1. Samuel knew the books of Daniel to Malachi, though some say from Hosea onward were called Minor Prophets because of their size in comparison with those of Jeremiah, Isaiah and Ezekiel (the Major Prophets). He often made this statement as a reminder to his listeners

that all the prophets were powerful men of God, regardless of the length of their books and that we must not think of them as inferior prophets.

Chapter Eighteen
1. Yuri Gargarin, a Russian name, can also be spelt Yuri Gagarin. His orbit of the earth lasted 108 minutes.
2. Sermon notes from the 1950s of Samuel Howells are scattered with references to revival and reports of revival from around the globe. These included revivals in Korea, the Belgium Congo, Tommy Hicks in Argentina and a sermon on the centenary of the 1859 Ulster Revival. A number of revivalists spoke at the Bible College of Wales Every Creature Conferences (and other meetings) including Duncan Campbell of Scotland (Hebridean Revival), Andrew Gih of China (who saw revival in China and other Asian countries), James A. Stewart of Scotland (who saw revival across Eastern Europe prior to WWII. He later moved to the USA). Norman Grubb saw revival in the Congo in the 30s and David Davies, a former student who also saw revival in his mission station in the Belgium Congo from 1953-57. The College was actively praying for revival. Some of these revivals are documented in *Revival Fires and Awakenings* by Mathew Backholer, ByFaith Media, 2009 and *Revival Fire – 150 Years of Revivals* by Mathew Backholer, ByFaith Media, 2010.

Chapter Nineteen
1. Reinhard Bonnke is the most fruitful, living active evangelist who as a first year student at BCW, after hearing of a 'deliverance' (answer to financial prayer) declared that he wanted to be like Mr Samuel – a man of faith. In one meeting in Nigeria, Africa, one million people made a profession of faith under the anointed preaching of Rheinard Bonnke, founder of CfaN. Bonnke also has a healing ministry and has seen many miracles in the name of Jesus Christ, by His shed blood in the power of the Holy Spirit. To God be the glory for the great things He has done! He has revisited the College on a number of occasions. In 1999, Rheinard Bonnke arrived with a film crew as he was documenting his life. The students, all dressed in their dirty work clothes, with no preparation or foreknowledge of his arrival by the College authorities, sang his favourite hymn (which no one knew) unaccompanied, one line at a time! It never made it into the final edit! In 2006, he secretly arrived and spoke to the students and gave his testimony. If his appearance was public knowledge, too many visitors would have turned up. Once, when a well-known healing evangelist announced on Christian television that he would be visiting the Bible College of Wales, BCW was inundated with phone calls as to the time and date. Unfortunately, this preacher had not informed BCW of his intentions and when he did, his request was politely turned down by the trustees.

Chapter Twenty
1. In December 2012, the Derwen Fawr Estate was sold to a Christian organisation. Renovation of Derwen Fawr House began in Dec. 2013.
2. This was a *very* common saying of Samuel Howells.
3. A saying, which he picked up from his father, Rees Howells.

Chapter Twenty-One

1. The publisher, as a staff member of the Bible College of Wales, distinctively recalls the long, loud, yet polite call of "Rrrruuuth" of Mr Samuel (as he was affectionately known). This was followed by the "I'm coming Mr Samuel" and the gentle footsteps of Miss Ruth Williams (who barely stood 5-feet in height) walking across the landing to his room. Miss Williams was born in 1918, thus making her five and a half years younger than Mr Samuel. She was his faithful secretary, then personal assistant until his death in 2004 in Ruth's eighty-sixth year!

2. The College relay system even transmitted into the main building of the Glynderwen site. This was a five-minute walk down Derwen Fawr Road from Derwen Fawr House; the site where services were held.

3. During the publisher's time as a student and then staff, BCW had thirteen services a week. One every evening from 7:30-9pm (Monday-Friday), with Saturday night free and the Sunday evening service was from 6:30-7:45pm, followed by the evening meal. Morning services were generally 30-45 minutes in duration (Monday to Saturday), beginning from 8:45-9:30am, except Sunday where the service began at 11:15am and concluded between 12:30-12:45, ready for lunch. In other eras, the morning services were held at different times. There was also morning prayers at 6:45am (Monday to Friday) when the men and women students had separate meetings, this was after Quiet Time, which was meant to be at 6am, though some students had their Quiet Time after breakfast or in the afternoon during study period. Breakfast was at 7:30am. Students also had fifteen lectures a week plus assignments!

Chapter Twenty-Two

1. Saturday and Monday mornings were 'workout' times. Not to be confused with exercise or sport as one new student in the late 1990s discovered. She turned up in her tracksuit, reporting for duty and enquiring what sport or exercise would they be doing? "Domestic duties" was the answer! Women students' duties were: cleaning, dusting, vacuuming, polishing, typing, washing, ironing and looking after the elderly staff members, the "old ladies" (who were in their early to mid-80s in the late 1990s) as they were affectionately known to distinguish them from the 'younger' staff members who were in their 60s and 70s, whilst the 'boy' staff members were in their 20s and 30s! Men students generally did manual work such as chopping wood, sweeping paths, painting and decorating, moving furniture and gardening. Incidentally, jam was only placed on the meal tables on a Sunday evening and this tradition went back to World War II when food was scarce and there was strict rationing. During WWII, the boarders were given their weekly butter ration in a jam jar. There was bread at every meal and margarine in the evenings. Tomato ketchup and brown sauce were introduced onto the student table in 1999; up until this time, it could only be found on the staff table. The workouts made the students practical in many new skills but also, helped keep the student fees down. The fees in 1998-2001 were £2,250 ($3,600) per annum, or £750 ($1,200) per term (which was near one third of actual cost, thus Samuel subsidised the other two thirds as an example of faith). Many other colleges in the UK charged similar or

larger amounts for tuition only! At BCW, day students of which there were never more than six to eight per year, were charged £2 ($3.20) per lecture.

2. Rule 8 forbade the prolonged fraternising of members of the opposite sex during term times. *Failure Is Never Final* by Lynda Neilands (1994) is the life story of Janny van der Klis who was a student and then staff member at BCW from 1959-1966. One section covers Rule 8 as she encountered it. From the 1990s, College rules also forbade you to enter into a relationship with a member of the opposite sex within the College community until you had known them for six months and both parties had sought permission from the dean of students. You were not permitted to get engaged until a year had elapsed (permission also had to be sought) but it was strictly forbidden to get married whilst still a student and this was punishable by expulsion. These rules may seem odd or even harsh from an outside perspective but were based on experience of living in a community. If a relationship broke down, there was nowhere to hide and everyday you would see that person at the meetings, at meal times and in lecturers.

3. *The righteous perisheth, and no man layeth it to heart: and merciful men are taken away, none considering that the righteous is taken away from the evil to come. He shall enter into peace: they shall rest in their beds, each one walking in his uprightness.* Isaiah 57:1-2 (AV). Edward Jeffreys, son of Stephen, praised Rees Howells and his team of doctors and nurses at BCW who attended to his dad during his last illness at Mumbles (*Stephen Jeffreys – The Beloved Evangelist*, 1946). The Jeffreys brothers (Stephen and George) were the greatest evangelists in Britain since the days of John Wesley and George Whitefield of the eighteenth century.

4. One of the OM (Operation Mobilization) ships docked in Cardiff in 2001 and a convoy of students in their cars and the BCW minibus arrived and had a tour of the ship and its wonderful facilities.

5. Jimmy Carter, 39th President of the United States (1977-1981) is an ardent Dylan Thomas fan. Carter visited Swansea in 1977 and again in 1995 in relation to the history of Thomas who was one of the twentieth century's best-loved poets and Swansea's most famous literary son. Samuel sat behind President Carter in August 1995 aboard *Logos II*.

Chapter Twenty-Three
1. The publisher found in the archives a list totalling £260,000 ($416,000) that was given away to a number of ministries across the world (including some former students) ranging in gifts of £500 ($800) to £5,000 ($8,000). Gifts of £1,000 ($1,600) and £2,000 ($3,200) were the most common. Upon making enquiries with the author, the publisher was informed that the year in question was believed to be 1989. Using the Bank of England's online inflation calculator, £260,000 in 1989 is the equivalent of £504,500 ($807,200) in 2012! Remember these were gifts given to the work of the Lord in just *one* year. Nestled in the archives are hundreds of receipts / cheques sent from both Rees & Samuel Howells to perhaps a hundred different organisations and individual workers.

In 1989, Samuel said, "We want to thank Him for all He has done. It's been the most expensive year since the inception of the work. The expenses have averaged about £10,000 ($16,000) a week (£520,000 / $832,000 a year). Where would we be but for the goodness of God? Where would you turn? We haven't held one deputation meeting. We haven't written a letter to any person. We can truthfully say that. Not to one person. All has been committed to God alone and if He didn't answer the thing would fold up. More has been given this year for the dissemination of the Word than in any year past. Oh the work of grace! This is what His servant (Rees) wanted to do, but He didn't have the opportunity of doing it. People have given to us sacrificially. Not the leftovers. Our hearts are full of praise to Him. We love lost souls. Think of the tens of thousands of them that have been saved this year!"

In 1991, Samuel said, "I believe the expenses now, including the ministry (of giving to others) average weekly about £12,000 ($19,200) (£624,000 / $998,400 a year). How can we deal with such a situation" without partners, fundraisers and appeals? "Only by the anointing of the Holy Spirit. Let alone all these other big prayers." Samuel had no newsletter, no list of donors he could appeal to, no radio or TV ministry to ask for partners and no wealthy benefactors. To teach the principle of faith to students by example, Samuel subsidised their fees by two thirds, making BCW the cheapest Bible College in the Western world!

Chapter Twenty-Four
1. Rees Howells paid 100,000 francs in 1938 (£10,000 / $16,000) which is worth £525,000 ($840,000) in 2012. The Maison de l'Evangile (The Gospel House) was first known in Britain as the Wakefield Bible College (*Fourth Every Creature Conference – Annual Report*, 1939).
2. The Deux-Chevaux economy car, known in English as a 2CV was built between 1948-1990. The original 1948 model only produced 9 hp with its tiny 435cc engine and had a top speed of just 40 mph (64 km/h).

Chapter Twenty-Five
1. These conscripts (drafts) were from the age of fifteen upwards.
2. For an account of the Argentine Revival (1982-1997), see *Revival Fires – 150 Years of Revivals* by Mathew Backholer, ByFaith Media, 2010.

Chapter Twenty-Six
1. The massacre was reported by the BBC on the 27th November 1987. New Adams Farm was in the province of Matabeleland, sixteen Christians were massacred / martyred, mostly missionaries and their children, including a six-week-old baby.

Chapter Twenty-Seven
1. In the 1960s, Emmanuel Grammar School was expanding with new buildings. There were four hundred and fifty children, fifty of them being children of missionaries, but as the years went on, the numbers of missionary children decreased each year. In the final year of the School, there was just one missionary child. Students were from four to eighteen years of age and were predominately from the local area. In the 1980s

until its closure in August 1994, Emmanuel Grammar School was running at a considerable annual loss. An Association ran the School for a year 93/94 but they too could not make the school financially feasible.
2. In 1989, gifts totalling £260,000 ($416,000) were given away by Samuel Howells to a number of ministries ranging in size from £500 to £5,000 ($800 to $8,000), some of whom were former students. £260,000 from 1989 is the equivalent of £504,500 ($807,200) in 2012!

Chapter Twenty-Eight
1. Before 1976, the dollar was the official translation of the Ethiopian *birr*. In 1971, five hundred Ethiopian dollars was the equivalent of £105 ($168).

Chapter Twenty-Nine
1. In Britain, the end of the financial year is the 5th April.
2. See *Revival Fires and Awakenings* by Mathew Backholer, 2009, chapters 19-20 for other prophecies and visions for the United Kingdom and Europe, including those of Smith Wigglesworth (1947), Tommy Hicks (1954) and Jean Darnall (1967).

Chapter Thirty
1. Ian Paisley came to Swansea in 1994 to open a church in Burry Port. Pisgah Chapel (in an out of the way location) has since closed.
2. The publisher was present on this most memorable of occasions, Samuel Howells' fiftieth year in charge. Mr Samuel (as Samuel Howells was known) unusually revelled in the excitement of being the centre of attention and for the publisher, is the memory he holds most dear of Mr Samuel as he looked his happiest. Mr Samuel was most obliging to the number of students who all wanted to take photos of him and to have their pictures taken with him.
3. Samuel Howells collapsed in 2000, which was a distressing time for many and the entire student and staff body were very concerned. On Good Friday 2001 Samuel collapsed at the pulpit whilst preaching, he held onto the pulpit and pulled it over. An ambulance was called for. Mr Samuel was quickly discharged from hospital. After that incident, the pulpit was screwed to the floor, and after some months, Mr Samuel was encouraged to preach from a chair, sitting down, which he did.
4. Alan Scotland became a trustee in 2001. Other trustees were installed in 1996, 2000 and 2001.
5. This talk on the bridge happened on or around the year 2000.
6. Friday afternoon evangelistic outreach in Swansea town centre was developed in the 1990s. It would include street preaching, singing, tract distribution, free Gospels of Mark and John, the use of a sketch board (in good weather) and the occasional mime or drama. Different nursing homes were also visited for a few weeks of the year in the winter months as the College students with accompanying staff and friends of BCW split into two or three groups and held a service in each of the homes. Door-to-door evangelism was rare. Once a year, the students split into four or five groups and held a week of evangelism associated with a church where various activities and evangelistic methods were used.

Chapter Thirty-One
1. In 1939, £100,000 ($160,000) was a sum the College was praying for as a gift to the Jewish people, as also described in Rees *Howells Intercessor* chapter 33. In May 1939, Rees Howells was prepared to sell the three sites of Glynderwen, Derwen Fawr and Sketty Isaf which had been valued at nearly £100,000 and then use these huge funds to look after a minimum of 1,000 Jewish refugee children, though they calculated they could take 2,000 children. One thousand children would cost £50,000 ($80,000) per year. Even the local newspapers reported on this 'Welsh George Müller.' Rees would be liable for the children's board, keep and education until their eighteenth birthday. Rees also stated in *God Challenges the Dictators* (chapter 6), that the College would need another £100,000 for all the new buildings to educate and accommodate so many children and staff. The School was going to move to Penllergaer but this never happened as the Lord never told Rees Howells to sell the three estates but saw that he was *willing*. Due to British Government restrictions on immigration, Rees Howells was unable to take in the large number of Jewish refugees that he wanted to save from the Nazi regime. Rees received more than a hundred letters (from 1937-1940) often accompanied with photos from parents (Jews and non-Jews) and older siblings across Europe, begging and pleading him to accept their children or younger siblings, yet his hands were tied. Many applicants wanted places for their child or children at the Boarding School, others just pleaded for asylum. It took months for the Home Office to grant decisions. The publisher has read some of these heart-wrenching letters (and some of the replies), especially as the fate of most of those concerned was sealed in the concentration camps of Europe. On the 18th September 1947, Grunhut of Vienna stayed at BCW for a holiday so reported a local newspaper. Twice Mr Grunhut escaped the gas chamber in a Polish concentration camp – forty-two of his relatives died in the Holocaust including his own parents. His two children came to Britain as refugees; BCW raised them – Herbert (the baby in the basket as seen in the photos from *Rees Howells Intercessor*, 1952 edition) and his older brother, Ervin.

A newspaper report of May 1948, stated that Rees Howells soon 'expects a gift of £100,000' – '19 times he has been right' and proceeded to state that up until that point they had received eighteen gifts of £1,000 and one gift of £10,000! The archives sermon notes reveal that Rees Howells and the Bible College of Wales were praying for at least three sums of £100,000, all for different projects / gifts and a number of figures for other works.

Chapter Thirty-Two
1. Alan Scotland was a student at BCW in the 1960s and a staff member in the 1970s. He became a trustee in 2001.
2. Alan Scotland became Director of BCW in January 2002.
3. The Welsh word *bach* is a term of endearment meaning 'dear.'

www.ReesHowells.co.uk

ByFaith Media Books

The following ByFaith Media books are available as paperback and eBooks, whilst some are also available as hardbacks.

Christian Teaching and Inspirational
Samuel Rees Howells: A Life of Intercession by Richard Maton is an in-depth look at the intercessions of Samuel Rees Howells alongside the faith principles that he learnt from his father, Rees Howells, and under the guidance of the Holy Spirit. With 39 black and white photos in the paperback and hardback editions.

The Baptism of Fire, Personal Revival, Renewal and the Anointing for Supernatural Living by Paul Backholer. The author unveils the life and ministry of the Holy Spirit, shows how He can transform your life and what supernatural living in Christ means. Filled with biblical references, testimonies from heroes of the faith and the experiences of everyday Christians, you will learn that the baptism of fire is real and how you can receive it!

Tares and Weeds in Your Church: Trouble & Deception in God's House, the End Time Overcomers by R. B. Watchman. Is there a battle taking place in your house, church or ministry, leading to division? Tares and weeds are counterfeit Christians used to sabotage Kingdom work; learn how to recognise them and neutralise them in the power of the Holy Spirit.

Holy Spirit Power: Knowing the Voice, Guidance and Person of the Holy Spirit by Paul Backholer. Power for Christian living; drawing from the powerful influences of many Christian leaders, including: Rees Howells, Evan Roberts, D. L. Moody and Duncan Campbell and other channels of God's Divine fire.

Jesus Today, Daily Devotional: 100 Days with Jesus Christ by Paul Backholer. Two minutes a day to encourage and inspire; 100 days of daily Christian Bible inspiration to draw you closer to God. *Jesus Today* is a concise daily devotional defined by the teaching of Jesus and how His life can change yours.

Biography and Autobiography
The Holy Spirit in a Man: Spiritual Warfare, Intercession, Faith, Healings and Miracles by R. B. Watchman. One man's compelling journey of faith and intercession – a gripping true-life story. Raised in a dysfunctional family and called for a Divine

purpose. Sent out by God, he left employment to claim the ground for Christ, witnessing signs and wonders, spiritual warfare and deliverance.

Samuel, Son and Successor of Rees Howells: Director of the Bible College of Wales – A Biography by Richard Maton. The author invites us on a lifelong journey with Samuel, to unveil his ministry at the College and the support he received from numerous staff, students and visitors, as the history of BCW unfolds alongside the Vision to reach Every Creature with the Gospel. With 113 black and white photos in the paperback and hardback editions!

Revivals and Spiritual Awakenings
Revival Fires and Awakenings, Thirty-Six Visitations of the Holy Spirit: A Call to Holiness, Prayer and Intercession for the Nations by Mathew Backholer. With 36 fascinating accounts of revivals in nineteen countries from six continents, plus biblical teaching on revival, prayer and intercession. Also available as a hardback.

Global Revival, Worldwide Outpourings, Forty-Three Visitations of the Holy Spirit: The Great Commission by Mathew Backholer. With forty-three revivals from more than thirty countries on six continents, the author reveals the fascinating links between pioneering missionaries and the revivals that they saw as they worked towards the Great Commission.

Revival Fire, 150 Years of Revivals, Spiritual Awakenings and Moves of the Holy Spirit by Mathew Backholer, documents in detail, twelve revivals from ten countries on five continents. Through the use of detailed research, eye-witness accounts and interviews, *Revival Fire* presents some of the most potent revivals that the world has seen in the past one hundred and fifty years.

Revival Answers, True and False Revivals, Genuine or Counterfeit Do not be Deceived by Mathew Backholer. What is genuine revival and how can we tell the true from the spurious? Drawing from Scripture with examples across Church history, this book will sharpen your senses and take you on a journey of discovery.

Reformation to Revival, 500 Years of God's Glory by Mathew Backholer. For the past five hundred years God has been pouring out His Spirit, to reform and to revive His Church.

Reformation to Revival traces the Divine thread of God's power from Martin Luther of 1517, through to the Charismatic Movement and into the twenty-first century, featuring sixty great revivals from twenty nations.

Understanding Revival and Addressing the Issues it Provokes by Mathew Backholer. Many who have prayed for revival have rejected it when it came because they misunderstood the workings of the Holy Spirit. Learn how to intelligently cooperate with the Holy Spirit during times of revivals and Heaven-sent spiritual awakenings.

Supernatural and Spiritual

Glimpses of Glory, Revelations in the Realms of God Beyond the Veil in the Heavenly Abode: The New Jerusalem and the Eternal Kingdom of God by Paul Backholer. In this narrative receive biblical glimpses and revelations into life in paradise, which is filled with references to Scripture to confirm its veracity. A gripping read!

Prophecy Now, Prophetic Words and Divine Revelations for You, the Church and the Nations by Michael Backholer. An enlightening end-time prophetic journal of visions, words and prophecies.

Heaven, A Journey to Paradise and the Heavenly City by Paul Backholer. Join one person's exploration of paradise, guided by an angel and a glorified man, to witness the thrilling promise of eternity, and to provide answers to many questions about Heaven. Anchored in the Word of God, discover what Heaven will be like!

Christian Discipleship

Discipleship For Everyday Living, Christian Growth: Following Jesus Christ and Making Disciples of All Nations by Mathew Backholer. Engaging biblical teaching to aid believers in maturity, to help make strong disciples with solid biblical foundations who reflect the image of Jesus Christ. The book's fifty chapters are split into six sections: Firm Foundations, The Call of God, World Missions, Evangelism and Teaching, Ministering in the Power of the Holy Spirit, and Ministry – Being Set Free and Delivered.

Extreme Faith, On Fire Christianity: Hearing from God and Moving in His Grace, Strength & Power – Living in Victory by Mathew Backholer. Discover the powerful biblical foundations for on fire faith in Christ! God has given us powerful weapons to defeat the enemy, to take back the spiritual land in our lives and to walk in His glory through the power of the Holy Spirit.

Historical and Adventure
Britain, A Christian Country, A Nation Defined by Christianity and the Bible & the Social Changes that Challenge this Biblical Heritage by Paul Backholer. For more than 1,000 years Britain was defined by Christianity, discover this continuing legacy, how faith defined its nationhood and the challenges from the 1960s onwards.

How Christianity Made the Modern World by Paul Backholer. Christianity is the greatest reforming force that the world has ever known, yet its legacy is seldom comprehended. See how Christianity helped create the path that led to Western liberty and laid the foundations of the modern world.

Celtic Christianity & the First Christian Kings in Britain: From St. Patrick and St. Columba, to King Ethelbert and King Alfred by Paul Backholer. Celtic Christians ignited a Celtic Golden Age of faith and light which spread into Europe. Discover this striking history and what we can learn from the heroes of Celtic Christianity.

Lost Treasures of the Bible: Exploration and Pictorial Travel Adventure of Biblical Archaeology by Paul Backholer. Join a photographic quest in search of the lost treasures of the Bible. Unveil ancient mysteries as you discover the evidence for Israel's exodus from Egypt, and travel into lost civilisations in search of the Ark of the Covenant. Explore lost worlds with over 160 colour pictures and photos in the paperback edition.

The Exodus Evidence In Pictures – The Bible's Exodus: The Hunt for Ancient Israel in Egypt, the Red Sea, the Exodus Route and Mount Sinai by Paul Backholer. Brothers, Paul and Mathew Backholer search for archaeological data to validate the biblical account of Joseph, Moses and the Hebrew Exodus from ancient Egypt. With more than 100 full colour photographs and graphics!

The Ark of the Covenant – Investigating the Ten Leading Claims by Paul Backholer. The mystery of the Bible's lost Ark of the Covenant has led to many myths, theories and claims. Join two explorers as they investigate the ten major theories concerning the location of antiquities greatest relic. 80+ colour photographs.

Short-Term Missions (Christian Travel with a Purpose)
Short-Term Missions, A Christian Guide to STMs by Mathew Backholer. *For Leaders, Pastors, Churches, Students, STM Teams and Mission Organizations – Survive and Thrive!* What you need to know about planning a STM, or joining a STM team.

How to Plan, Prepare and Successfully Complete Your Short-Term Mission by Mathew Backholer. *For Churches, Independent STM Teams and Mission Organizations.* The books includes: mission statistics, quotes and more than 140 real-life STM testimonies.

Budget Travel – Holiday/Vacations
Budget Travel, a Guide to Travelling on a Shoestring, Explore the World, a Discount Overseas Adventure Trip: Gap Year, Backpacking, Volunteer-Vacation and Overlander by Mathew Backholer. A practical and concise guide to travelling the world and exploring new destinations with fascinating opportunities.

www.ByFaithBooks.co.uk

Social Media
www.facebook.com/ByFaithMedia
www.instagram.com/ByFaithMedia
www.youtube.com/ByFaithMedia
www.twitter.com/ByFaithMedia

www.BibleCollegeOfWales.co.uk

ByFaith Media DVDs

Revivals and Spiritual Awakenings
Great Christian Revivals on 1 DVD is an inspirational and uplifting account of some of the greatest revivals in Church history. Filmed on location across Britain and drawing upon archive information, the stories of the Welsh Revival (1904-1905), the Hebridean Revival (1949-1952) and the Evangelical Revival (1739-1791) are brought to life in this moving 72-minute documentary. Using computer animation, historic photos and depictions, the events of the past are weaved into the present, to bring these Heaven-sent revivals to life.

Christian Travel (Backpacking Style Short-Term Mission)
ByFaith – World Mission on 1 DVD is a Christian reality TV show that reveals the real experience of a backpacking style short-term mission in Asia, Europe and North Africa. Two brothers, Paul and Mathew Backholer shoot through fourteen nations, in an 85-minute real-life documentary. Filmed over three years, *ByFaith – World Mission* is the very best of ByFaith TV season one.

Historical and Adventure
Israel in Egypt – The Exodus Mystery on 1 DVD. A four year quest searching for Joseph, Moses and the Hebrew slaves in Egypt. Join Paul and Mathew Backholer as they hunt through ancient relics and explore the mystery of the biblical exodus, hunt for the Red Sea and climb Mount Sinai. Discover the first reference to Israel outside of the Bible, uncover depictions of people with multicoloured coats, encounter the Egyptian records of slaves making bricks and find lost cities. 110 minutes. The very best of *ByFaith – In Search of the Exodus*.

ByFaith – Quest for the Ark of the Covenant on 1 DVD, 100+ minutes. Join two adventurers on their quest for the Ark, beginning at Mount Sinai where it was made, to Pharaoh Tutankhamun's tomb, where Egyptian treasures evoke the majesty of the Ark. The quest proceeds onto the trail of Pharaoh Shishak, who raided Jerusalem. The mission continues up the River Nile to find a lost temple, with clues to a mysterious civilization. Crossing through the Sahara Desert, the investigators enter the underground rock churches of Ethiopia, find a forgotten civilization and examine the enigma of the final resting place of the Ark.

www.ByFaithDVDs.co.uk